Vacationing on the
Jersey Shore

Vacationing on the
Jersey Shore

Guide to the Beach Resorts
Past and Present

CHARLES A. STANSFIELD JR.

STACKPOLE
BOOKS

Published by
STACKPOLE BOOKS
5067 Ritter Road
Mechanicsburg, PA 17055
www.stackpolebooks.com

Printed in China

10 9 8 7 6 5 4 3 2 1

FIRST EDITION

Design by Beth Oberholtzer
Cover design by Caroline Stover

Picture credits:
Photographs by the author and illustrations from the author's collection, unless noted below

Atlantic City Convention & Visitors Authority, cover, 181.
Atlantic County Historical Society, 117, 161 (bottom).
Batsto Citizens Committee, Inc., 203.
Joel Bernstein, 109. Photo ©1979 Joel Bernstein.
Delaware River & Bay Authority, 85.
Dover Publications (from **Early Woodcut Views of New**
   York and New Jersey*), 18, 37, 62 (both), 63, 66, 67.*
Hasbro, Inc., 177. MONOPOLY® & ©2003 Hasbro, Inc. Used with permission.
Library of Congress, 102, 103 (both), 104, 105.
Dick Scott photo, 46 (both).
Tuckerton Seaport, 135, 150, 151 (top).
United States Geological Survey, 34.
Urban Archives, Temple University, Philadelphia, 199.
Kyle R. Weaver photo, 41 (bottom), 80, 190, 191, 208 (bottom), 212 (top), 213 (both), 230.
Kyle R. Weaver Collection, ii, 6 (both), 7 (bottom), 33, 41 (top), 118 (left).

Library of Congress Cataloging-in-Publication Data

Stansfield, Charles A.
    Vacationing on the Jersey shore : the past and present, with a guide to the beach resorts / Charles A. Stansfield Jr.
        p.   cm.
    Includes bibliographical references (p.   ) and index.
    ISBN 0-8117-2970-2
    1. Atlantic Coast (N.J.)—History.   2. Seashore—New Jersey—History.
3. Beaches—New Jersey—Atlantic Coast—History.   4. Vacations—New Jersey—
Atlantic Coast—History.   5. Atlantic Coast (N.J.)—Social life and customs.
6. Atlantic Coast (N.J.)—Guidebooks.   7. New Jersey—History.   8. New Jersey—
Social life and customs.   9. New Jersey—Guidebooks.   I. Title.

F142.J4S73   2004
974.9'00946—dc21

                                                        2003008244

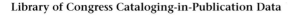

*For my wife, Diane, the belle of my beach,
my constant companion on the great field trip of life;
and for my grandchildren—Jordan Elizabeth,
Aidan Charles, and David Bryce—through
whose eyes I may see afresh the wonders
and beauty of the world.*

Contents

Maps

Preface

The purposes of this guidebook are to describe and interpret the beauties and pleasures of the Jersey shore, to encourage your own explorations of the remarkably varied and interesting region, and to increase your appreciation of the area.

A full, true appreciation of any part of the world suggests that you first develop a sense of place, a basic understanding of that area, and how it came to be that way. An intimate knowledge of a place requires the establishment and identification of reference points, guideposts, in both time and space. The Jersey shore was created by nature but also shaped by people. It certainly did not always look and feel the way it does now. The New Jersey seashore did not always have the power, or the means of access, to attract millions of vacationers every year. It is a region that came to be over centuries, and it is still a work in progress, a little different from year to year, just as it is from place to place.

A sense of time and place is vital, and a good measure of our awareness and thinking capacity. As a patient regains consciousness from the effects of anesthesia, two questions routinely are asked to determine his or her level of awareness: "Do you know what day it is?" and "Do you know where you are?" In the hospital setting, the answers are very specific. In your life experience, the answers are more broadly philosophical, but just as fundamental. Appreciating a place—fully enjoying its unique flavors and pleasures, its "personality"—means understanding its nature, its historic roots, and its process of development. The first three chapters of this book help you establish the guideposts or reference points of this delightful resort region in time and space.

The following four chapters each focus on a section of the Jersey shore—the North Shore, Central Shore, Atlantic City region, and South Shore. Each region is a unique blend of nature, history, and character, and each has its own special characteristics, advantages, and appeals, each a collection of different resort "personalities."

This guide focuses upon the reasons to visit each region and gives suggestions for how best to enjoy being there, depending on your interests. However deep-rooted or recent your experience, whether you know one town or a dozen, this book is intended to add to both the depth and breadth of your appreciation of New Jersey's shore in all its varieties and moods.

What this guide does not attempt to do is list specific establishments in which to stay, eat, drink, or carouse. Choices of this nature are highly personal, influenced by one's own budget, taste buds, lifestyle, and values. And nothing, absolutely nothing, changes faster than a restaurant's reputation, menu, service, or prices. We're talking nanoseconds here, relatively speaking. Most everyone has had the experience of introducing guests to a favorite restaurant, only to have a memorably bad experience due to new owners, different cooks, or plain old off days. For specific recommendations, refer to one of the frequently updated guides with professional evaluations of visitor accommodations and eating places.

This book begins with the how and why, as well as the results of the continuing development of the great variety of seaside resorts along New Jersey's beaches. Each resort is then described so that you can select one that meets your desires and tastes, and learn more about old favorites. Read, travel, and enjoy!

Acknowledgments

I was most fortunate to find in my editor, Kyle R. Weaver, another fan of the Jersey shore. Kyle was not only enthusiastic about the proposal for this book and supplied reassuring support during its development, but also happily provided photos and postcards from his collection to help illustrate it.

Patricia Martinelli, a longtime friend, former student, and typist on many past projects, once again proved her uncanny ability to decipher my handwriting and made many valuable suggestions on the manuscript. Joyce Bond did a splendid job on the copyediting.

Rowan University's Campbell Library is blessed with a knowledgeable, friendly, and most helpful professional staff. I especially want to thank Maryann Gonzalez, Joyce Olsen, and William Garrabrant of the Stewart Collection of New Jersey materials. My former Rowan University colleague, Herb Richardson made his great postcard collection available for my use and gave good advice.

The supportive environment at Rowan University owes much to the dynamic and visionary leadership of its president, Donald J. Farish. I must also thank my many stimulating colleagues and interested students at Rowan, who listened critically and receptively to my thoughts on the Jersey shore.

The knowledgeable and friendly staff of the Atlantic City Convention & Visitor's Authority was most helpful. Special thanks to Karen DeRosa of Tuckerton Seaport for her hospitality and invaluable assistance with photos. My old friend Wade Currier accompanied me to Atlantic City and shared his insights into the casino industry.

My dear wife and favorite field trip companion, Diane, traveled with me from Cape May to Sandy Hook; her enthusiasm and support were constant. She more or less forgivingly accepted my conversion of our newly decorated dining room into what looked like a small library that had recently undergone a small earthquake.

1

Beginnings

The natural charms of New Jersey's seashore haven't changed much over the thousands of years that people have lived in the neighborhood. The waves still rhythmically crash up onto the beach, only to slide back down the gentle slope to rejoin the ocean. Currents and waves still build beaches and destroy them, fill in old inlets and open others, a few grains of sand at a time. Late summer just as likely brings fierce storms, the last blows of hurricanes, to reshape the edge of the ocean in faster, more dramatic ways. Gulls still scurry along the waterline, somehow always evading the incoming wavelets.

Summer is the season when the shore has the greatest appeal to us. From late morning to dusk, cooling breezes move from sea to land—nature's air-conditioning. There is a soothing timelessness in the regular rhythm of breaking waves—nature's tranquilizer. The power of the sun is gentled by the refreshing coolness of the water. The bounty of nature is evidenced in the abundance of shellfish and finfish.

This is the place where the largest of immovable objects, the continent, meets the ultimate irresistible force, the ocean. The shoreline is the bumper, the shock absorber, between the two. The coast also is the front door of the nation. Until the past century, everything and everyone entering or leaving the continent did so by sea. The oceans once provided our only connections to other lands and peoples.

Cape May Lighthouse,
built in 1859.

For much of its history, however, New Jersey's 127 miles of ocean shore-line have been more like a blank wall turned to the sea than a busy entryway. Everything that makes the Jersey seashore so inviting to vacationers—the gently shelving shoreline with shallow waters safe for bathers, the surf line of waves breaking along ribbonlike islands, the beach protection effect of offshore sandbars—puts up a large danger sign for boats, especially ships under sail. To a sunbather, this is paradise; to a sailor, this is not exactly hell, but close enough to it in a storm.

The great seaports of this part of the world grew at the northern and southern flanks of this glorious realm of sand and surf. And no wonder. Ships need safe harbors, protected from the often powerful and dangerous combination of wind and waves on the open ocean. Deep water close to land is an asset too. These ships' requirements are missing between Sandy Hook and Cape May. And so great cities first arose, not along the New Jersey shore, but to both north and south, on the Hudson and Delaware Rivers.

When the United States was born, the Jersey shore was not considered a very attractive place. Only small vessels could safely navigate its shallow bays and shifting inlets. The grassy marshes and sand beaches were not all that productive for farming. Seashore land was cheap, but there were few buyers. Around 1700, a man sold all of Five Mile Beach and Two Mile Beach for £9 to buy his wife a dress. Five Mile and Two Mile Beaches today are

The Hamburg-American Line Piers, Hoboken, N. J.

Hoboken Piers, early 1900s. Good harbors offer protected, deep-water shorelines.

Absecon Inlet. The seashore's shallow, shifting channels are usable only by small craft.

known as the Wildwoods. Most permanent inhabitants of the region—and there were very few of them—were either lighthouse keepers or those who made their living from the sea: whalers, fishermen, oystermen, clammers, and crab catchers.

Within two and a quarter centuries after the nation's birthday, this picture of a desolate, unproductive, and almost empty land has been turned

Island Beach State Park. The pre-development seashore.

upside down. For many living in other states, New Jersey's seashore is the most familiar part of the Garden State. Walt Whitman commented, "To me, it is the seaside region which gives stamp to Jersey." What was once the remote edge, a zone of little interest or importance, has become an almost continuous string of popular resorts. Where once a few dollars would buy an entire island, today small oceanfront lots offered at a million dollars are considered great bargains. Crowding during the summer season rivals that of the highest-density neighborhoods of metropolitan centers. Atlantic City has reclaimed its position as a world-class attraction, a super-star among resorts, while the sleepiest of seaside communities undergo real estate booms of dazzling prices.

What caused this amazing transformation, this reversal of values and images of the shore? In a word, transportation. The easier, faster, and cheaper it was to get from the big cities—especially New York and Philadel-phia—to the seashore, the more people came. While the natural qualities of the shore have changed only in minor detail, people's appreciation of the seaside has changed immensely.

Beach Location and the Market

Not all beaches are born equal. Some are much better than others—wider, more gently sloping into the water, composed of softer, finer-grained sand, or located in warmer, sunnier climates. There are world-class beaches and there are just so-so beaches.

But the most spectacular of natural beaches, everyone's dream beaches, do not always become world-famous resorts. And some less-than-wonderful beaches support widely known resort communities, towns that attract large crowds in season, and real estate prices that would stagger millionaires.

Why? Because of geography. There's the geography of the natural resources, the beaches themselves, and the geography of beachgoers, the market demand for these natural resources. These two geographies do not necessarily always overlap.

Under ideal circumstances, in a more perfect world, broad, beautiful beaches would be conveniently next to dense concentrations of wannabe beachgoers: a perfect geographic match of a top-quality natural resource with concentrations of people looking for a tan and a relaxing good time. But sometimes people must compromise in their search for the absolute best beaches due to practical considerations like distance away from home. No matter how great the beach may be, if it takes too long to reach it or the trip is too expensive, some other, closer beach will have to do.

The New Jersey shore is a happy combination of an excellent natural resource for recreation with a nearby massive concentration of people looking for quality recreational environments.

A Place of Infinite Variety

Just what do you want? Is your idea of a trip to the seashore one of long, lazy days quietly working on your tan? Then nearly all the resorts will please you. Perhaps you'd rather gamble. If so, Atlantic City is the place for you, with its quarter slot machines and the highest-stakes games east of Las Vegas. Are you into thrill rides? Seaside Heights and Wildwood will fulfill your dreams. History and architecture buffs might prefer Cape May or Ocean Grove. Avid fishermen will find many opportunities.

In some New Jersey beach towns, short-time visitors encounter high fees for daily beach badges (often even higher

The New Jersey shore in its regional setting.

on weekends) in combination with a conspicuous lack of short-term visitor conveniences like beachfront restrooms, parking, or snack bars. If you don't own a cottage or rent for the season in these towns, then you just don't belong.

In other towns, day-trippers are welcome as volunteers to be processed by that well-known entertainment factory, the boardwalk. There, vendors will swap fast food, cold drinks, candy, popcorn, thrill rides, video games, and T-shirts decorated with quasiobscene slogans for cash. The sunburn is free. This seafront assembly line will be the center of visitor-oriented retailing and services, the locale of all action. So enticing are these commercialized boardwalks that Americans actually walk, rather than drive, from attraction to attraction. Even more amazing, they do so as families.

In the smaller, quieter towns of both permanent and seasonal residents, many retirees, and truly stratospheric real estate values, the boardwalk may be a simple oceanfront promenade unadorned by candy, hamburger, or pizza stands and with no mechanical amusements in sight. At the other extreme are the noisy, glittery boardwalks like those of Atlantic City, Wildwood, and Seaside Heights. Glitz may not have been invented on the Jersey shore, but it was perfected there. Tom Wolfe once described Las Vegas as Wildwood, New Jersey, entering heaven.

Memories and Appreciation

Family photo albums, home movies, and home videos feature many beach scenes. Playing by the sea must have very special appeal. Both the oldest and newest of family photos include family groups sunning on the beach. Toddlers squint happily at the camera, posing by their best-ever sand castle or frolicking among the wavelets. Bigger children brave the breakers, reassured by Daddy's arms. Teenagers eye both the competition and the prospects, in between improvised ball games at the water's edge. The older generation gossips in the shade of beach umbrellas, observing the present and remembering past beach scenes.

Do you have cherished memories of the Jersey shore, or are you exploring the seashore for the first time? Are you revisiting a town that holds many fond memories, or are you still looking for the perfect match of your lifestyle with one of the many coastal communities?

Every place has a history and a geography, both of which have shaped the place, contributing to its unique character. When we look at any part of the Jersey shore, what we see now is like a still photo from a movie, the lat-

Seashore snapshots, 1940s and '50s

1970s

1980s

est frame of many. That snapshot in time can be fully appreciated only if we've seen the movie up to that point; similarly, some general historical background helps us understand the present.

As real estate agents like to joke, "The three most important things about a property are location, location, and location." Understanding the location of the seashore towns relative to neighboring great metropolitan centers, as well as the physical qualities of their locations—beaches, ocean, bay, and marsh—contributes to a greater appreciation of the enticing Jersey shore.

Life Is a Beach: Our Love Affair with the Seashore

Anyone driving home from the beach on Labor Day evening knows that many, many people (too many, it sometimes seems) love the beach. Really, really love it. Just look at the time, money, and effort that millions are willing to devote to beachgoing. And look at the effect that the magic words "seafront" or "beachfront" have on real estate prices. Oceanfront locations have a few extra zeroes before the decimal point when compared with less blessed interior locales. Ocean*view,* a fine distinction from ocean*front,* may still add a zero or two over equally luxurious homes, condos, or hotel rooms a few blocks inland. Bargain-hunting vacationers quickly discover the fiscal delights of "offshore" motels and campgrounds that lie further inland.

Why are so many willing to lay out extra dollars for a window on the surf? It's true that oceanview condos or hotel rooms are the most prestigious, up-to-date, and luxurious available, but that simply reflects the need to milk the most profit out of the most expensive real estate. This cost reflects competition for the cachet of a "sea view."

Some rather pretentious academics argue that people may have deeply embedded memories of the likely fact that early humans favored seashore

Place Names by the Sea

Only a handful of American Indian place names survive along New Jersey's shoreline: Mantoloking, Tuckahoe, Metedeconk, Manasquan, and Absecon Island (Atlantic City and its neighbors). Early non-Indian place names often honored explorers, pioneers, or early landowners: Ludlum's Beach (Sea Isle City), Bradley's Beach, Peck's Beach (Ocean City), Tucker's Beach (now underwater), Loveladies (Captain Lovelady), Cape May (explorer Captain Mey), and Harvey Cedars (who else, Harvey). Physical features are commemorated by Highlands, Bayhead, Point Pleasant, Sandy Hook, and Island Beach (State Park).

Resort founders often wanted to mention the basic attraction, thus Ocean City, Surf City, and Spray Beach. "Sea" or "seaside" are part of five place names, and there is one "harbor" (Stone Harbor) and one "port" (Longport).

Two resort towns, Margate and Ventnor, are named for older resorts on England's southern coast and in Wales. Avalon evokes the mythical glamour of King Arthur's Court. Barnegat is the region's only Dutch name. It means "inlet with large waves."

(or lakeshore) environments for their homes. There they could enjoy the greatest possible variety of foods and materials from both land and sea. The animals and plants of land were on one hand, and on the other, fish, shellfish, even the odd whale or dolphin washed ashore.

Or maybe it's just that we see the seashore as a near-perfect fun place, a gift of nature designed for the enjoyment of leisure. From an early age, we naturally like to play in water—as any parent knows. The giant sand-box of the beach simply adds to the pleasures of wading in shallow water, swimming, fishing, frolicking in surf, or boating.

It doesn't matter to most of us exactly why we love the seashore; what matters is that our image of a summer paradise is reflected by the New Jersey shore.

Welcome to New Jersey

People tend to see new places in terms of their personal values and goals. If the place happens to have what they wanted to see, they're happy. What doesn't seem useful at the time probably will get little attention.

The American Indians were the first people to see this shoreline, but they left no written records of their experience and observations.

The first European explorer to see New Jersey for sure was Giovanni da Verrazano. (John Cabot may have sailed this far south in North America, but some historians dispute that.) Verrazano's 1524 voyage along much of the East Coast produced only vague descriptions of places, and his records of longitude and latitude were more guesstimates than scientifically accurate. It was possibly along the Jersey coast that the explorer was mooned by the locals. According to Marc Mappen in *Jerseyana,* on July 8, 1524, an explorer's crew (almost certainly Verrazano's) witnessed a show of contempt from a group of Indians who turned away and "stuck out their buttocks." Welcome to New Jersey! But worse things happened to Verrazano than that: In 1528, on a voyage to the Caribbean, he was captured and eaten by cannibals.

Verrazano, an Italian working for the French, reported that the land along the Jersey coast was "green with forests" and that the area around Lower New York Bay was "hospitable and attractive," but he said little about the future Jersey seashore. These were mostly long-distance observations— Verrazano didn't bother getting off the ship to look at what is now New Jersey. He did send some men in rowboats to explore New York Bay, but it is not clear if they went inland any distance. Verrazano was looking for a route to the Indies, and he quickly lost interest when he didn't find it here.

The Europeans were less than excited by Verrazano's 1524 reports on this part of the world. It was not for eighty-five more years that another European took a closer look at what we know as New Jersey.

It was in small, fragile wooden sailing ships, like this one from a seventeenth-century map, that Europeans first explored the area that is now New Jersey.

In 1609, Henry Hudson, an Englishman working for the Dutch, undertook a more detailed exploration. In *Land and People*, Peter Wacker writes that Hudson's first impression of the Jersey shore was "a white sandy beach and drowned land within"—his description of salt marshes and bays.

Although present-day Americans would be favorably impressed by lovely white sand beaches to play on, these early explorers were far more interested in deep, spacious harbors, not to mention gold mines. They found excellent harbors in both the Delaware Bay and New York Bay, but not along the Jersey shore, so they had little to say about the seashore.

Henry Hudson, surely one of the most thorough and adventurous of explorers, came to a bad end. In discovering Hudson Bay in Canada, his ship became locked in the ice over an entire winter. His terminally bored crew revolted and set him adrift in a small boat, and he was never heard from again. He probably wished he had stayed in New Jersey.

Discovering the Seashore (Again)

The ancient Romans, at least the rich ones, certainly knew how to indulge themselves in the more physical types of pleasure. Those inventive Romans were experts at having a really good time. And there is plenty of historical and archaeological evidence that, for the aristocracy, good times frequently had a seaside setting. Several emperors spent their summers on the Isle of Capri. Their example was followed by many other wealthy and influential Romans, who built beautiful marble villas at the seaside. Group nude bathing was popular, accompanied by other group nude indulgences. Use your imagination—the Romans did.

That the wealthiest Romans enjoyed the seashore is no surprise. All the necessary ingredients were in place: sunny summers tempered by sea breezes, with sea temperatures mild enough to entice bathing; access to seashores (the whole empire focused on the sea); plenty of leisure time among the rich; and the peace and security necessary to allow people to relax at the beach, free of worry about exposure to seaborne raiders or pirates.

When the empire collapsed, the seaside lost the image of security, fewer folks had the required combination of money and leisure time to build vacation villas, and the new religion frowned on the more excessive expressions of physical pleasures.

One Roman cultural expression and social habit—traveling to mineral water spas or baths—remained popular with Europeans, even through the long centuries when the seashore was pretty much a no-go zone. The Romans believed in the curative effects of drinking from and bathing in mineral-rich waters found in some natural springs, especially hot springs. Ever since the Romans, many people have maintained this confidence in mineral springs up to the present.

"Taking the waters" was a good excuse for getting away from home, relaxing, and socializing. For the more puritanically minded, it provided the necessary cover story for taking a vacation: "It's for my health." Drinking mineral water from uncontaminated springs probably was good for people who otherwise drank little water. Water from shallow wells or rivers was so often contaminated that a general avoidance of water was a wise move. Bathing, a daily ritual at spas, was something most people in Europe usually did far too little of by modern standards. No doubt, daily bathing contributed to a feeling of good health.

In eighteenth-century England, doctors began to recommend bathing in, and drinking from, the ultimate "mineral water" source—the sea. Chemists proved that seawater contained every mineral that could be found in any mineral springs. Seawater was much more readily obtained, as most British were closer to salt water than to a spa. Bathing in seawater was good for you, and so was drinking some salt water. Actually, drinking salt water (mix it yourself with tap water and table salt) does have a predictable, sometimes desired, effect on the digestive system. It sort of moves things along.

Clean sea air and sunshine are still touted as good for one's health, long after the vogue of drinking seawater has died away. In general, getting away from it all and visiting the seashore does help people feel better, if only psychologically.

Sea Monsters, Raiders, and Pirates

The beaches of Normandy, France, have a far different image, at least to those familiar with World War II history, than the beaches of New Jersey. Instead of visions of life at its best, with sun umbrellas, surfboards, beach chairs, and sunbathers, mention of the beaches of Normandy suggests pictures of landing craft, offshore warships, artillery, and brutal death. The shivers of dread that images of French Normandy beaches in wartime induce are in stark contrast with the anticipation of delights suggested by, say, New Jersey's Normandy Beach (just south of Mantoloking). No New Jersey beach has been invaded by any force more threatening than jellyfish, at least since the War of 1812. Americans understandably have very positive ideas about living at the beach. But French Normandy's 1944 experience of the beach as a hazardous war zone is much more representative of human history than our present-day love affair with sand and surf.

For most of the human experience, ocean beaches were not very safe places to live. They were hazardous places to be avoided, what with hurricanes, winter gales, treacherous sandbars, and shifting channels, not to mention real sharks and imagined monsters. Pirates and raiders made the beach a dangerous place, too. Sightings of Viking longboats produced terror for centuries along seacoasts from Scotland to Sicily. Equally feared were the skull-and-crossbones flags of marauding pirates.

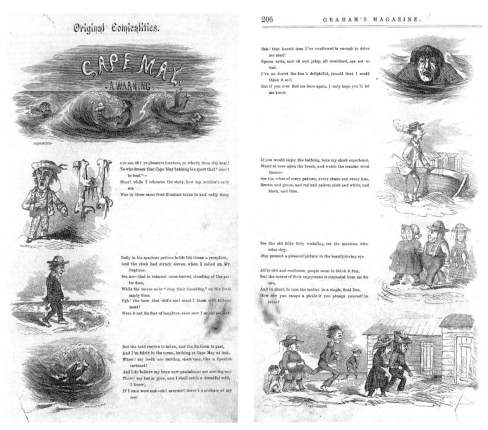

Cape May was already popular enough in 1854 to be the subject of this comic.

It was only in the nineteenth century that the beaches of Europe and America began to be regarded as natural playgrounds rather than war zones. Sailors and fishermen still looked for safe havens—bays and river mouths—for their workplaces and residences, not the shallow waters off beaches. Sailors and fishers know all too well the power of storm waves and currents, and seldom wish to live where the waves can reach.

Popular attitudes about the beach have undergone a radical reversal, from negative to positive, only in the past two centuries or so. The playground image developed only after the shore was safe from pirates and the emergence of railroads allowed for speedy, cheap connections between big cities and the surf.

The Birth of New Jersey's Seashore Resorts

Americans seem fascinated by "firsts"—first landing place of the Pilgrims, first European child born in America, first brewery in New England, and so on. And so the question comes up, which was the first seashore resort in America?

New Englanders like to believe that the very first such place was near Boston. New Jerseyans know better. Besides, New England already claims more than its share of important historical firsts, like that vital first brewery.

The historical picture is a little murky and arguable, even among New Jerseyans. North Jerseyans point to Long Branch, while South Jerseyans favor Cape May. Either way, we're talking about the late eighteenth century, ancient history for most Americans.

Partisans of either Cape May or Long Branch as the very first seashore resort in New Jersey, and possibly the nation, could prove their respective cases through judicious selection of sources. According to William Nelson, in *The New Jersey Coast in Three Centuries*: "Long Branch was the first distinctively summer resort of the New Jersey coast to win the favor of the pleasure seeking public, and for many years it was the only one known to society at home and to travelers from abroad. . . . In 1792 Herbert and Chandler were operating a hotel at Long Branch (then called Shrewsbury) and erected bathing houses on the beach. In 1806 the property was sold to Joshua Bennet who enlarged the building so as to accommodate 250 guests." A steamboat connection between Red Bank and New York City was established in 1828, with stage connections to Long Branch. "About 1850 wealthy people of New York began to pay great attention to Long Branch and thronged there in great numbers."

John Cunningham, in *The New Jersey Shore*, reports that Cape Island's (Cape May's earlier name) claim to be the oldest resort is based partly on an

---

New Jersey Shore
"Firsts" and "Mosts"

First boardwalk "rolling chairs": First rolled out at a seashore resort in Atlantic City in 1884, these were man-powered, three-wheeled wicker chairs holding one (sometimes two) footsore vacationers. By 1948, Atlantic City's rolling chairs were electric-powered, limited to four miles per hour. Now, human-powered chairs are back in style.

First seaside casinos: No, not in Atlantic City. Before Atlantic City existed, both Cape May and Long Branch had open, if not legal, gambling by the 1830s. But by the end of the nineteenth century, they were gone.

First televised indoor football game: With the many domed football stadiums now functioning, indoor football is commonplace. But in December 1964, Utah and West Virginia met in the Liberty Bowl (since moved to Memphis) inside Atlantic City's 1929 Convention Hall. Utah won, 32–6.

First nationally known beauty pageant: The Miss America Pageant, September 1921.

Largest St. Patrick's Day parade in New Jersey: South Belmar.

Tallest lighthouses in New Jersey: Barnegat Light, at 172 feet, and Absecon Light (Atlantic City), at 171 feet.

Oldest operational lighthouse in the United States: Sandy Hook Light, 1764.

Oldest lifesaving station: The first federally sponsored lifesaving station in America was at Island Beach State Park in 1848.

---

advertisement placed in the *Pennsylvania Gazette* in 1766 by one Robert Parsons, offering for sale his Cape May plantation "within one mile and a half of the Sea Shore, where a number resort for health and bathing in the water."

As quoted in the Federal Writers Project's *New Jersey's First Summer Resort,* in 1801, Cape Island's postmaster, Ellis Hughes, advertised in the Philadelphia *Daily Aurora:* "The subscriber has proposed himself for entertaining company who use sea-bathing. . . . The slope of the shore is so regular that persons may wade a great distance. It is the most delightful spot the citizen may retire to in the hot season." *Historical Collections of the State of New Jersey,* an 1844 volume by John Barber and Henry Howe, observed: "The village of Cape Island is a favorite watering place. . . . It began to grow into notice as a watering place in 1812, at which time there were but a few houses there. It now contains two large hotels, three stories high and 150 feet long—and a third lately erected, four stories high and 100 feet in length; besides numerous other houses for the entertainment of visitors."

〜〜〜〜〜〜〜〜〜〜〜〜〜〜〜

First wireless telegraph experiments: Conducted by Guglielmo Marconi at Atlantic Highland's "Twin Lights," 1895–99.

First indoor helicopter flight: In November 1970, the first indoor helicopter flight took place in Atlantic City's old Convention Hall. The ceiling is 137 feet above the floor. It was a very short flight.

Most visits by U.S. presidents: Long Branch—Ulysses S. Grant, Rutherford B. Hayes, James A. Garfield, Chester A. Arthur, Benjamin Harrison, William McKinley, and Woodrow Wilson; Cape May: Franklin Pierce, Abraham Lincoln (but before he was president), Ulysses S. Grant, Benjamin Harrison.

First female lifeguards on the U.S. East Coast: Wildwood, 1933 (Atlantic City waited until 1975).

First Easter parade at the shore: Atlantic City's Boardwalk, April 16, 1876.

First Ferris wheel: Built of wood in Atlantic City by William Somers in 1891.

First municipal airport in the United States: Atlantic City's Bader Field in 1919. Also, first usage of the term *airport* to designate a permanent landing field for aircraft.

First ship-to-shore telephone call: From Atlantic City to a ship at sea, December 8, 1929.

First organized crime bosses' conference: May 14, 1929, at Atlantic City. Attendees included Al Capone, Louis "Lepke" Buchalter, "Dutch" Schultz, Frank Castello, Meyer Lansky, and "Lucky" Luciano.

Oldest fishing port on the East Coast: Belford, with more than two centuries of fishing.

An Empire of Sand

Geography rules. It is neither by accident nor luck that New Jersey's ocean shoreline has become one of the most intensively developed, densely populated (in season), virtually continuous strips of resorts in the world. The Jersey shore has few rivals, in nature or in culture.

Three sets of facts must be considered, evaluated, and appreciated in their geographic relationships. The New Jersey seashore is an economic phenomenon, as well as a cultural icon and a social phenomenon. The linear resort complex we know as the Jersey shore is a product of supply, demand, and technology.

First let's look at the geography of supply. Beaches are a fun environment, at least the sandy beaches that slope gently into an apparently tame and gentle sea, which seem made for recreation in many forms. Technically, beaches are those areas along a coastline where an accumulation of

Best of the Jersey Shore

Widest beaches:	The Wildwoods
Tallest lighthouse:	Barnegat Light
Tallest sand dunes:	Avalon
Best amusements:	North Shore: Seaside Heights South Shore: Wildwood
Most spectacular skyline:	Atlantic City
Best preservation of townscape:	Ocean Grove and Cape May
Most picturesque lighthouse:	Sandy Hook
Greatest beach restoration effort:	Sea Bright
Most user-friendly museum:	Atlantic City Museum and Arts Center, Garden Pier, with free admission and free parking
Oldest, still-functioning hotel:	Chalfonte, Cape May
Best use of state taxpayer money:	Island Beach State Park
Best use of federal taxpayer money:	Sandy Hook; Brigantine Wildlife Refuge
Most handicapped friendly:	Island Beach, with its "dune buggy" wheelchairs
Most successful revitalization:	Atlantic City
Most interesting shopping areas:	Schooners Landing/Bay Village, Beach Haven; Washington Street Mall, Cape May; Park Place (formerly Ocean One), Atlantic City; Historic Smithville, Smithville
Greatest potential for redevelopment:	Asbury Park
Most heartwarming places:	Popcorn Park Zoo, Forked River; Marine Mammal Stranding Center, Brigantine
Best outdoor museums:	Tuckerton Seaport; Cold Spring Village
Best fine-arts museum:	Noyes Museum, Oceanville
Best environmental education center:	Wetlands Institute, Stone Harbor
Most historic site, modern technology division:	Marconi's "wireless telegraph," Twin Lights Museum, Highlands
Most historic site, popular music division:	The Stone Pony, Asbury Park

Best aquariums:	Jenkinson's, Point Pleasant Beach; Ocean Life Center, Gardner's Basin, Atlantic City
Best nearby attraction:	Batsto Village
Most haunted place:	The Spy House, Port Monmouth
Best neon landscape:	Wildwood
Best walk-through tin elephant:	Lucy, Margate
Special award for free beaches:	Atlantic City; Wildwood

sediment is in motion. Geologists and physical geographers often describe beaches as though they were alive—they are created, they grow, they erode away and sometimes disappear. Very little about beaches, if anything, remains constant for long. Living on beaches requires facing this sometimes unpleasant reality.

Beaches are not always made of sand, but most popular and desirable beaches are. Other than sand, beaches can be made of pebbles, small stones, larger rocks called cobble, or some combination of these materials. The characteristic in common for all beach materials is that they are made of fragments of a larger whole. New Jersey's beaches are mostly grains of quartz, tiny pieces of the continent. Farther south, in Florida, the beach materials are mostly fragments of dead animals, the skeletons of millions of once-living coral animals.

Beach coastlines made up of sediments—eroded, transported, and deposited chunks of tough materials—are called depositional coastlines. Erosional coastlines, like those along much of New England and the U.S. West Coast, feature steep cliffs, sea caves, sea arches, and sea stacks—isolated columns of resistant rock surrounded by the surging sea.

Because people see sandy beaches as user-friendly environments, great for many forms and styles of leisure and recreation, it's a piece of good luck that sand beaches and barrier beaches—the long, skinny islands typical of the central and southern parts of the Jersey shore—are the rule on America's Atlantic and Gulf coasts. Sandy beaches stretch from Long Island, New York, to the Mexican border with Texas. Such a long stretch of sand beaches is unusual in the world; barrier islands and beaches occupy only about 10 percent of the world's coastlines.

So, the physical geography of coasts has provided an unusually long line of highly desirable sand beaches—thirty-one hundred miles' worth—along the U.S. East Coast and the Gulf coast. This is the geography of supply.

Now let's look at the geography of demand—the geography of people who do not live at the beach year-round, but want to visit the beach and can match this desire with both time and money; people who have the time for leisure and recreation and enough income to spend some money to get there and stay awhile without busting the budget.

Desire to go to the beach doesn't put you there; desire must be accompanied by both time and money. What provides both time and money above that required to provide necessities? A good job, if not a rich parent. The industrial revolution eventually provided the leisure time and the greater buying power required to translate desire into action. It also provided the advanced transport technology necessary to connect—cheaply and quickly—the demand with the supply.

The geography of supply in New Jersey is a long, slightly bowed, but fairly straight line of beaches extending from Sandy Hook southward to Cape May. The geography of local demand is not just one city, but a string of them. This geographic phenomenon was christened "Megalopolis" in a 1961 book by geographer Jean Gottmann. Megalopolis, which means "super city" in Greek, is a term that has entered common usage; you don't have to be a professional geographer to realize that it refers to a huge, sprawling, interconnected metropolitan area.

In his landmark study, Gottmann pointed out that something very interesting was happening on the northeastern seaboard, from the southern New Hampshire suburbs of Boston to the Virginia suburbs of Washington, D.C.; that this had not happened ever before, anywhere; and that it certainly was going to happen again and again, elsewhere. And what was this impressive

Already a prospering city in 1844, Newark was typical of the growing urban need for recreational opportunities.

The rapid expansion of industrial cities like Newark by the early 1900s led to nearby resort growth as well.

new phenomenon? It was a gigantic chain of cities—small, medium, large, and very large—that were growing toward one another. This interconnecting growth was forming a complex region of cities, suburbs, and open space stretching over five hundred miles and containing, at the time, 20 percent of the nation's people—on average the richest 20 percent.

Interconnection is the key observation in comprehending Megalopolis. As Gottmann pointed out, a great city expanding outward in every possible direction is not news. Great cities have been doing that since the days of the ancient Roman and Chinese empires. What *was* news was that a *series* of already large and medium-size metropolitan areas—Boston, Hartford, New York, Newark, Jersey City, Trenton, Philadelphia, Wilmington, Baltimore, Washington, D.C.—appeared to be merging, not in an official or political sense, but in an economic and land use sense.

Cities tend to grow by expanding outward at their edges. This process looks like the spreading, ringlike patterns caused by tossing a rock into a lake. The newest growth rings are on the outer edge, with older areas in toward the center, much like the growth rings of trees.

These urban growth rings are not as neat as those of trees. Maps showing built-up areas, as opposed to open land in farms or forest, often portray a starlike pattern rather than a circle. There are good reasons for the irregular growth edge. Housing developments, shopping centers, apartment complexes, and industrial parks all prefer locations near high-speed highways. These highways pull such urban land use farther out from the center along their routes, leaving less-accessible land open, at least for a while.

Why do suburban locations have greater appeal, for most purposes, than central locations? Money, convenience, and quality of life are the answers. Suburban land usually is cheaper than city land. Suburban land usually requires less preparation for construction than urban land, which commonly requires expensive acquisition and demolition of old structures before building can begin. Real estate taxes in the suburbs almost always are cheaper—much cheaper—than big-city real estate taxes. The convenience factor can be summed up in one word: parking. There also are biological advantages of suburbs over cities—basically less pollution, a result of less concentration. The key to the success of a suburb in attracting residents and businesses is in achieving a balance between accessibility to a nearby city for economic advantages and sufficient distance from that city to enjoy the suburban lower costs and environmental amenities. In other words, ideally, suburbs should be close, but not too close.

Megalopolis is about suburban growth around big cities, but suburban growth that is *channeled.* Suburban growth at the edge of one metropolis is pulled farther from the center in the direction of another big city. After all, accessibility to metropolitan markets and metropolitan labor forces is doubled by locating between, let's say, Philadelphia and New York, or between Baltimore and Washington, D.C. This "growth corridor" linking the major centers of the Megalopolis is served by excellent (if overcrowded) highways as well as railroads, another superior advantage in location.

The northeastern Megalopolis has been redefined over the years to stretch from Portland, Maine, to Richmond and Norfolk, Virginia. Currently, this enormous urban-suburban region contains about 16 percent of all Americans. It includes the nation's political capital, Washington, D.C., and its economic capital, New York City. Megalopolis has a northeast-southwest orientation, roughly paralleling the seacoast, but not all of its great cities are located directly on the open ocean. True, Boston, New York, Jersey City, and Newark are saltwater ports, but Philadelphia (America's largest freshwater port), Baltimore, Washington, and Richmond lie about fifty to seventy miles from the actual seacoast. So some Megalopolitan centers, like New York City, have their own beaches on the Atlantic, but many do not.

The backbone of Megalopolis is Interstate 95 and U.S. Route 1, the earlier "Main Street" of this region. A much smaller version of Megalopolis, running down the New Jersey shore, has developed. Just like the original Megalopolis, this is a long, linear, urban region, this time a chain of small cities and towns, occupying every inch of seacoast not within state or fed-

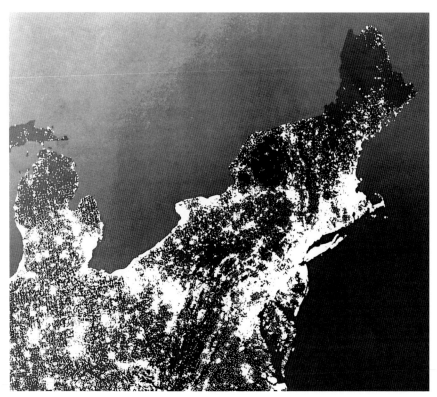

A negative of a census map shows population distribution in the Northeast similar to the way that bright lights outline cities and suburbs at nighttime.

eral control and reserved as public open space or wildlife refuge. Its spine is the Garden State Parkway and, before that, old Route 9. While Megalopolis is composed of great industrial centers, seaports, and administrative nerve centers, the smaller version of interconnected urban centers is built of resorts. While Megalopolis works hard at industry, commerce, and government, the pint-size version along the seacoast of New Jersey makes a living more focused on tourism and recreation.

What could we call this "fun in the sun" offspring of Megalopolis that we can see along the Jersey shore? Oceanopolis? Beachopolis? Leisureopolis? Maybe we shouldn't worry about a name yet. The important thing is recognizing that it's there—a kind of small-scale "shadow Megalopolis" that is on the supply side of recreational space to Megalopolis's market demand for such.

Megalopolis is where millions work up a sweat at work; "Leisureopolis" is where they cool off and work on their tans. Only one thing had to happen before Leisureopolis arose to fulfill the vacation and leisure time requirements of the nearby earlier-established Megalopolis, and that was

〰〰〰〰〰〰〰〰〰〰〰〰〰〰〰〰〰

Profits from Sun, Sand, and Surf

In proportion to their states' permanent populations, in which state does tourism make the largest contribution to the state's economy: Florida, California, Texas, or New Jersey? All those answering "New Jersey" can take a bow. Per capita, tourism brings in more money in New Jersey than in such popular resort and vacation states as Florida or California. Not all of New Jersey's tourist dollars are earned along its seashore; the Garden State also has mountain resorts, including ski resorts, but the seashore clearly is the main attraction. Speaking of Garden State, New Jersey agricultural products add up to only 3 percent of tourist revenues, which in turn are half as important in the state's economy as manufacturing. How does New Jersey's tourist industry compete with Florida or California in local importance? It helps that the miles of beautiful sandy beaches in New Jersey are only a short distance from some of America's largest metropolitan centers.

The major trend that will favor the New Jersey seashore over other vacation destinations is that shorter, more frequent vacations are becoming common. In the United States, the average vacation trip averages under five nights' duration, and fully half of all vacation trips are limited to weekends. The Jersey shore is highly accessible in terms of weekend getaways; it is within a day's drive of almost all of the residents of the northeastern seaboard Megalopolis.

providing the necessary connections—the transport links between the Megalopolis market for fun and the roughly paralleling ribbon of recreational resorts of the Jersey shore.

The Resort Cycle

Most resort towns along the Jersey shore can trace their history as a community back to the great railroad-building era of the 1870s and 1880s. If the beach was their mother, the railroads served as fathers. And so the majority of Jersey resorts now are about 120 to around 135 years old. A few, such as Cape May and Long Branch, are much older, and there are towns that were mostly empty lots until seventy or eighty years ago, but the majority are well into their second century of life.

Much like people, some relatively old resorts, Cape May in particular, have aged well. They still look good, despite their advanced age. Other towns look decrepit, worn-out, and beaten down by the years, even if the

The 1870s were a time of rapid resort growth. Bathhouses, such as this one at Ocean Grove, 1878, sprang up along the Jersey coast.

Ocean Grove has aged gracefully through careful preservation of its Victorian cityscape.

actual years don't add up to advanced age. Like a once-great athlete who has stopped training and gotten into bad habits, drugs, and alcohol, some towns appear to have sagged into premature old age. Neighboring towns, founded at about the same time, like Asbury Park and Ocean Grove, have aged very differently. If an urban community can look senile, in poor condition and much neglected, much of Asbury Park unfortunately appears to fit the description. Next door, Ocean Grove's Victorian buildings are, in contrast, well maintained and still attractive, like an aging but well-preserved movie star.

These comparisons of people and resort towns are interesting and suggestive. People and towns have much in common. People are born; resorts are created. People grow up from infancy and get bigger and stronger; resorts also grow from birth into maturity. People appear to age at different rates, with variable success at keeping their looks, their appeal, and their ability to control their immediate environments; so do resort communities. People follow a predictable sequence of stages in life—infancy, childhood, adolescence, maturity, and late maturity or old age. Resort towns seem to follow a life cycle of sorts also. They are born, they grow up, they gradually age into adulthood and eventual old age. Can they die? If towns "die," can they be reborn? It is common for people to discuss the "death" and "resurrection" of neighborhoods or even entire cities. Such terms certainly were applied to Atlantic City, before and after casinos.

Asbury Park, N.J., Arcade and Beach.

Entering its golden age, Asbury Park was a thriving resort with new facilities in 1906.

Asbury Park at the end of decades of urban decay.

Applying the life cycle concept to resorts could help in understanding the growth, expansion, maturation, and possible eventual death (or at least widespread decay) of resort towns.

In infancy, resort towns, like people, are full of potential, but they score low on achievement. Mostly empty lots, they require some imagination to foretell their future appearance. In childhood, a period of rapid growth occurs. Just as humans repeatedly double their weight during their first year, new construction rules a resort's first decades. In adolescence, resort towns begin to foreshadow their mature characteristics. Adolescence is a yeasty time, for both people and resorts. For resorts, it is a period of expanding visitor service facilities—new and better roads, new and better public transportation, new and better hotels, motels, restaurants, entertainment complexes—just new and better and bigger everything. And *new* is a magic word for Americans. Advertisements for just about any product or service always use large, bold type for "new" and "improved." The resort in adolescence is approaching the high point in its reputation; it has successfully appealed to its market.

In maturity, it appears that all is well, even if it isn't quite. In earlier stages of the resort life cycle, there were strong incentives for reinvestment and new investment, of both public and private funds. Local governments were paving new streets, building new water and sewer systems, erecting new schools, fire stations, libraries, and city halls. Private businesspeople were modernizing and expanding their hotels, restaurants, and entertainment facilities—all of which were in the latest fashion and technologically up-to-date. But in maturity, there is a tendency to cut back on continuous modernization and reinvestment of profits in favor of sitting back and enjoying the profits, consuming rather than reinvesting. Business "cash cows" are being milked as much as before, but they are not being fed and cared for as well as they had been. And the "cows" are approaching retirement and replacement.

Somehow, the customers notice, before the owners and managers see it, that the paint is fading and the carpets are threadbare. The style, not just the physical condition of facilities, is becoming obsolete. What thrilled your grandparents now is boringly old-fashioned to your eyes.

Most likely, private enterprises no longer are owned and operated by local entrepreneurs, people who had a personal commitment to the town and a local reputation to uphold. Large, distant corporations will have succeeded local ownership and may not care about much beyond the "bottom line" of this year's profits. The rich and famous move on to newer, more glamorous resorts. Their patronage is replaced by the less rich and not-so-famous. In this period of decline, the short-term view nudges aside the longer-range view. Resorts can't afford to live in the past and neglect the present. If both public and private facilities are neglected and not kept in first-class condition, the resort may enter a downward spiral in reputation, prestige, and income.

A view of the parlors of the Arlington at Ocean Grove depicting the genteel comfort demanded by the rising middle class in the nineteenth century.

Making Money by the Sea

Making money—by operating businesses, providing visitor services, and renting hotels, motels, and other property—has always been what the seashore is all about. To the American Indians, however, going to the shore meant making money in the most literal sense. Among their motives for seasonal trips to the shore was the opportunity to make wampum—the closest thing they had to cash. The Algonquin tribes, including New Jersey's Lenape, used wampum beads, strung on skin or sinew, to pledge treaties or agreements and as a medium of exchange. White beads were made from conchs or whelks, and the more valuable purple beads came from the insides of clamshells. The painstaking cutting, polishing, and drilling of tiny holes through each bead involved a lot of time and labor. This limited supply and enhanced value. Strings of wampum were assembled into breast plates that covered the chest or, more commonly, into wide belts worn as jewelry. The tedious labor involved made the American Indians really appreciate a wampum belt.

Increasing competition within the tourism industry and among resorts produces a cycle of ever-growing investment requirements. New standards are established in the increasing scale and sophistication of tourist facilities and attractions. Hotels, restaurants, and entertainments become ever more lavish. Competing businesses, resort towns, and even entire resort regions are challenged to either match or top the competition, to stay competitive or drop out of the race and accept a permanently second-rate, obsolete status thereafter. Such "can you top this" leaps in investment requirements are illustrated dramatically in the history of the casino resort industry in Las Vegas, but the basic lesson of Las Vegas's experience is one that all resorts, not just legalized gaming resorts, must learn from.

The Dreadnought Concept

Gaming industry expert Eugene Martin Christiansen (as quoted in Charles Stansfield's "From East Coast Monopoly to Destination Resort") calls dramatic advances in scale of investment, degree of sophistication, and level of lavish accommodations and sheer spectacle—clear challenges to the competition—"dreadnoughts." A little history is in order here; be patient.

Before World War I, there was a determined and expensive naval power race among all of the great military powers. France, Japan, Italy, Russia, and the United States all participated, but the major contenders were Britain and

The Buildings of Your Dreams

The point of traveling on vacation is to get away from it all. "It all" includes your job, your home, and your daily routines. People want different experiences while on vacation, even when their budget requires but a brief escape from their everyday world.

As a result, the design of successful resort attractions often features fantasy architecture—buildings that look really different. Outrageous shapes, exotic themes, and vibrant colors help assure visitors that, yes, they are not in Kansas anymore. Or Staten Island, or Trenton.

Eye-catching buildings are intended to stand out from their background. There is a long tradition of such buildings in resort environments. In the early 1800s, the English resort of Brighton was made famous when the future

The Royal Pavilion, an early 1800s palace in Brighton, England, is a good example of fantasy architecture at a resort.

Germany. The British Navy was determined to remain number one in size and power. The Germans decided to challenge that position. The Germans would launch a battleship; the British would launch two. The Germans would build two more; the British would build four. Finally, the British response was to design an entirely new class of battleship. "Dreadnought," rather antique language for "fear nothing," was the first of this new type of battleship. Dreadnought outclassed every other battleship afloat—it was bigger, faster, better armored, and had more powerful guns. The day it was launched, it made every other battleship hopelessly obsolete, an expensive heap of scrap iron. Dreadnought changed all the rules, set new standards, and issued a challenge—match it or surrender quietly now.

A "dreadnought" has become a metaphor for any similar level of challenge in a competitive environment—something so far superior that, at least for a time, it is the unquestioned leader and dominates the field. Incidentally, the Germans did respond by building their own versions of the dreadnought, and then upped the ante by building a super-dreadnought. Even dreadnoughts don't reign supreme for long, either in naval power or in any other context. Were you taking notes? Good. Now back to the tourism business.

Taj Mahal Casino in Atlantic City continues the tradition of exotic architecture.

King George IV chose the seaside town as his "getaway" vacation residence. He acquired a modest classical mansion (think Monticello on the back of nickels). This graceful mansion was remade into a fantasy of Asian architecture, complete with onion-shaped domes topped by Islamic minarets. It was not just a coincidence that Britain was then in the midst of conquering a vast empire in India, and things Oriental were much in fashion. Notice that, in the photos, this half-Indian, half-Chinese palace could be considered a direct ancestor of Atlantic City's Taj Mahal, although this was not deliberate.

Maybe the most memorable fantasy building is the Margate elephant, nicknamed "Lucy" (see page 190). This sixty-five-foot-tall elephant was built in 1881 as an attraction for a real estate subdivision. Lucy was intended as a truly memorable landmark, and that she is.

The first dreadnought of the experience of Las Vegas's casino industry appeared in 1946. The casinos in the 1930s and early 1940s mostly had catered to locals and transients passing through, usually headed to or from Los Angeles. By modern standards, these downtown casinos were small, short on amenities, and undistinguished. Just the opportunity to gamble legally was enough of an attraction to bring in the customers; frills seemed unnecessary in a political and cultural environment in which Nevada had a nationwide monopoly on legal gambling. At the time, casinos offered gambling, period. While a few were fancier in decoration and had high minimum wagers to discourage small-time amateurs, most depended on a high volume of low-limit players looking for a little action. The high-volume day-tripper-oriented, nonluxurious gaming houses were known as "sawdust joints" as opposed to classier "carpet joints." But joints they were, carpeted or not, and most did have sawdust on bare floors.

And then the first casino dreadnought, Bugsy Siegel's Flamingo, opened its doors. The 1946 Flamingo first of all was on the highway to L.A., not in the traditional "Glitter Gulch" of downtown. Bugsy pioneered the now-famous "Strip" with plenty of free parking. The Flamingo literally was a "carpet joint"—a beautiful carpet, too, and dealers wore tuxedos. As part of its high-class image, the Flamingo forbade patrons to wear hats at the tables—a move that angered old-timers in town. Everything was first-class, including the top-name entertainment. The ostentatious Flamingo seems to have pioneered the freestanding, immense, gaudy electric signs that towered higher than the buildings they advertised. One of Bugsy's major contributions to American popular culture was twin, eight-story-tall, neon cocktail glasses with mammoth neon bubbles appearing to rise up to burst above the rims. Talk about class! The Flamingo was an instant success, a model for all to follow. A dreadnought had been launched.

Twenty years afterward, Caesars Palace introduced a new level of opulence. This innovative blend of fantasy theme park and casino once again challenged the competition by greatly escalating the scale and cost of casino resorts.

The latest super-dreadnoughts on the scene are the so-called megaresorts, launched in 1989 when the $630 million Mirage opened in Las Vegas. A fake volcano "erupted" on schedule, accompanied by special-effects imitation earthquakes; live sharks cruised in huge tanks in the lobby. This fantasy blend of Hollywood special effects, "family" entertainment, circus, shopping mall, and Disney-quality theme park was the first of a series of megaresorts, which have shaped a spectacular new skyline for Las Vegas.

The reason for this new, gigantic leap in scale of investment? Nevada's monopoly on legalized gaming in the United States, first broken by Atlantic City in 1978, is now but a fading memory. Legal casinos seem to be popping up everywhere, like weeds on suburban lawns after a soaking rain. Casinos on midwestern riverboats, casinos on Indian reservations—casinos, it seems soon, on everyone's doorstep, or at least in day-trip distance from a lot of doorsteps.

Now that the availability of legal gaming in itself is no longer a unique attraction, casinos must offer much more than just gaming in order to remain destination resorts—that is, to pull in tourists over long distances. It worked for Las Vegas to offer the megaresort experience, and it will work for Atlantic City too.

How to Read the Boardwalk

Not every Jersey shore town has a boardwalk, although most do. Those few communities where there are no public beaches are exceptions. When private homes front directly on the beach, mostly in North and Central Shore communities, there are no boardwalks. "Boardwalk" has become a generic term for a seafront promenade, even where it is not actually built with boards. In most cases, though, visitors understand and anticipate that the boardwalk will be more than just a pedestrian convenience, a kind of broad, slightly elevated sidewalk along the seafront. Most boardwalks are more than just a place for people to stroll along the beach without getting sand in their shoes, though that was pretty much the reason for the very first boardwalk.

In a very few cases, like Sea Bright, there is no continuous seafront promenade simply because there is no room for it. Along some sections of the Jersey shore, beach erosion has been so severe that the parallel zones of the sea-to-land sequence consist of ocean, seawall, seafront road, and then structures (houses, condos, or motels), rather than the much more characteristic New Jersey sequence of ocean, beach, boardwalk, structures, road, then more structures. There are two variations on the typical sequence. The Cape May model is ocean, beach, boardwalk (including piers or structures built on pilings on the ocean side), oceanfront drive, then a paralleling row of hotels, motels, retail businesses, and houses. The Atlantic City model, in contrast, is ocean, beach, boardwalk with oceanside piers, a strip of retail businesses and entertainments along the landward side of the boardwalk, backed by hotels, motels, condos, and so forth, without any paralleling roadway immediately behind the boardwalk.

Learning to "read" the boardwalk will tell tourists just what kind of resort they're visiting. The character of the town is summarized graphically in the character of seafront development. If there simply is no public seafront—neither boardwalk nor drive—due to private ownership and control of beach and ocean access, that certainly is revealing about the community's social and economic character.

Where the boardwalk is sandwiched between the beach and oceanfront drive, the resort almost certainly dates to the prerailroad era. Vacationers in those early days were rich enough to arrive in their own carriages, or at

This view of Sea Grove, circa 1878, now Cape May Point, shows the great hotels and splendid cottages of the wealthy, typical of new resorts. Notice the boardwalk between the beach and the road.

least to rent such private transportation in order to enjoy seafront drives. Atlantic City broke that mold, as in that resort's first fifteen years, the rail bridge was the only bridge across the bays, channels, and marshes separating Absecon Island from the mainland. The Atlantic City model prevailed in most of the other resorts created by railroads.

Because boardwalks attract crowds of people with both money and wants and desires, most boardwalks are seen by entrepreneurs as good business locations. Boardwalks, especially those in larger resorts catering to a high percentage of day-trippers, have become business districts. The makeup of these very specialized business districts provides a clear picture of the kind of people who make up the bulk of the resort's clientele. The pedestrians-only nature of these commercialized boardwalks both echoed the marketplaces of long ago and anticipated the suburban malls.

First of all, boardwalk business districts are not merely suburban malls in a unique setting. Neither are they like the traditional downtowns that regional malls have largely replaced. No one goes to the boardwalk to shop for car batteries, light bulbs, computer printers, or frozen turkeys. There are items and services that we really need—things like spaghetti sauce, toothpaste, or a set of screwdrivers. We know where to go to shop for these, and it's never a boardwalk. With the exception of meals, snacks, and beverages, we don't really *need* the things we buy on the boardwalk. We want them, but we don't need them. So boardwalk varieties of businesses emphasize two sets of retailers and services. Food services—restaurants,

VIEW OF BOARD WALK AND BEACH, ATLANTIC CITY, N. J. 7/7/06

G-6 ILLUSTRATED POST CARD CO., N. Y.

The Boardwalk at Atlantic City in 1906.

The boardwalk at Ocean City, 1960.

pizza parlors, snack bars, candy stores, and drinks (seldom alcoholic)—are available on the boardwalk because people spend a lot of time there and on the adjacent beach, and they'll patronize food and drink establishments that are handy rather than walk for blocks inland or get their cars out of the parking lot.

But notice the other retailers and services that pay the high seasonal rentals along the boards: No hardware stores, no auto parts, no appliance stores. No insurance offices, dentists' offices, or used-car lots, either. What people will spend money on along the boardwalk, other than to satisfy their stomachs, lies firmly in the category of, as economists say, discretionary spending. This spending is on things or services that we don't absolutely need, at least at the moment.

The boardwalks' nonfood-service establishments usually offer an array of souvenirs, beach gear—chairs, umbrellas, and towels—bathing suits, toys, and T-shirts, and a variety of other leisure clothing alongside amusements and entertainments. The customers are almost 100 percent vacationers rather than year-round residents. Most of the merchandise available on the boardwalk is bought on impulse. Shopping on the boards is just another leisure pastime—it is shopping for fun rather than shopping to acquire necessities. Boardwalks are recreational service business districts, in effect.

The contents, qualities, styles, and prices of souvenir stands and leisure clothing stores on the various boardwalks will reveal more about the economic and social status of vacationers than would reams of sociological data. Just for fun someday, browse those types of stores on your favorite boardwalk and come up with a rough guesstimate of the average price of the goods.

2

Nature and Us at the Shore

Purely natural environments, untouched by people, are not common these days. The Jersey shore is no exception. The traces of human activity, of human decisions about managing the environment, seem to be everywhere, like the sticky fingerprints of active children. Sometimes these "fingerprints" are all too obvious to even the most casual observer, as in a big-city environment. Other times and places, the impact of people is difficult to even imagine, as in wildlife preserves or the great parks along the shore. But it is there.

All of the natural physical and biological forces, excepting people, which shape and reshape the physical world can be grouped as *nature*. *Culture* is the term that includes all the past and present effects of people, individually and collectively. The influences and effects of people can range from almost too little to observe to massive reshaping of the natural world. People's degree of impact on nature is a product of three key factors: attitude, numbers, and tools.

Attitude sums up a human society's view of the relationships between people and nature—both the relationships that exist and those that should exist, ideally. It would be fair to say that for most Americans, the attitude is aggressive, active, and ideally, responsible.

An aerial view of Stone Harbor showing the elimination of some beach dunes and the eradication of the bayshore marshes by dredge and fill.

The Bible clearly directs people to "be fruitful and multiply, and replenish the earth and subdue it" (Genesis 1:28). Now, we've gotten the "multiply" part down all right—just look at Labor Day crowds on any New Jersey beach. Multiplying our numbers is something we've done well. Notice the Bible's use of that active verb, to subdue. Even those who seldom open a Bible would agree that our mission on the planet, as members of the human race, has been to tame nature. The underlying idea is that nature can be hostile and dangerous, that people must work to subdue it. To subdue is to dominate and control. So, as a group, we've been control freaks when it comes to nature. It's just part of who we are that we see our relationship with nature as a contest, a contest we must win.

It is very American, patriotic almost, to take pride in rearranging nature to suit ourselves, such as at the Jersey shore. Take a close look at a dollar bill, a classic American symbol. The reverse side of the bill shows the Great Seal of the United States, and that seal bears two mottoes in Latin. *Novus ordo seclorum* ("A new order of the ages") refers to the new political system created by the American Revolution and the Constitution. In the ecological sense, though, a different kind of new order was deliberately imposed on the land and upon its ecosystems. Gone forever was the very light impact on the land made by the American Indian's Stone Age hunting, gathering, and agricultural society. This land was our land—to claim politically, use more intensively and productively, and reshape with our more powerful tools. The other Latin motto, *Annuit Coeptis,* is translated as "He [referring to the Divine Creator] has smiled on [or favors] our undertaking." In other words, we are going to change things, and God wants us to, so there!

Numbers are important here. There are a lot of us people on the planet in general, and specifically at the Jersey shore (remember how enthusiastically we've learned to multiply). Simply, more people per square mile equals more potential energy and capability for reshaping nature.

The tools available in subduing nature are very important too. One person driving a bulldozer makes a bigger impression than one person wielding a clamshell.

In regard to subduing nature, we Americans have it all—strong, long-established traditions of motive, relatively large numbers of people in one place, and excellent tools and engineering talents. We're quite prepared to shove Mother Nature around, for better or for worse.

Qualities of two aspects of the natural environment are especially important to us at the seashore: landforms (beaches) and climate (mild sea breezes). Of the two, people have made a determined effort to control and influence local landforms, by building or at least retaining beaches. We've consciously set out to manipulate landforms; we may find out that we've accidentally influenced climate as well, in the form of global warming. We need to take a quick look at the landforms and climate characteristics of the New Jersey seashore in order to appreciate both their meaning to us and our impact on nature.

Shifting Sands

The key to understanding beach erosion, erosion control, beach "replenishment" or restoration efforts, and both short- and long-term physical changes in New Jersey's beaches is to remember one fact: This is a mobile shoreline. Unhindered by human efforts at stabilizing and fixing in place the wandering sands, nature would constantly and smoothly reshuffle the material, shape, and location of beaches like a pack of playing cards in the hands of a professional blackjack dealer. Just between 1820 and 1920, it is estimated that New Jersey lost 5,521 acres of beach to the ocean. It was happening before 1820, and certainly, it has continued since 1920.

As Karl F. Nordstrom et al., a group of expert scientists, observed in *Living with the New Jersey Shore,* "A beach is a place where sand stops to rest for a moment before resuming its journey to somewhere else. That 'somewhere else' can be north or south to an inlet, offshore during a mild storm, or up the beach, over the dunes, through houses, and into the street during serious storms. In New Jersey, beaches have been moving since they first were formed, despite the best efforts of those who would have them stay in one place."

"Those who would have [the beaches] stay in one place" include, foremost, property owners along the shore. Imagine paying at least in the high six figures or low seven figures for a beachfront or even beach block

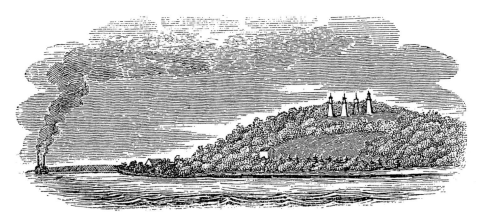

Highlands of the Navesink, the highest elevation along the shoreline, has long been the site of lighthouses and, in this 1844 print, a telegraph station.

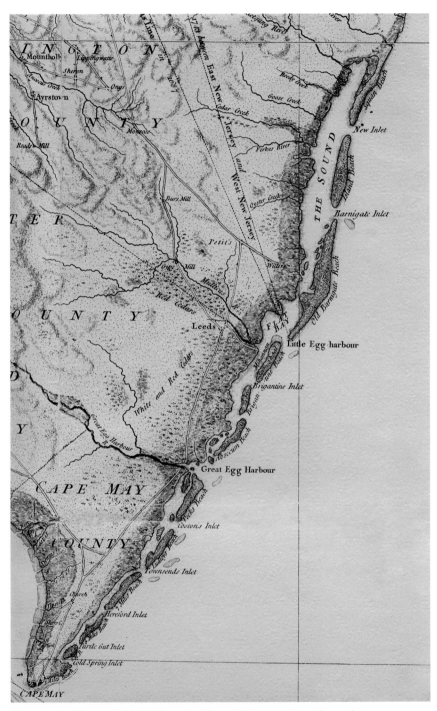

A comparison between this 1777 map and a contemporary map shows that, among other changes, Turtle Gut, Brigantine, and New Inlets have filled in.

lot, and then erecting a house or condo on it for a further quarter to a half million or so. Getting the poststorm news that your house is gone with the wind and your lot is now part of an inlet would be bad news indeed.

Wind, Waves, and Currents

New Jersey's beaches, like those everywhere, are shaped and reshaped by the natural forces of wind, waves, and currents. These forces of nature are connected with one another. Wind causes waves. The only ocean waves *not* produced by winds are rare events caused by underwater earthquakes. Such earthquake waves, or tsunamis, are much more common in the Pacific than in the Atlantic. Ocean currents reflect and affect the angle at which waves strike the shore; they also affect the movement of sand along the shore. Waves transport sand up, down, and along the beach. In addition to winds, the temperature and saltiness of seawater are both causes and effects of ocean currents, which are also affected by the contours of the seafloor and the shape of the coastline.

It may all sound complicated, but the important thing to remember is simply that all the forces of nature concerned, and all the products of these forces, are connected. Each influences the others in some way. Each responds to any new developments in these natural agents of change. Usually, winds, waves, and currents, nature's engineers, mesh gears rather

The famous bluffs of Long Branch have been severely eroded over the years.

Lifeguards

Venturing into the surf always has been part of the fun at the seashore. Indeed, braving the breakers, a relatively safe brush with danger, produces a little thrill, like riding nature's own roller coaster. But the risk of drowning, however remote, is tragically real.

In the early years, no official lifeguards existed, at least if we don't count dogs. An 1845 visitor to Cape May noted that two huge Newfoundlands splashed into the surf whenever the alarm was raised, having been trained to retrieve people rather than ducks. There is no record of whether the dogs were on the town payroll.

After thirteen people drowned off Atlantic City's beaches in 1865, hotel proprietors and bathhouse owners in early resorts, all too aware of the dangers to their customers, chipped in to hire private lifeguards. In early Atlantic City, the Camden and Atlantic Railroad supported lifeguards, supplemented by public donations. Unofficial volunteers also patrolled the beaches, motivated by the custom of being well rewarded by grateful rescuees. According to Harold Wilson in *The Story of the Jersey Shore*, an 1869 newspaper story reported that one gentleman, safely dragged ashore by one such volunteer, gave only 50 cents to his rescuer. The insulted rescuer gave him back 49 cents in change, remarking that he never accepted more than the person's life was worth.

A rescue at Atlantic City, circa 1910.

Ocean City Beach Patrol, 1950. The same types of patrol booths and boats are used in Ocean City today.

Some hotel owners provided rescue ropes, cables strung from beach flagpoles and anchored beyond the breakers, with vertical ropes suspended from the cables every nine feet. This allowed the hotels to boast of safe bathing beaches for their clientele.

By the 1880s, many a resort had added lifeguards to the police payrolls. In 1892, Atlantic City's first separate beach patrol was organized. Most other resorts had official lifeguards by 1900. Wildwood hired the Jersey shore's first female lifeguards in 1933, but Atlantic City maintained an all-male patrol until 1975.

Echoing the Newfoundlands of early days, many beach patrols had dogs as mascots by the 1930s. Wildwood's lifeguards once even had an injured, flightless seagull as their mascot. Reportedly, Oscar thrived on his unofficial salary of tomato and lettuce sandwiches.

The beach patrol in North Wildwood today.

smoothly. They work together as they always have, moving sand continuously if usually gradually. Beaches, offshore sandbars, dunes, inlets to the back bays, salt marshes, all are built, shifted, destroyed, and rebuilt over time. Details of the coastline change seasonally as well as continually over the years. On your first visit of the season, you may think you are stepping onto exactly the same beach that you visited last Labor Day. But it isn't. For one thing, some of the sand is certain to be different than last year's, though it might look the same.

Waves are a form of energy transmission across the water's surface. How much energy is derived from wind, and how it affects wave characteristics, depends on the surface distance over which the wind blows, the wind speed, and the duration of that speed.

Ocean waves transmit energy across the water, but they do not transport huge volumes of water over great distances (although currents do). If great masses of water actually traveled across oceans as quickly as waves do, navigation would not be possible. Imagine that you could label just one little drop of water and watch its motions as a wave passes over it. You would observe that that drop, like all the water around it, simply bounces up and down in a generally circular motion. It would rise up as the crest of the wave passes over, then bounce down in a circular movement as the crest moves forward and the trough, or lowest part of the wave, follows behind the crest. As the crest of the next wave follows, the droplet completes the circle, rising upward again. All of the action is at, or at least near, the surface. Observe the distance between wave crests. Almost all the "action" or water movement takes place only one-half the wavelength down into the water. Far below the surface, a submarine could cruise steadily on, unaffected by even a hurricane on the surface.

You create a wave motion when you crack a whip, a rope, even a drapery cord. Take hold of one end of the rope or cord and give it a good shake. Your wrist action is up and down. The "wave" motion travels along the cord to the other end. No fiber or particle of the rope actually moves from one end to the other; rather, each segment moves up and down with the waveform as it passes along. The same thing happens with ocean waves.

The reason that waves coming in to shore "break" is that the water at the bottom of the circlelike vertical movement of a passing waveform

Most visitors to Atlantic City have experienced relatively flat beaches such as this one.

These beachfront townhouses at Hereford Inlet have no beach left, only a rock-and-concrete seawall.

begins to touch the seafloor. The crest of the wave begins to travel faster than the bottom, now dragging on the ever-shallower seafloor. As the crest rushes forward, it falls forward on its face like an ice skater whose blades just struck a patch of grit on the ice.

The breakers move sand up and down the slope of the beach. The forward surge of incoming water up the beach slope is called the "swash"; the drain of water back down the beach slope is the "backwash." There, now you know.

Alongshore Currents

Alongshore currents move sand along the coast. For New Jersey's coastline, this means that sand is carried either northward or southward. This also means that beaches tend to move either northward or southward.

By learning to "read" the beach, you can tell which way the sand is being moved by the alongshore current. That means you can predict which way the beach will "move"—that is, which end, north or south, will add more sand and extend its breadth, and which will lose sand and gradually disappear.

Stand with your back to the boardwalk or oceanfront drive, looking out to sea. Watch the crests of waves as they come in to the beach. They might come marching in, line after line, parallel to the waterline. But most likely

The Saga of Tucker's Island

The story of Tucker's Island, or Tucker's Beach, is typical of New Jersey's changing shoreline. Waves and currents twice separated this island from Long Beach Island, twice rejoined it, and now have reduced the island to a submerged sandbar. Reuben Tucker, who once owned the whole island, opened his home in 1765 for the "health and entertainment" of visitors. His boardinghouse stayed in business until 1823. Tucker's Island, also known as Sea Haven or Short Beach, thrived as an early resort because a stagecoach once connected Philadelphia with Tuckerton, on the mainland behind Tucker's Island. A boat trip then completed the journey to Tucker's Beach, or Short Beach, which is now extremely short, being underwater. Tucker's Beach was a popular resort until 1900, when severe erosion forced its permanent inhabitants to retreat to the mainland. The local combination lighthouse and lifesaving service station, which rescued the survivors of some two hundred shipwrecks, was the last building to fall into the sea, in 1935. By 1955, the island was gone. Waves and currents willing, the island could arise again, evidence of this shifting shoreline.

A short-lived cliff in the sand that resulted from a winter storm at Ocean City in 1992.

The northward alongshore current at Deal traps sand on the south side of the groin.

these incoming crests, while nearly perfectly parallel to each other, are approaching land at an angle. The swash moves forward at less than, or more than, a right angle to the general waterline. But when the water drains back toward the ocean, it responds to gravity, moving downslope at a true right angle to the shoreline.

Imagine that you could identify one particle of sand and follow its movement as it is repeatedly picked up and dropped by waves. Picked up by the incoming swash, it will be carried up the beach, then carried downslope by the backwash. But if the sand is moved onto the beach in an area with a southward alongshore current, that particle of sand will be carried in, not from the east (on a north-south oriented coastline), but from the northeast. Moved again by the backwash, it will travel due east, then be picked up again by the swash out of the northeast, and so be moved not only westward (up the beach), but southward as well.

But you don't need to tag a sand grain and measure its travels to know if you're dealing with an alongshore current. Play in the breakers for an hour or so, ride incoming waves, get knocked off your feet, wade back in, encounter another breaker, and repeat the experience. It won't take an hour for you to become aware that, looking back to the beach, you have moved relative to your beach umbrella. If there is a northbound alongshore current, you will emerge from the ocean north of where you entered it, and vice versa.

The southward alongshore current of Cold Spring Inlet has deposited sand on the north side (Diamond Beach) of the twin jetties, but eroded the shore to the south side (Cape May).

An aerial view of New Jersey's southern tip at Cape May Point showing the effect of multiple groins along the shoreline.

There is another way to spot north or south alongshore currents without getting wet. On a beach that uses "groins," fairly short barriers of rocks, wood, or sandbags constructed into the water at right angles to the shoreline, you'll notice that sand builds up on one side of these groins, which were indeed designed to trap sand that otherwise would move along the coast. Sand accumulates on the upstream side of groins. If the alongshore current is southward, then sand is trapped on the north side of the groins.

A northward alongshore current will result in a sand buildup on the south side of groins.

Groins and jetties are not the same. Jetties are usually longer and commonly used in pairs to keep inlets and channels open for boats. Groins trap sand to build beaches. Seawalls parallel the shoreline, rather than run at right angles to it, and are meant to protect against further erosion.

As seen from the air, multiple groins produce a waterline that resembles a series of shark-fin-shaped beaches. It's like a "good news, bad news" joke. The good news is that sand is trapped on one side of each groin, but the bad news is that sand is eroded from the other (downstream) side. Groins interrupt what amounts to a natural conveyor belt of waves and currents carrying sand along the coastline. Groins are always bad news for downstream beaches, which then do not get replacement sand for the sand that is constantly being eroded away.

Northward of about Barnegat Inlet, the alongshore current is moving, and transporting sand, northward toward Sandy Hook and Raritan Bay. Southward of Barnegat Inlet, the alongshore current is moving southward toward Cape May and Delaware Bay.

Stabilizing the Unstable

The almost inevitable next step after groins, which ultimately fail to stabilize a wide beach, is to construct seawalls. These massive engineering efforts can be seen at some places scattered along the Jersey shore, from Sea Bright to Cape May, although they seem more common along the North Shore. Seawalls are rigid structures of rock and concrete; they create a "hard" shoreline in contrast to the soft shoreline of a natural beach. Seawalls, no matter how solidly (and expensively) built, will be pounded to pieces some day—it's just a matter of time. The force exerted by typical Atlantic Ocean waves averages more than two thousand pounds per square foot; the force during storms is even more powerful. When such enormous pressures hit solid objects, like seawalls, the resulting shock is huge. Water from incoming waves is forced into a crack or cavity, compressing air in those openings. When the wave falls back, the highly compressed air now expands explosively, enlarging the cracks and crevices, and slinging rock fragments into the oncoming waves. Now the powerful waves, carrying those sharp rock fragments, act like a power sander equipped with very coarse sandpaper.

In contrast, incoming wave energy is absorbed and dissipated by sand beaches. This is the principle of the punching bag. If the great power of a punch thrown by a professional boxer is received by a relatively rigid structure like a human skull, bad things can happen to the opponent's face. If the fist is not protected by a heavy glove, bad things happen to the hand, too. But when a boxer practices with a heavy, suspended sandbag, neither the bag nor the fist sustains significant damage. Punching bags, like sand beaches, absorb and spread out the shock. Unlike a rigid surface such as a seawall or a gypsum board drywall, they don't shatter under attack. Sand is, in effect, "preshattered." Most beach material along the Jersey shore is quartz sand. Quartz sand is very hard material that cannot be further disintegrated by forces like ocean waves. It survives and dominates beaches after weaker materials have disappeared under wave attack. Sand makes the ideal shock absorber.

Beach replenishment, building (or rebuilding) beaches by dumping new sand brought to the beach site from somewhere else, is an alternative or substitute to groins and seawalls. Beach replenishment sand usually comes from the back bays, navigation channels, or offshore submerged sandbars, or it is brought in from sandpits on the mainland. The type of sand, in grain size, is important. Sand pumped from the bottoms of bays or supplied from dredging navigation channels in bays and inlets often is fine-grained. This type of imported sand will wash off beaches quickly in storms. Also, dredging sand off the bottoms of bays affects ecosystems there. Moving sand from deposits on the ocean floor is seldom a permanent fix, either. If this sand once formed offshore submerged sandbars, then their function of helping to protect the shoreline from storm waves is lost. Dredging the ocean bottom also produces changes in currents that might speed up beach erosion. Beach replenishment, sometimes called beach nourishment, can

In areas of severe erosion, such as Sea Bright, high seawalls are needed to protect valuable real estate.

Beach replenishment projects can restore a wide beach, at least temporarily.

Beachfront houses have little defense against the next storm.

cost many millions of dollars per mile of beach, and it is not rare for replenished sand to disappear through erosion in one stormy night. Beach replenishment is not a one-time fix. Replenishment must be ongoing or repeated on some regular cycle.

So why do we bother to try so expensively to stabilize what in nature is mobile and temporary? Money. Beaches are the basic resource for the tourist industry along the seashore. Despite long-range, frustrating failures, why keep on going back and building more groins and seawalls and pumping more new sand? Experts Nordstrom et al. view the situation with a little cynicism: "The cause is a well-known coastal phenomenon that dictates that the person who builds a house closest to the water wins. These winners get to see the ocean firsthand; sometimes they even get to feel the ocean firsthand as it passes through the living room on its way out the back door. When this happens, the beachfront owners call for public assistance, and the county, state and federal governments trip over each other trying to save the day with emergency bulldozers, new sand and more rocks."

Beach Profiles

A cross section of a typical "barrier beach" (any long, narrow island of sand, a barrier between the open ocean and the continent) is shown on page 52. Though it is low, it isn't flat. Wind, one of nature's busiest construction engineers, will blow sand to form a ridge of dunes back from the high-tide line. This dune actually is nature's line of defense along the narrow islands,

The Big One

Just as San Franciscans, when discussing earthquakes, refer to the April 1906 quake as "the big one," New Jersey shore residents with long memories refer with suitable awe to the March 1962 storm as their "big one." This Ash Wednesday storm caused 14 deaths and about $100 million worth of damages to the Jersey shore. It was most unusual and memorable in that fearsomely destructive storms typically are late summer–early fall hurricanes. Hurricanes hit, or rather, sideswipe, New Jersey's shoreline an average of about once every eight years. The hurricanes of the years 1938, 1944, 1954, and 1960 were particularly destructive; among them they caused 750 deaths and upward of $500

million in damages along the entire northeastern coast. While the U.S. Gulf coast and South Atlantic coasts see far more hurricanes, those affecting the New Jersey coast move faster, and thus it is tougher to predict their future paths more than a day ahead.

Ruins of concrete pier supports at Atlantic City testify to the power of storm waves.

limiting or preventing storm waves from washing right over the island and into the lagoon or back bay. Sometimes there will be a second line of dunes paralleling the first, separated by a gentle, wavelike trough. Actually, the profile of sandy beaches changes seasonally, affected by complex dynamics of waves, winds, and currents that need not concern us in detail. The summer profile commonly includes a very low, temporary ridge of sand called a berm, which runs parallel to the waterline and is located just landward of the average high-tide line. In winter, the stronger, storm-driven waves coming into the beach eliminate the berm and build a shorter, steeper beach profile.

Most of the dunes that nature built along the Jersey shore no longer exist. The very high value of seashore land proved to be an irresistible temptation to people, who bulldozed most of the dunes flat. Leveling the dunes provided the raw material for making land, a former monopoly of nature. The width of the barrier beach islands varies from about four miles at Wildwood to less than a football field's length at many locations. The

After Long Beach Island was underwater in the March 1962 storm, new building regulations required stilt construction to reduce future flood damage.

The March 1962 storm was the result of high spring or new-moon tides being driven ashore by persistent gale-force winds ranging up to sixty miles an hour. Waves as high as twenty feet pounded ashore. Several islands were overwashed, meaning that ocean waves washed completely across the island into the back bay. Reconnaissance flights reported that all of Long Beach Island, from Barnegat Light to Beach Haven Inlet, was underwater for a few days. To the south, the comparatively small community of Sea Isle City alone lost 285 homes to the storm waves. On Long Beach Island today, over 80 percent of the structures date since the 1962 storm.

It is estimated that if another storm of that severity were to strike again, damages to property would be in the neighborhood of $1.5 billion. Inflation of real estate values and the fact that many more structures have been built since would make for an even more destructive "big one."

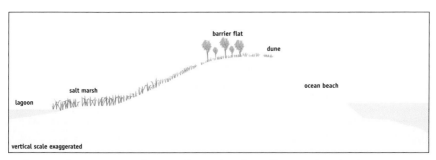

A diagram showing a typical natural barrier beach profile. Some beaches have a secondary line of dunes as well.

bayside edge of the island is (or was) fringed by salt marsh and very shallow water.

Truck sand from the dunes and dump it in the marsh along the bayshore. Result: additional acres of building lots, more money in local pockets, more tax revenues to local governments, and more happy vacationers. But also, no more natural line of defense against washovers in severe storms.

The storm-defense functions of dunes, now officially recognized and valued, have led to efforts to maintain existing dunes and re-create lost ones. Dunes are stabilized by plants growing on them. To prevent destruction of plants and the erosion that would follow, beachgoers are asked to cross the dunes only on plank walks (back to the original boardwalks!). Newly rebuilt dunes may be of bulldozed sand into which are embedded discarded Christmas trees, which help hold the dunes in place against wind erosion. Narrow slats of wood wired together vertically, with open spaces between the solid strips, long have been used as snow fences. These fences slow wind speed near the ground, causing snow to accumulate at the fence line rather than on a nearby road. The same principle is applied to help accumulate blowing sand along the dunes, with snow fences recycled as sand fences.

Tides

Tides are massive movements of the oceans produced by the gravitational effects of the moon and the sun in relation to the earth. Tides are a fact of life along every ocean shoreline. They seldom are of any real concern to visitors, unless those visitors are operating small craft in shallow channels of back bays, or in some other situation where rising and falling water levels could affect them. Tides cause, or are one of several causes, of some currents as water surges in or out of the inlets between barrier beaches, so small boat operators learn to pay close attention to their tide tables. Anyone relaxing on the beach becomes aware of tides as the sea level keeps changing. A place for the beach blanket, once safely out of the reach of waves, can suddenly be underwater if the beachgoers haven't been paying attention.

The gravitational attractions of both the sun and the moon cause the oceans, the atmosphere, and even the land to be pulled in the direction of the sun, moon, or both. We can't see the tidal bulges of the atmosphere, though they are there. The tidal stretching of solid land also exists, but it is extremely slight and can't be observed or measured except by sensitive scientific instruments. Just so you know, there are tidal bulges or stretches on the side of the planet *opposite* from the direction of the sun and moon, too, but don't worry about *why*—we're concerned here with effects. Every day, there are two high tides and two low tides. High tides are called flood tides. Low tides are called ebb tides.

Although the sun obviously is much larger than the moon, it also is much farther away from the earth, so the sun's effect on tides is only half that of the moon. When earth, sun, and moon are lined up in a row, the combined pulls create a kind of double tide effect known as a spring tide. "Spring" is used here as in "spring forth," not as in the season. Lower

Earning Their Salt

Did you know that the word *salary* comes from the Latin word *sal,* meaning salt? Roman soldiers were paid, in part, in salt—they literally were worth their salt. Not only do we enhance the taste of most foods with salt, but salt is an industrial raw material used in, among other things, gunpowder.

In Colonial times, the British government had a monopoly on salt, which was taxed. Some independent-minded Jerseyans realized that they were living near an ocean full of salt for the taking, and many small—and illegal—salt works were set up in out-of-the-way spots along the coast.

When the Revolutionary War began, these salt works became essential to the war effort, as making gunpowder requires salt. Seawater was boiled over a fire until the water evaporated away. The Continental Congress subsidized salt works near Toms River, and salt makers were exempt from military service. Other salt works were at Barnegat, Absecon Beach, Forked River, and on both Great and Little Egg Harbors. By 1800, seawater production of salt could not compete with inland, underground salt mines, and the local industry died.

Salt Marshes: Wasteland or Wonderland?

Salt marshes line the bayshores of both mainland and offshore barrier beaches from Mantoloking on Barnegat Bay to Cold Spring Harbor on Cape May's north end. The wide mouths of the Navesink, Shrewsbury, Shark, Manasquan, Metedeconk, and other rivers along the shore also are bordered by broad salt marshes.

These salt marshes are a mingling of water and land. Oozy, squishy mud anchored by marsh grass, almost underwater at high tide, veined with twisting channels of very shallow water, the many acres of salt marsh are poorly understood. Are they a wasteland of no value, just waiting to be drained or filled with trash, to be magically transformed into valuable building lots? Or are they valuable in themselves?

In the past, the attitude seems to have been that the marshes, neither land nor sea, should be "improved" by either filling them with the sand from leveled dunes or using them as dumps. Solid, buildable land could thus be "made." Waterfront land at that. A popular technique was "dredge and fill"—scooping out channels navigable by small pleasure craft, and dumping the resulting sand and debris alongside in order to create building lots.

Salt marshes do, in fact, provide two valuable services. First, a marsh acts like a giant, spongy shock absorber, breaking up and absorbing wave energy that otherwise would erode a more solid shoreline. High tides and storm surges are held and then slowly released as the water level in the bays drops.

Second, the shallow channels mix salt and fresh water and the nutrients each carries. The decaying vegetation and fertile mud, the swarms

than average, or neap, tides are produced when the moon moves to a position at right angles to the sun's position relative to the earth. Spring, or unusually high, tides occur at both new and full moons. Neap tides occur at the moon's first and third quarters. The combination of spring tides and storm-driven waves can be disastrous.

The timing of daily high and low tides changes by about fifty minutes per day, just as the timing of moonrise shifts fifty minutes per day. The tidal range—the difference in sea level between two successive tides (one high and one low)—differs from place to place along the seashore. This is because of the shapes of bays and channels, the season of the year, and other complications. Most daily tidal ranges are only a few feet, but where

Salt marshes serve as sponges, absorbing the wave energy of storm tides and providing valuable wildlife habitat.

of insects, and the occasional dead sea creatures stranded there all add up to a rich buffet for oysters, crabs, clams, and many finfish. It is said that each acre of salt marsh produces more food, high-quality protein at that, than the best-quality farmland. Salt marshes also are naturally protected environments, nurseries for the young of many species of shellfish and finfish.

Think of the salt marshes as seafood factories that also help protect bayshores from the full force of waves.

a funnel-shaped bay magnifies tidal effects, tidal ranges of thirty-five feet can occur, as at Nova Scotia's Bay of Fundy. A few locations around the world have much higher tidal ranges.

The Climate of the Seashore

Weather forecasting for the Jersey shore is quite accurate, at least for about two days in advance. This high predictability is due to a combination of two facts. First, the technology supporting forecasting is amazing—satellite images, radar, and the like. But what really makes weather predicting so successful here is that our weather systems, primarily huge low-pressure areas, or cyclonic storms, come to New Jersey from the west (or northwest or southwest). As long as we know what is happening, weather-wise, to the west, and how fast that weather is traveling toward the east, weather forecasting is a piece of cake. Well, almost. New Jersey "imports" its weather. In winter, the Jersey shore's weather is dominated by cold air masses originating to our northwest, over western and northern Canada. In summer, air masses originating over the Gulf of Mexico and the Atlantic dominate.

How many times have you heard the weather forecaster on television news programs say, "The high temperature today was ten degrees cooler than normal," or "The low temperature was twenty degrees higher than it should be at this time of year." As you may have noticed, temperatures and precipitation figures actually are seldom "normal" or "what they should

〰〰〰〰〰〰〰〰〰〰〰〰〰〰〰〰〰

The Gulf Stream

What does New Jersey have in common with places like Ireland and Norway—in fact, with much of northwestern Europe? All are influenced to some degree by the Gulf Stream.

The Gulf Stream was described by pioneering oceanographer Matthew Maury as a "river in the sea," and it really matches that description. The second largest among the world's ocean currents, the Gulf Stream originates in the warm waters of the Gulf of Mexico. As this warm current exits the Gulf through the Florida Straits, it is racing along at a rate of about 140 miles a day. Its volume is at least fifteen hundred times (some sources say eighteen hundred) the flow of the Mississippi at New Orleans. The stream is about 50 miles wide and extends downward into the ocean from the surface to about three thousand feet below sea level. The Gulf Stream's speed slows as it advances northward. Off the Carolinas, it is moving at about 40 miles per day; off Newfoundland at 10 miles per day. As it both spreads out and slows down, the Gulf Stream is renamed the North Atlantic Drift, if you catch the drift.

Benjamin Franklin was the first to identify and map the Gulf Stream. As Colonial postmaster, he noticed that some westbound mail packets, in contrast to most merchant ships going from England to Colonial ports like Boston, New York, or Philadelphia, took about two weeks longer for the same voyage, while all eastbound ships on the same route made better time. His cousin, a Nantucket ship captain, told him that the westbound mail packet captains just didn't know the secrets of the location of a great eastbound current. Ben and his helpful cousin published the first map of the Gulf Stream in 1770.

be." This is because words like "normal" are mistakenly used for "average," which is a very different thing. Climate is described and measured by long-term averages for temperature and precipitation data. The more years of data available, the better. But the figures are still averages. Remember the old joke, if you have one foot in a bucket of near-boiling water and the other foot in a bucket of ice, on the average, you're comfortable!

Climate is what you expect; weather is what you get. So forget "normal"—averages may actually seldom be the same figure as current weather (today as opposed to long-term average conditions). Even average climate data may vary from source to source due to different time spans used to calculate averages.

Climate is one of the natural appeals of the New Jersey shore. On average, seaside places are a little cooler in summer than inland places a short

Other than to sailors, the great importance of the Gulf Stream is that it provides places like Ireland, England, and Norway with much warmer climates than would be normal that far from the equator. West winds carry the warmth and humidity of the Gulf Stream onto the northwestern coasts of Europe. Although the Gulf Stream's average location (it varies) is about ninety miles off the Jersey coast, it doesn't have as great an influence on New Jersey's climate as it does in northwestern Europe. This is because, for New Jersey, upper atmosphere winds mostly are moving out of the northwest—*off* the coast rather than *onto* the coast. However, lower-level winds associated with the great cyclonic or low-pressure cell storms that dominate New Jersey's weather for more than half a year often do come off the sea, out of the east-northeast. Still, the large temperature contrast of Gulf Stream waters with New Jersey coastal waters does help keep the coast, though not the rest of the state, a bit warmer in winter. And the heat energy of the stream helps power the notorious "northeaster" storms that sweep down on the coast occasionally.

The Gulf Stream's warm waters help keep coastal New Jersey a bit warmer in winter. This river in the sea of tropical water moves at better than thirty miles a day about ninety miles off the Jersey shore.

distance away. Also, seashore locations are noticeably warmer in winter than interior locations nearby.

For example, the January average temperature at Atlantic City is 34 degrees F, while Philadelphia's January average is 30 degrees F. Not a huge difference, but a critical one. Ask yourself, would you rather drive on wet roads at 30 degrees F or at 34 degrees F. Can you say, "ice"? Cape May, surrounded on three sides by open water, has a January average of 39 degrees F.

Average temperatures for July, the warmest month, show coastal locations just a little cooler than nearby inland places. July in Philadelphia averages 77 degrees F; Atlantic City, 74 degrees F; Cape May, 75 degrees F. At the northern shore, Long Branch's January and July averages are 32 degrees F and 74 degrees F; nearby Newark, on the bay rather than the open ocean, averages 31 degrees F and 76 degrees F for its coldest and warmest months.

The climate data in the table "The Seashore's Mild Climate" show two important facts. First, all three seashore locations—Atlantic City, Cape

"To Your Health": The Seashore Will Cure What Ails You

For many of the older generations of Americans, the idea of traveling just for fun—pure, plain fun—made them a little uncomfortable. Maybe it was the Puritan legacy. Puritans once were described as those who deeply feared that somewhere, somehow, somebody was having fun.

Or maybe it was just the idea that serious, hardworking, upright people needed a purpose—a socially admirable purpose—for a trip. An ancient tradition in Europe was that of traveling to spas—mineral water springs—to "take the waters." These mineralized waters were drunk, bathed in, or both to "cure" a wide variety of complaints. Colonial Americans eagerly adopted the British enthusiasm for spas, especially hot springs. Many hot or cold mineral springs were discovered in the Appalachians of Virginia. Martha Washington liked to visit Berkeley Springs. More than two centuries ago, doctors on both sides of the Atlantic were advising sea bathing as a health measure. The early popularity of the shore was related to these recommendations of doctors.

As late as the 1960s, Atlantic City was publishing brochures on the health benefits of sea air and saltwater bathing, in case you still needed an excuse to visit. But don't try to tell the IRS that your seashore visit is a medical expense.

The Seashore's Mild Climate: Monthly Averages in Temperature and Precipitation

Place		January	February	March	April	May	June	July	August	September	October	November	December	Annual Average
Atlantic City	T	35	35	41	50	60	69	74	74	68	59	48	38	54
	P	3	3	4	3	3	3	4	5	3	3	4	4	41
Cape May	T	39	34	43	53	60	67	75	75	67	54	48	40	55
	P	3	3	4	2	5	3	1	3	3	2	1	4	34
Long Branch	T	32	33	40	50	60	70	74	73	67	57	46	35	53
	P	3	4	4	4	4	3	4	5	3	3	4	4	45
Trenton	T	32	33	41	52	62	71	76	74	67	57	46	35	54
	P	3	3	4	3	3	3	5	4	3	3	3	3	40
Harrisburg	T	31	32	41	51	62	71	75	73	66	55	42	30	50
	P	3	2	3	3	4	4	4	3	3	3	3	3	36
Chicago	T	26	27	37	47	58	68	74	73	66	55	42	30	50
	P	3	3	4	3	3	3	5	4	3	3	3	3	40

All data rounded to nearest full degree Fahrenheit or inch of precipitation.

May, and Long Branch—are very similar to each other. Second, as you go inland and away from the influence of the seacoast, the winters get colder and the range of high and low monthly average temperatures increases. Inland from the shore, not only are the winters colder, but the summers are about as hot as those along the seashore.

The big reason that the seashore is slightly warmer in winter, and also slightly cooler in summer, than locations more distant from the ocean is that the ocean has a huge balancing effect on seasonal temperatures. In contrast to land, water stores heat energy in summer. The sea gets warmer in summer much more slowly than the land heats up. Even by the end of summer, ocean temperatures in the surf may be 20 degrees F cooler than the beach or boardwalk, making for a refreshing dip. In the autumn, as temperatures fall quickly over land, the ocean cools off much more slowly, gradually giving up its stored heat from summer.

This is why bathers can enjoy comfortably warm water well into September and boardwalk strollers needn't bundle up until mid-October. Thanks to the ocean's "slower to warm up, slower to cool off" nature compared with land, autumn is delightful along the shore. Also delightful are the cheaper hotel-motel rates after the school year begins.

3

Connections

T wo if by land, one if by sea." Paul Revere's Revolutionary wartime message can be adapted to describe early travel to the Jersey shore. Land transportation, which required ferries across either the Hudson from New York City or the Delaware River from Philadelphia to the seaside, was a two-day effort from Philadelphia, but only one day was required by the early, primitive steamboats. Philadelphia, unlike New York, had no nearby oceanfront beaches. Connecting Philadelphians with the nearest sand and surf always was a longer trip. On the other hand, New York City's greater population size has meant that New Yorkers long have sought out beaches less crowded than their own Brooklyn's Coney Island or other nearby Long Island beaches.

Though many from the metropolitan areas that sprawl around New York and Philadelphia now are within a few hours' drive of their favorite Jersey shore resort—at least, if they avoid driving on major summer holidays—such trips once were painfully slow. The earliest visitors to the seashore must have been a rugged lot. Jersey wagons or oyster wagons were graceless boxes on wheels. The wheels were wide to avoid sinking into the soft sands of many early roads. The "springs" were wooden. At least one passenger called them "atrocities of wheeled vehicles." They hauled oysters most of the year, switching to passengers in summer. The passengers complained a lot more than the oysters. The overland trip from

Navesink Highlands, 1874.
Note the steamboat landing below
the Twin Lights. The boats connected
to the railroad to Long Branch.

Mullica Hill, 1844. Horses and wagons like this once connected towns. Note the large sign for an inn, the early equivalent of motel, restaurant, and service station along the highway.

Philadelphia to Cape May took two days, requiring an overnight at a road-side inn on the way.

The agonizingly slow, bumpy wagon ride was made even worse by the clouds of mosquitoes, greenhead flies, and gnats that pestered the tourists. It was said that at the end of two days' travel in a Jersey wagon, many passengers had to be helped to crawl from their "rolling coffin," as they were called. No doubt, these early seashore vacations required stamina and a lot of determination to get there. Women, then patronizingly called the "weaker sex," were advised not to undertake such excursions.

Philadelphians usually began their trips to the shore with the Camden ferry.

Stagecoaches were a big step forward. Sprung on thick leather straps, the more comfortable stages set speed records compared with the old wagons. Philadelphians would take an early ferry to Camden to catch the stagecoach, leaving at 4 A.M. They were delivered to Cape May around midnight of the same day, if they were lucky.

Stages also carried Philadelphians from Camden to Tuckerton on Little Egg Harbor. There, they caught a boat to Long Beach or Tucker's Beach. This was a two-day trip, as was the Philadelphia–to–Manahawkin stage line.

At the northern end of the Jersey shore, New Yorkers would take a boat southward from Manhattan to Red Bank, followed by a six-mile jaunt by wagon or stage to Long Branch. An alternative was a boat to Sandy Hook, then a wagon to Long Branch.

Steamboats to the Shore

Clearly, an all-water route to the seashore would be a lot more comfortable than one involving wagons or stagecoaches. As long as ships still depended on wind, though, keeping to a tight schedule was impossible. Because winds were unpredictable and could be countered by currents and tides, sailing ships did not necessarily always save time over land travel by wagon or stage. Generally, though, going by water was more comfortable, except for people prone to seasickness.

The era of steamboat travel made the trip both faster and more comfortable. Steamboats revolutionized the resort industry everywhere, especially for Cape May and Long Branch. By 1823, steamboats departed Philadelphia in the morning, calling at New Castle, Delaware, to pick up Baltimoreans and Virginians, who had used Chesapeake Bay steamboats and a short rail-

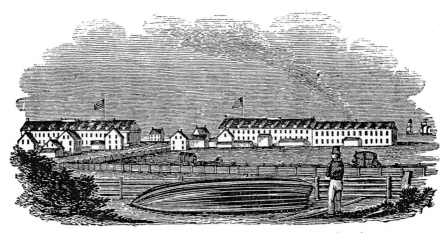

Large hotels, built as early as the 1840s, are testimony to Cape May's early success.

Oysters "R" in Season

Everyone has heard the advice to eat oysters only in months containing an "R" in their names. This "R" requirement eliminates May, June, July, and August. Because oysters, prior to refrigeration, were notoriously likely to spoil in warm weather, this was good advice. In early New Jersey, avoiding oysters in the warmer months was more than common sense—it was the law. As early as 1719, raking for shellfish was forbidden from April 10 to September 1. In fact, in 1765, the Colonial government was asked to ban carrying *any* fish, finfish, or shellfish to markets between June 20 and August 20, the season when the catch was most likely to spoil en route. Shellfish gone bad are so deadly that U.S. and Soviet spy agencies once used these concentrated toxins as secret weapons.

The summer ban on taking oysters, which spawn in summertime, was a conservation measure as well as a public health precaution. In 1820, New Jersey prohibited nonresidents from gathering any shellfish, and even New Jerseyans were forbidden to use dredges, tongs, or rakes in areas of declining production. Also, as oysters reproduce in summer, not taking them at that time logically increases the size of the next generation.

Temporarily, oysters are not being taken in New Jersey waters. This is a conservation measure to allow the oysters to recover from two serious diseases that have greatly reduced their numbers. Suppliers also advise against consumption when oysters are spawning, as the taste is not up to par.

road from the upper bay across the Delmarva Peninsula. Everyone arrived at Cape May by six in the evening. In 1828, steamboats began a through service from Manhattan to Long Branch, with no cumbersome land transfers to slow the trip.

At the northern end of the Jersey shore, the geography of resorts and resort customers was very different than in the Philadelphia-oriented South Shore. For seashore-bound vacationers from Philadelphia and vicinity seeking the shortest, most direct route to the sand and surf, they looked eastward or southeastward across New Jersey. For southeastern Pennsylvanians, a direct link to the beach is a land route.

In contrast, if New Yorkers wanted to visit the Jersey shore, their most direct route would take them southward. Going directly south from Manhattan suggests a water route. Indeed, a mostly land route, which required crossing the Hudson River, would take New Yorkers in a big half circle,

In the early 1900s, Jersey City piers served coastal steamers, including those for Sandy Hook and Raritan Bay points.

Steamer Monmouth, early 1900s. The geography that made the water route a direct course from Manhattan to Sandy Hook Bay kept steamboats in service until about 1940.

first crossing the Hudson, heading west, then turning south, then east to finally reach the beach.

This may explain why steamboats remained important, and patronized, on the New York–Sandy Hook or Long Branch routes until the late 1930s, while earlier railroads ran steamboats out of business for the Philadelphians who were heading for the beach by 1913.

The Railroad Era

It would be difficult to overemphasize the scale of the revolution brought about by railroads in American life. Their importance in the nation's economic development was matched only by their significance to our national lifestyle, including American recreation and tourism.

The New Jersey seashore would not—could not—have been transformed from a near-wilderness into some of the state's most valuable real estate without railroads. Without railroads, the great majority of rapidly expanding populations never could have fulfilled their dreams of a day by the sea.

Railroads made day trips to the seashore possible, building on the shoulders of a process begun by steamboats, especially on the North Jersey shore. Day-trippers were those who had little time or money for leisure activities. Factory workers, shop clerks, domestic servants—they and their families never could have aspired to visits to seashore resorts without the magic of the railroads. This magic had two expressions, time and money, which are related to one another. Time was money to working-class vaca-

Railroads created a new urban landscape with their bridges, tunnels, and underpasses. Every part of American life was affected.

Railroads revolutionized transportation in the 1840s. Note the top hat on the engine driver of this early train from the 1840s.

tioners, because they could not afford overnight accommodations at the place where they played, relatively far from home. They could only afford to be day-trippers, traveling to and enjoying their chosen resort, then traveling home again, all within a day. Railroads made the one-day, home-resort-home connection possible with their speed. The direct importance of money lay in the relatively low fares that railroads could charge and still pile up the profits, for passenger services were a volume business for the railroads. Transporting passengers at a mile a minute meant that each seat in a railcar could be filled, and sold, many times a day. The railroad's equipment and labor force easily made several round-trips a day from places like Philadelphia to the shore, in contrast to the older, slower transport systems. A Jersey wagon, its horses, and driver could handle only a few passengers at a time and took several days to bring this handful to a resort. This meant tying up equipment and labor force, resulting in less than two round-trips per week in most cases. Railroads were far more efficient in using their labor force and equipment.

The rigid schedules necessarily followed by the railroads made clock watchers, and pocketwatch owners, out of nineteenth-century Americans. The whole nation's play schedules, as well as work schedules, became "on time." Americans' social lives, including their leisure habits, were just as affected as their work schedules by what John Stilgoe, in *Metropolitan Corridor: Railroads and the American Scene,* memorably terms "organized haste."

At least until about 1910, trains were the fastest things on earth. Passenger service was provided on virtually every one of the 258,000 miles of track that existed in the United States in 1900. Unlike the then-dawning age of private automobiles, train travel meant that, as John Jakle says in *The Tourist: Travel in Twentieth-Century North America,* "departure, move-

〰〰〰〰〰〰〰〰〰〰〰〰〰〰〰〰〰

New York versus Philadelphia Connections

The various resorts along New Jersey's shoreline appeal to visitors from all of America's northeastern quarter, and from eastern Canada as well. The closer the visitors' "home base" is to the seashore, the more likely is a Jersey vacation, especially for seasonal rentals or second-home ownership.

Located between neighboring metropolitan centers, New Jersey long has had a split orientation between New York and Philadelphia. This is true of the whole Garden State, but it is especially noticeable at the shore. In fact, when the colony of New Jersey was founded in 1664, it was one huge condominium—the whole colony was owned jointly by two friends of the duke of York, brother of England's King Charles. These two condo owners didn't agree on much, so they decided to divide the colony into two equal parts. The key word here was "equal"—not just in square miles, but in quality of the land and resources, and general value of the real estate. The solution was to survey a boundary between East Jersey and West Jersey. A line was surveyed, starting at a point on the seashore at Little Egg Harbor, behind Long Beach Island, and running directly to the extreme northwest corner of New Jersey. This boundary would give each former condo owner a slice of each major physical envi-

ment, and arrival defined a rhythm of travel tied to fixed routes and fixed schedules."

As wonderfully fast and cheap as train travel had become, in contrast with earlier transport technologies, individualistic Americans were happy to switch to private autos, which departed on the owner's schedule, not the railroads' timetables, and offered a variety of routes.

The Special Challenges of the Seashore Railroads

Although seldom thought of as such, New Jersey is a peninsula. The state's only land boundary, with New York State, forms but 12 percent of New Jersey's total boundaries. In other words, 88 percent of interstate connections by land transportation require bridges, tunnels, or ferries. It's a general rule in transportation that the use of ferries to connect rails or highways across a water barrier is much less desirable in the long run than the more expensive to construct, but more efficient to use, bridges or tunnels. Ferries interrupt the smooth flow of traffic. They are bottle-necks in the movement of both freight and passengers. There are no rail

ronment—seashore, pinelands, farmlands, and mountains. Because of inaccurate maps and faulty surveying, the exact location of this boundary was argued in courts until 1855. This old Colonial boundary looks amazingly like the general division within New Jersey between the Philadelphia versus New York orientations of the state.

Other things being approximately equal, people tend to choose the closer of competing shopping centers, entertainments, and resorts. No big surprise there. New Yorkers favor Jersey's North Shore, while Philadelphians just as naturally gravitate to the South Shore. Closer means less cost in time and money. When steamboats brought most visitors, New Yorkers were delivered directly to Long Branch starting in 1828. Steamboat service from Philadelphia to Cape May was inaugurated in 1823. Even in the railroad era, the southward advance of rails directly from New York ended at Tuckerton, 16 miles north of Atlantic City. Although it was possible then for New Yorkers to reach Atlantic City by rail, this required a dogleg inland to Winslow Junction. Cost was a factor, too. In 1889, a New York–to–Long Branch ticket cost $1.50; New York–to–Atlantic City cost $4.50.

New York license plates are the most common out-of-state plates in resorts north of Long Branch State Park; Pennsylvania plates dominate to the south. Atlantic City's casinos make that South Shore resort an exception—that city serves both metropolitan centers, and way beyond.

bridges or tunnels between Pennsylvania or Delaware and New Jersey south of Philadelphia. The very busy railroad "Megalopolitan spine," carrying through traffic between New York and Philadelphia, crosses the Delaware River at Trenton rather than Philadelphia. As late as the early 1950s, most Philadelphians bound for Cape May County resorts by train crossed the Delaware River by ferry to Camden. New Yorkers could not avoid ferries in their train trips to the Jersey seashore until 1910, when the Pennsylvania Railroad opened its Hudson River tunnels directly connecting its New Jersey rails with Manhattan.

In 1833, one of the earliest major railroads in the country, the Camden and Amboy, built the first through connector between New York and Philadelphia. This line pioneered the still-busy New York–Newark–Trenton–Philadelphia route, which still functions as the rail backbone of the northeast Megalopolis. Both freight and passenger traffic (think Acela, Metroliner, and Amtrak's fastest trains) is heavy here.

To the south and east of this heavily traveled corridor lie New Jersey's seashore resorts and the rail's "seashore" lines. These seashore railroads have always had to cope with a special geographic situation—that of dead-ending at the shore. This dead-end situation means that no through traffic exists to help pay for maintenance costs.

Railroads typically have high initial costs of land acquisition and construction that must be paid regardless of later traffic volume. Ideally, construction costs can be spread across many trains per day. The roadbed, bridges, tunnels, signal equipment, and so on cost the same to build whether two trains or twenty use that route daily. Even maintenance costs do not rise in proportion to frequency of use. Both through traffic and local traffic are important to building revenues. But unlike the Megalopolitan corridor, the seashore railroads had no through traffic, originating elsewhere and bound for destinations beyond the local rail system. The New Jersey Pinelands, which lay across the path of rails crossing southern and central Jersey, were a notoriously unproductive, sparsely populated region. As a result, little freight or passenger demand was generated within the Pinelands, and sparse local traffic produced little additional revenue.

By the 1920s, few railroads were making profits on passenger service, and they subsidized their passenger trains with freight revenues. Chilling drop-offs in numbers of passengers gave railroads across the nation a head cold. In the case of the seashore lines, so heavily dependent on seasonal passenger revenues, it was more a case of pneumonia.

The Railroads Create Resorts

The steam locomotive was the true father of most Jersey seashore towns. From a two-day trip via wagon, stage, or sailboat on the Philadelphia–Cape May route (the New York–Long Branch route, being shorter, was usually a one-day event), transportation time was reduced to two or three hours. By the twentieth century, the trains were even faster. In 1920, of the sixteen fastest trains in the world, thirteen were in the Atlantic City service.

Railroads changed the rules about "closest" ocean beaches to Philadelphia. When steamboats were the preferred means of delivering Philadelphians to the seashore, Cape May was the first place on the open ocean accessible by water. But cross-state railroads made Atlantic City the closer beach, with vacationers traveling for the first time in a straight line. At first the rails were less revolutionary in transporting New Yorkers to the North Jersey shore, as the nearly straight-line route from Manhattan to Long Branch still was a steamboat to Sandy Hook, connecting to a railroad to Long Branch. A direct rail route from Jersey City's Hudson Ferry terminals to Long Branch was not completed until the mid-1870s. While the railroads dominated the traffic from Philadelphia to the seashore by the 1870s, the Manhattan–to–Sandy Hook (or Highlands) steamers continued to provide service until nearly World War II.

In 1854, the Camden and Atlantic Railroad was built between Camden, opposite Philadelphia across the Delaware, and Absecon, opposite the future Atlantic City across the bay. The trestle across the bay to Atlantic City was completed the following year. It was a risky enterprise. The Camden and Atlantic necessarily crossed the Pine Barrens, a land of few people and low productivity, a land that would not, in itself, generate much profitable passenger or freight business. The rails dead-ended at what was then an almost empty shoreline. And seasonal passenger traffic would be, at best, highly seasonal.

Five years after the railroad made it into Atlantic City, the city's permanent population was only seven hundred. Railroad revenues were so disappointing that the company went bankrupt in 1857 and was reorganized. Fortunately for the stockholders, the railroad's wholly owned subsidiary, the Camden and Atlantic Land Company, had been spun off as a separate company, and land at the now reachable

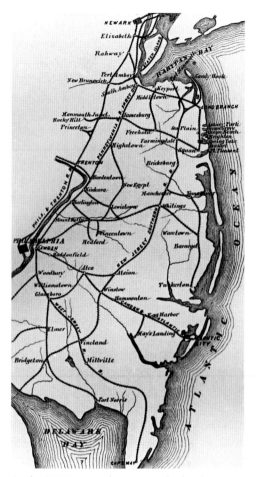

By the 1870s, most shore resorts had rail service.

beach was where the money was. The shareholder profits were enormous.

Absecon Island, the site of Atlantic City, had been almost worthless before the rails came. By 1900, land that sold at $10 an acre in 1854 was selling at $500 to $800 a front foot. Atlantic City real estate was valued at $50 million at the dawn of the new century. By 1873, the Camden and Atlantic ran six round-trip trains to Atlantic City, with two extras on Sundays. The Philadelphia and Atlantic Railroad introduced competition on the route in 1877, followed by a third line built by the Pennsylvania Railroad in 1880. Competition cut the price of round-trip tickets from $3 to $1.

This real estate bonanza offered a role model to other investors. If a rail connection between a beach and a concentration of would-be beachgoers could create Atlantic City, why not repeat this moneymaking miracle on

Wildwood Railroad Station, 1908. Railroad stations in resorts were the busiest places in town early in the twentieth century.

Wildwood Railroad Station, 1971. This abandoned station testifies to the death of passenger service for most central and southern shore resorts after the 1960s.

every stretch of sand and surf? Not every still-empty beach would become another Atlantic City, but not for a lack of effort.

A railroad was completed into Cape May in 1863. These trains conveniently ran directly to a large hotel, which had been built by the railroad—a common tactic by the railroads to make a double profit from their seasonal passengers. Unlike the Camden and Atlantic's literal creation of a city, the Cape May line simply served an already popular resort, competing directly with the steamboats then serving as the vital "connection" from the vacationers' homes.

As was the case at Cape May, the first railroads to the North Shore lagged behind the construction of the line to Atlantic City because the steamboats already provided service to established resorts like Long Branch. A rail line connected the steamboat wharf at Sandy Hook with Long Branch by 1865; an all-rail route to Jersey City was built a few years after. Manasquan got its rail connection in 1867.

The decade of the 1880s saw most of the future resorts directly connected with both New York and Philadelphia. Not a surprise, the rapid expansion of railroads to the seashore reflected the state's general experience with the "iron horse." Within the whole state, railroad mileage just about exactly doubled from 1850 to 1860, then doubled again from 1860 to 1870. Mileage grew 50 percent from 1870 to 1880, then expanded by another 20 percent by 1890. The peak year for New Jersey's total rail mileage was 1920, with 2,352 miles. By 1987, it had steadily declined to 1,331 miles, a 43 percent drop.

Everything about the seashore resorts—their permanent populations, their hordes of vacationers, their real estate values—all grew explosively during the era of railroad building. In 1850, the last census before rails reached the shore, the total population of the four coastal counties was 55,706. By 1885, it had doubled. Before the railroad, all of Absecon Island held about two dozen people; by 1860, it was 700. Between 1870 and 1886, Atlantic City's permanent resident population grew at the rate of 425 percent!

How Railroads Helped Shape Resort Towns

The street plan of a typical seashore resort follows the familiar grid or waffle-iron pattern. Parallel straight streets cross other straight streets, again parallel with one another, at right angles. The resulting building lots are on a checkerboard of squares (actually, mostly rectangles). Nothing unusual, so far. However, it's an interesting fact that both of the oldest resorts, Cape May and Long Branch, have oceanfront drives paralleling the beach. In the majority of resorts, the somewhat younger resorts created by railroads, it is common for those streets of the grid that run at right angles to the beach to dead-end at a boardwalk.

Driving on Ocean Ave. West End, Long Branch, N. J.

At Long Branch, in the early 1900s, the seafront drive was the scene of daily parades of fine carriages displaying their owners' wealth.

This seafront pedestrian boardwalk, rather than a vehicular street, seems to have started with Atlantic City, the first true railroad resort. This lack of a seafront avenue for horse-drawn vehicles was a major departure from earlier and long-established seaside resorts. All of the classic European seaside resorts—think French Riviera or the many English resorts—follow the beachfront boulevard or scenic drive pattern.

But the older seaside resorts had more than oceanfront streets in common. These early resorts catered to elites—those relatively few who had both the time and the surplus cash to be on vacation far from home. Some arrived in their own carriages. Naturally, they liked to take drives along the seafront to enjoy the fresh air and scenery. Like the owners of expensive sports cars today, they liked showing off their fancy carriages and sleek horses. For these people, a seafront boulevard was a requirement.

When the Camden and Atlantic Railroad created Atlantic City in 1854, its passengers were mostly working men and women who didn't own carriages. When they got off the train, they walked. No showy carriage rides for them. They needed a pedestrian promenade, safe from vehicular traffic.

As far as the railroad was concerned, there was no big hurry to build, or encourage municipal authorities to build, bridges, causeways, or elevated roadways across the broad belt of shallow water and marshes sepa-

Bradley Beach, circa 1910, followed the Long Branch and Cape May model, with a wide oceanfront drive and a few tourist services directly on the beach.

Atlantic City Boardwalk, circa 1910. The exclusively pedestrian—or rolling chair—nature of Atlantic City's seafront became the model for many American seaside resorts.

〰〰〰〰〰〰〰〰〰〰〰〰〰〰

Stretching the Season

As with resorts everywhere, New Jersey's seashore towns must cope with strong seasonal rhythms of business. As predictably as the ocean's tides, the number of visitors and seasonal residents ebbs and flows by the calendar. Some shore resort entrepreneurs optimistically talk about a Memorial Day to Labor Day season, but the actual high season is more like early or mid-June through Labor Day. As much as anything else, the summer season is limited by the school calendar. Young families must limit their

Miss America, 1927. The famous beauty contest, traditionally held a week or two after Labor Day, is a classic attempt at stretching the season.

rating the resort islands from the mainland. From 1855 to 1870, the railroad trestles and bridges were the only access to Atlantic City except by boat. Vacationers wealthy enough to own carriages would have had a difficult and expensive time bringing their own transportation, even if they wanted to share the beach with factory workers and shop clerks.

In an interesting coincidence, Atlantic City's first Boardwalk (it's always a capital "B" in Atlantic City) was built in 1870, the year that carriages and wagons could first drive directly into the city. What about Cape May's claim to have built boardwalks before Atlantic City? Cape May's pioneer-

seasonal rentals to schools' summer vacations. College students, and not a few schoolteachers, are available as seasonal help according to the same two-and-a-half- to three-month block of availability.

Hotels, motels, restaurants, and the like, operating near capacity during the season, empty quickly as vacationers clog the roads home Labor Day night. Many businesses simply close for the season; witness the almost total boarding up of small-town seafront businesses. For the desperate business operators, any business in the off-season is almost pure profit.

How to stretch the season? There are three basic strategies: conventions, special events and festivals, and attractive off-season bargain pricing. Off-season conventions clearly are a win-win situation: Convention goers get first-class accommodations at knockdown prices; there are no waiting lines at fine restaurants or theaters and showrooms. Business investments earn less than they would in summer but a lot more than nothing. Every sizable town has constructed a convention hall, though none rival Atlantic City's gigantic Boardwalk facility, whose most famous moment of glory was the 1964 Democratic National Convention.

The classic season-stretching special event is the Miss America Pageant, Atlantic City's invention. Begun in 1921, the pageant at first brought together the winners of city contests, later reorganized to feature the choices of state contests. The timing, conveniently, was a week or so after Labor Day. It is possible that this fading Atlantic City creation could be relocated soon.

The "graying" of America, with large numbers of seniors, many blessed with decent pensions, has produced an eager market for bargain-priced off-season vacations. As many retirees can testify, September is the seashore's best-kept secret in terms of both pleasant weather and bargain prices. The seniors market for accommodations and entertainment obviously is sensitive to cost, but not to school schedules or traditional vacation months. Everyone is a winner in stretching the season.

ing boardwalks apparently were designed to bring vacationers over the dunes and down toward the water's edge. Laid directly on the sand, these "walks" were mostly perpendicular to the waterline, not parallel as in the Atlantic City version.

The Atlantic City pattern of a pedestrian promenade lined with shops, fast food, and amusements, and not paralleling any seafront drive, was copied by almost every other railroad-era resort community. Boardwalks are so American. Democratic and unpretentious in character, they reflect the fact that railroads brought average citizens to play by the sea.

Planes, Trains, and Automobiles

Although the North Shore and Atlantic City are served by trains to this day, the railroad era is essentially over. Present train service, oriented to commuters, not vacationers, is only a shadow of what it once was. The peak year for passenger rail traffic in the United States was 1920. It's been pretty steadily downhill since then. Reasonably frequent service to shore points continued until the end of World War II, which was a kind of last hurrah for the excursion trains. The decade of the Great Depression, during the 1930s, made purchases of new cars less likely for the majority. Then, during the war, new cars simply were not available and gasoline was rationed. But when people could tear the ration stickers off their windshields and buy that new car, train ridership fell abruptly. New rail links directly to the seashore had not been built since 1897, when a trestle was extended to Brigantine Island north of Atlantic City. That trestle was wiped out in a storm in 1903, and never rebuilt.

By 1923, more vacationers were arriving in Atlantic City by car than by train. The switch in focus from trains to cars seems to have happened faster than the long-ago switch from steamboats to trains. The first vacationers to arrive by car in Atlantic City drove there in a French-built electric car in 1899. That same year, "Diamond Jim" Brady, a sporting gentleman who was

Tourist sightseeing, 1906. In the infancy of automobiles, resort visitors took local sight-seeing rides, for many their first ride in an automobile.

Sand sculpture. By 1910, cars were of great popular interest and were reshaping America.

never bashful about showing off his money, brought six electric cars to Long Branch. Evidently, he wanted to make sure that at least one was always charged up and ready to roll. By 1910, New Yorkers and Philadelphians were organizing group outings to drive their cars to their favorite resort.

More cars led to better roads. The early motorists lobbied for paved, marked, wider, and faster roads. Seashore merchants and hotel owners, recognizing a potential market when they saw it, joined in the demands for road improvements. The Camden–to–Atlantic City White Horse Pike, modern U.S. Route 30, was graveled by 1904 and completely paved by 1921. Ocean County's first graveled road was between Lakewood and Point Pleasant in 1904.

The 173-mile-long Garden State Parkway, built between 1952 and 1957, is the main access to Jersey shore resorts from the north. One of the country's safest and most scenic divided, limited-access roads, the Parkway is the twentieth and twenty-first centuries' counterpart to the nineteenth-century railroads. As early as 1984, as many as 1,131,000 vehicles a day used the Garden State Parkway. August is the busiest month, typically seeing over 30 million vehicles. Connecting Philadelphia's New Jersey suburbs with Atlantic City, and feeding into the southernmost Parkway, is the Atlantic City Expressway, a 44-mile-long toll road completed in 1965. Over 35 million cars per year pass through its tollbooths.

The concentration of population in New Jersey and its near neighbors means that about one-sixth of the nation (and a lot of Canadians as well) can reach the Jersey shore on one tank of gas. New Jersey's shoreline has become one long sunny patio and backyard swimming pool for this chain of cities and suburbs stretching from New Hampshire to Virginia.

The summertime flood of vacationers brings joy to shore towns' parking lot operators. Traffic jams occur even on the splendid new high-speed, limited-access superhighways. The almost complete dependence on private cars to convey vacationers from their home to their favorite seaside resorts often overwhelms those towns that were products of the

The Canadian Connection

"Bienvenue aux Canadiennes" (Welcome Canadians) read many signs in shop windows and on motel marquees in New Jersey seashore towns. Cape May and Atlantic Counties, in particular, exchange large amounts of Canadian dollars, according to the Philadelphia branch of the Federal Reserve Bank, far more than their population size and distance from Canada would suggest. Montreal is only about thirty miles north of the U.S. border, via Canadian Route 15. Southbound Montrealers then pick up Interstate 87 to the New York Thruway to the Garden State Parkway. With no stoplights and a total distance of just over five hundred miles, Montreal to Atlantic City, it is possible to complete the trip in one day.

Why do so many Canadians make that drive? Fact A: Canada has many scenic and recreational attractions, but bathing beaches with people-friendly ocean temperatures aren't among them. Fact B: It's more fun to bathe in ocean water that doesn't instantly turn you blue. Fact C: In the northeastern United States, wide, sandy beaches are pretty rare north of Long Island, New York. Fact D: Do you really want to fight traffic and crowds to get to Long Island beaches? Fact E: It's easy to stay on the Parkway until you (a) see signs for casinos or (b) run out of road. Welcome Canadians!

The name of this motel in Wildwood reflects the impact of Canadian vacationers at the resort.

101:—Broadway, Ocean Grove, N. J.

By the late 1920s, more vacationers were arriving by car than train, creating traffic and parking problems, as illustrated in this view of Ocean Grove in 1927.

railroad era. Narrow streets of short blocks, perfectly suited to pedestrian visitors just off the train, simply were not designed for the auto age. Atlantic City may be the best example of this antiquated street plan and its modern consequences.

Surprisingly, the air age has had little impact on the ongoing growth of the New Jersey seashore. Atlantic City's Bader Field was the first municipal airport in the country. Air service from New York was established by World War I. But no truly metropolitan-scale airport has been built along the shore.

Except for visitors to Atlantic City, whose relatively recent rebirth as a world-class resort draws folks from distant locales as well as the traditional visitor-supply centers nearby, typical Jersey shore vacationers just don't live that far away. Fortunately for New Jersey's seashore resorts, upward of 16 million people live close enough to drive there in two or three hours or less. For these beachgoers, airplanes are not an attractive alternative to the convenience of their own cars. The hassle of getting to and from airports, plus air traffic and security-related delays, eats up most of the airplanes' advantage in speed when the trip involves relatively short distances. When travelers do board an aircraft, it is for longer flights where the tremendous speed advantage over automobiles really counts. Once on the plane, why not go to Florida or the Caribbean for a little beach time, figure residents of nearby cities.

The Economics of Commuting

Commuters are a mixed blessing for railroads. It might seem as though large numbers of commuters would be a railroad executive's dream. Commuters provide a predictable, essentially nonseasonal demand for transportation services. As they likely chose their residence based on the convenience of commuting to their place of work, commuters are not prone to seeking out an alternative mode of commuting—driving their own cars or using a bus. Seldom is any particular "bedroom suburb" readily accessible to the big city by a competing railroad, so it looks like a sure thing for railroads. And because railroads in earlier days chose the locations of passenger stations, railroads commonly made a lot of money in real estate by first buying up land, then increasing the value of that land by increasing its accessibility. However, long-established railroads have, by now, sold off their suburban land, the profits from which were realized long ago.

While it certainly is true that a large number of commuters adds to the profitability of a rail line that otherwise is busy, commuters in themselves are not necessarily a profit source. Most commuter railroads in the country are subsidized by the state or local governments concerned, and for good reason. When the costs of adding new lanes to existing highways, or even constructing entirely new highways, are considered, existing railroads look, in comparison, to be highly efficient people movers. Not only is highway congestion en route to the city center reduced, but so are congestion and parking demands in the destination city relieved. But if commuters must pay the full cost of railroad operations, the high-ticket prices might well encourage their switch to car commutes.

Why would the cost of operating a commuter railroad, in situations where profits are not augmented by other uses, be high? The basic reason is the daily rhythm of demand for seats. A busy commuter line with little or no other income from freight or through traffic has to buy and maintain enough locomotives and passenger cars to meet the demands of morning and evening rush hours. But in between, before and after these daily rush hours, and on weekends and holidays, there is a much-reduced need for all that rolling stock. From 6 to 9 A.M., and again from 4 to 7 P.M., every seat in every railcar might be filled. But from 9 A.M. to 4 P.M., and from 7 P.M. to the next morning rush, most of the rolling stock is unneeded and unused. In other words, out of 168 total hours in one week, a commuting railroad's capital equipment investment is earning money for about 30 hours.

Worse, labor costs are high for commuter runs. The trains must be running both before and after normal work hours, but most trains are not necessary during midday. No union worth its dues would allow management to require its engineers and conductors to report for work in time to service the morning rush, then go off the clock for about six hours, then resume work to service the evening rush. No way. The alternatives are either expensive overtime or two different shifts, take your pick. Is this any way to run a railroad? Realistically, it is the only way to run a commuter-oriented railroad, and so some form of government subsidy toward operating costs is virtually a necessity.

Major Roads Serving the New Jersey Seashore

Both then and now in the history of New Jersey's shore resorts, the connections are an important influence on vacationers' choices of resorts. Distance plays an important role, but the time and effort needed to travel from home base to specific resorts have always been more important than distance alone.

With the important exceptions of the commuter-oriented train service on the North Shore and the newly upgraded service between Philadelphia and Atlantic City, roads rule in transporting seashore-bound travelers. Fortunately for everyone, there are some excellent highways to the sand and surf.

The majority of the Jersey shore's visitors originate in the central sector of the northeastern Megalopolis: the giant urban sprawl of greater New York–northeastern New Jersey, Trenton and central New Jersey, and the greater Philadelphia area, including large parts of southeastern Pennsylvania and South Jersey, and down to Wilmington, Delaware. Thus most shore-bound vacationers are traveling south, southeast, or east toward their favorite beaches.

This means that metropolitan New Yorkers' and North Jerseyans' preferred route is the Garden State Parkway, which runs essentially north-south from the New York state line, where it connects to both the New York State Thruway system and the Palisades Interstate Parkway, all the way to New Jersey's southern tip at Cape May. Interstates 80 and 78 feed into the northern sections of the Parkway from the west, supplemented in Monmouth County by interstate-quality (in part) State Route 18. Interstate 195 connects the Trenton area with both the New Jersey Turnpike and the Garden State Parkway. From the Philadelphia metropolitan sprawl, the fastest road is the Atlantic City Expressway, which intersects the shore-paralleling Garden State Parkway just outside Atlantic City.

The Pennsylvania Turnpike, I-76, from the west, and the Pennsylvania Turnpike's Northeast Extension, from northeastern Pennsylvania, connect to the Atlantic City Expressway via Philadelphia's Schuylkill Expressway to the Walt Whitman Bridge to the Route 42 Freeway to the Atlantic City Expressway. *Note:* The Schuylkill Expressway is known locally as the "Sure-Kill" due to very heavy traffic and occasional *left* exit ramps. Be alert.

If you prefer to bypass the newer, faster roads and their tolls, and are perhaps ever so slightly masochistic, there are alternative routes. For north-central New Jersey, State Route 9, interstate quality between Jersey City and

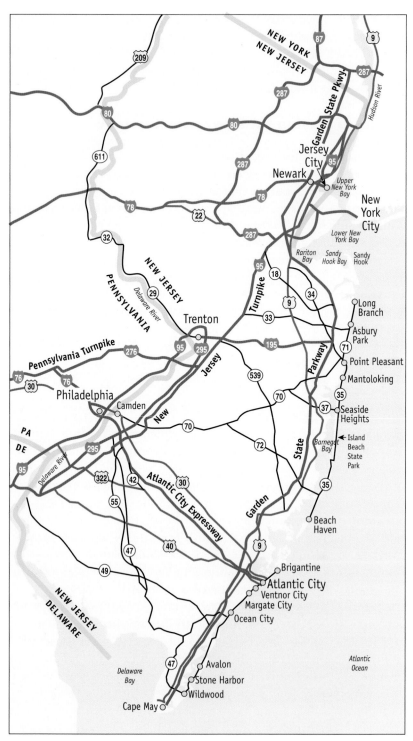

The major contemporary routes by which vacationers reach the shore.

Newark—the Pulaski Skyway—and a multilane road from Newark south to about Lakewood, is a very heavily traveled, frustrating but kind of interesting alternative to the Garden State Parkway. From Lakewood south to Cape May, Route 9 mostly follows the old Shore Road, and it will reward your patience with views of quaint old villages and interesting buildings.

For those headed for the South Shore from the Philadelphia area, State Route 55 looks like a great, toll-free alternative to the Atlantic City Expressway and Garden State Parkway. But look carefully at the highway map. Interstate-quality highway will whisk you from Philadelphia's Jersey suburbs quickly past Vineland and Millville, but it comes to a skidding, screeching halt near old Port Elizabeth. There, four lanes of superhighway suddenly

The Cape May–Lewes Ferry

For the adventurous approaching the South Shore from Delaware, try a short ocean cruise on the Cape May–Lewes, Delaware, ferry. Food and drink are available on board. In season, there are eleven sailings daily, with six additional crossings each direction on weekends. One-way voyages take an hour and ten minutes; round-trips are three hours. Photo IDs are required for all drivers and foot passengers. For information and schedules, call the Cape May Terminal, 609-889-7200, or Lewes Terminal, 302-644-6030. To guarantee space aboard for your vehicle, reservations should be made at least twenty-four hours in advance; vehicles must check in at least thirty minutes prior to departure.

The long tradition of southern visitors to the Jersey Cape is facilitated by the fast, modern Cape May–Lewes ferry across the mouth of Delaware Bay.

〰〰〰〰〰〰〰〰〰〰〰〰〰〰〰〰〰〰〰

New Jersey's Coastal Heritage Trail

Most transport route ways, such as railroads and highways, are planned in consideration of two separate sets of factors: the geographic locations that are to be linked, and the intertwined considerations of physical and economic geographies of the general route way. The ideal route, from an economic standpoint, is one that achieves some equilibrium among physical qualities of slope, drainage, and soil stability—and the costs of engineering solutions to environmental obstacles, plus the cost of land for the right-of-way.

New Jersey's Coastal Heritage Trail is not economically motivated. Neither did it require new construction or reconstruction. The goal of the Heritage Trail is to connect a variety of unique historic, cultural, and ecological sites that are examples of New Jersey's coastal heritage. Following the Coastal Heritage Trail will take you from Perth Amboy, the Colonial capital of East Jersey, all the way down the Atlantic coast to Cape May Lighthouse; to Salem, the first English port in New Jersey, and a city older than Philadelphia; and to Finn's Point National Cemetery, where the dead include over twenty-four hundred Confederate soldiers captured at Gettysburg. Parts of Middlesex, Monmouth, Ocean, Atlantic, Cape May, Cumberland, and Salem Counties are included in the trail.

The point of the Coastal Heritage Trail is not to get you from one place to another quickly and efficiently. Rather, it is to connect those sites that best illustrate the region's economic and cultural history and its variety of natural environments. The trail is a trip through time as well as across space. It is truly the scenic route, one that emphasizes appreciation and depth of understanding, a trail to be savored and revisited.

Congress authorized the New Jersey Coastal Heritage Trail in October 1988 to "provide for public understanding and enjoyment of sites and resources associated with the coastal area of New Jersey." This trail is a cooperative effort uniting federal, state, and local agencies with private groups and institutions. There are five interrelated themes: maritime history, historic settlements, relaxation and inspiration, coastal habitats, and wildlife migrations. The trail is divided into five regions: from north to south, Sandy Hook, Barnegat Bay, Absecon, Cape May, and Delsea (the Delaware River and Bay Coastal area). Free guides and maps of the regions can be obtained from National Park Service, N.J. Coastal Heritage Trail Route, P.O. Box 568, Newport, NJ 08345, telephone 856-447-0103, www.nps.gov/neje; or the New Jersey Office of Travel and Tourism, P.O. Box 826, Trenton, NJ 08625-0826, telephone 609-777-0885, fax 609-777-4097, www.visitnj.org. For a more detailed and personalized background for your tour, read Mark DiIonno's *New Jersey's Coastal Heritage*.

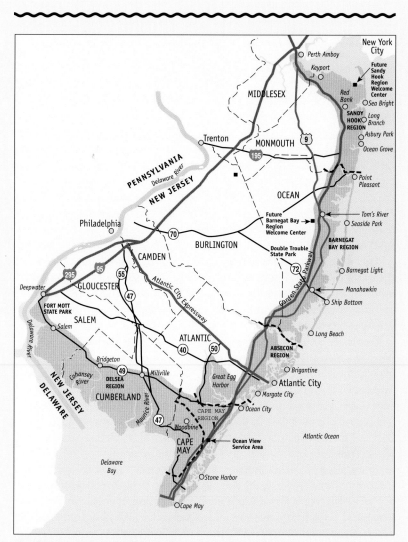

*The New Jersey Coastal Heritage Trail allows visitors to recognize that their
seashore jaunts are rooted in history.*

become two lanes of winding, scenic, snail-paced (in high season) State
Route 47. This old route was laid out originally by the Lenape Indians, who
doubtless never got behind a concrete mixer or motor home. This is a
highly scenic road, but it's incredibly slow in summer.

Other old roads roughly paralleling the Atlantic City Expressway from
Philadelphia to Atlantic City are U.S. Route 30, also known as the White
Horse Pike, and U.S. Route 322 (joined by U.S. Route 40 between McKee
City and Atlantic City), also known as the Black Horse Pike. The White

A Seashore African-American Heritage Trail

African-Americans have an interesting historic and cultural legacy at the shore.

Red Bank is the site of the Jazz and Blues Festival on the Navesink, an annual three-day celebration of music, food, and arts with an African flair. Concerts are held year-round at the 1926 vintage Count Basie Theater, named after the Red Bank native and noted big-band-era musician and composer. An interesting historic site is the home of T. Thomas Fortune, influential editor of a late-nineteenth-century nationally distributed black newspaper and founder of the Afro-American League, a civil rights group that was a predecessor of the NAACP.

The Heath Farm in Middletown, Monmouth County, was a center of the state's African-American agricultural history. The farm was established in the 1870s by a former slave. Call 732-671-0566 for a schedule of tours and demonstrations, or visit the website heathfarm.tripod.com/peacelane/index.html.

On Route 9, just off Exit 6 of the Garden State Parkway, is Whitesboro, an African-American community founded by the last black congressman of the Reconstruction era, George White of North Carolina. Seventeen hundred acres were purchased and resold to African-Americans eager to move north for greater opportunities around 1900.

Less than a mile east of Bridgeton, New Jersey's largest historic district, is Gouldtown (part of Fairfield Township), founded around 1700 as a community of free African-American landowners.

Atlantic City's resort industry early attracted a large African-American population. (New Jersey was second only to New York in the size of its pre–Civil War African-American population.) Visit the All Wars Memorial on Adriatic Avenue, which honors all African-American war veterans, and the Civil Rights Garden on Martin Luther King Boulevard, a monument to the ongoing struggle for civil rights by African-Americans. Call 609-407-9612 for information. From 1900 to the 1950s, "Chicken Bone Beach," between Missouri and Mississippi Avenues, was a segregated beach restricted to African-Americans. It is now the site of free jazz concerts sponsored by the Chicken Bone Beach Foundation.

Also check out the annual two-day Asbury Park Jazz and Gospel Festival. The PNC Bank Arts Center in Holmdel often showcases African-American performers and holds a variety of ethnic festivals, including African heritage celebrations. For more information, call 800-VISIT-NJ, extension 2977.

〰〰〰〰〰〰〰〰〰〰〰〰〰〰〰〰

A Seashore Asian-American Heritage Trail

Nearly half a million Asian-Americans make their home in New Jersey. Many more visit from out-of-state. The New Jersey Vietnam Veterans Memorial and Vietnam Era Educational Center are located at the PNC Arts Center in Holmdel. The Center often features ethnic festivals honoring various heritages. There is a Japanese Garden with a traditional teahouse at Georgian Court College in Lakewood. Atlantic City's large Vietnamese community features several excellent restaurants.

The Seabrook Educational and Cultural Center has exhibits on the World War II era, when Japanese-Americans were relocated from internment camps here to work on vegetable farms. Over five hundred families came to Seabrook voluntarily by 1946. The community still has a Buddhist Temple and Community House.

Seabrook is located on State Route 77, twenty miles south of Cherry Hill and four miles north of Bridgeton. For more information, call 800-VISIT-NJ, extension 0003.

and Black Horse Pikes are Colonial-era routes. They got their names from famous taverns that lay along the early roads. Following English tradition, early taverns had pictorial signs in an age when many couldn't read. The sign showing a white horse advertised the White Horse Tavern, and so on. These early taverns were important, functioning as hotels, restaurants, livery stables, bars, and post offices—basically providing all the services for travelers now found at modern interstate exits. The two old pikes are bordered by a variety of restaurants, derelict motor courts (individual tiny cabins), and elderly motels, along with some truly unique old buildings.

One of the delights of the old Black and White Horse Pikes is the opportunity, heading home from the shore, to stop at farmers' stands along the road. Fresh blueberries, strawberries, peaches, sweet corn, squash, asparagus, and absolutely the world's best tomatoes—ask anyone who's tried them—can still be had at very reasonable prices. Even the Atlantic City Expressway's official rest stop just west of the 17W interchange has a farmers' market attached. Take advantage and enjoy!

All of these South Jersey highways cross the Pinelands, a region of low population density and lots of woods, where deer are a frequent hazard, especially near dusk or dawn. Deer can frequently be seen along the Atlantic City Expressway, for example, often in the central divider.

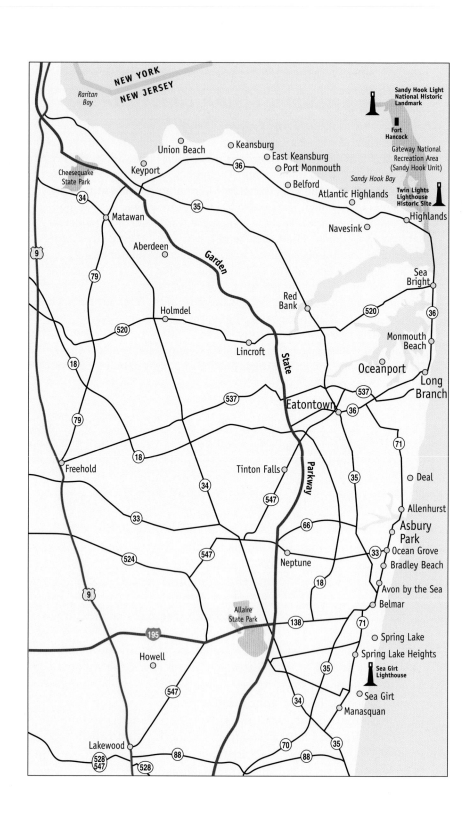

4

The North Shore

The North Shore region runs from Sandy Hook on the northern tip of the Jersey shore to Manasquan Inlet. The resort communities, north to south, include Navesink Beach, Normandine, Sea Bright, Monmouth Beach, North Long Branch, Long Branch, Elberon, Deal, Allenhurst, Asbury Park, Ocean Grove, Bradley Beach, Avon by the Sea, Belmar, Spring Lake, Spring Lake Heights, Sea Girt, Manasquan, and Brielle.

The largest portion of this shoreline is a mainland shore, that is, the ocean beaches are not located on offshore barrier beaches, but front directly on the continent. Exceptions to this mainland shore situation are the area from Monmouth Beach to the foot of Sandy Hook. Here, ocean currents long ago built ribbons of sand across the mouths of rivers, which once directly entered the sea. Now, instead of flowing eastward to the sea, the Navesink and Shrewsbury Rivers flow northward behind the sandy barrier to enter Sandy Hook Bay. Shark River, between Avon by the Sea and Belmar, only maintains its course eastward to the sea because large jetties there prevent the northward alongshore current from depositing sand in the inlet and closing it. The lakes just behind and perpendicular to the beaches of the North Shore—Lake Como, Spring Lake, Wesley Lake, Sunset Lake, and Fletcher Lake—are the remnants of rivers that, blocked by the strands deposited by ocean currents and waves, no longer meet the Atlantic head-on.

An unfortunate characteristic of much of the North Shore is that beaches there tend to be narrower and steeper than those to the south. Of

The North Shore consists of coastal Monmouth County from Sandy Hook to the Manasquan River.

North Shore Beach Facility Profiles

Facility / Phone Number	Accommodations	Amusements	Bathhouses	Beach Fee	Boardwalk	Fishing	Lifeguard	Picnicking	Rafting	Surfing	Tennis Courts	Garden State Parkway Exit
Allenhurst 732-531-2757			•	•	•	•	•		•	•	•	102 S/100 A-N
Asbury Park 732-775-0900	•		•	•		•						102 S/100 A-N
Avon by the Sea 732-502-4510	•		•	•	•	•	•	•		•		100 B-S
Belmar 732-681-3700	•	•	•	•	•	•	•	•	•	•	•	98
Bradley Beach 732-776-2990			•	•	•	•	•	•	•	•		100 B-S
Deal 732-531-1454			•	•		•	•	•		•	•	105
Loch Arbor 732-531-4740			•			•	•					102 S/100 A-N
Long Branch 732-222-0400	•		•	•	•	•	•	•	•	•		105
Manasquan 732-223-1221	•		•			•	•	•			•	98 S
Monmouth Beach 732-229-2204			•		•	•	•					117 S
Ocean Grove 732-988-5533	•		•	•	•	•	•	•	•	•	•	100 B-S/100 N
Sandy Hook 732-872-5970			•		•	•	•			•		117
Sea Bright 732-842-0215	•		•	•	•	•	•			•	•	117 S/109 N
Sea Girt 732-449-9335			•	•	•	•	•	•	•		•	98 S
Seven Presidents* 732-229-0924			•	•	•	•	•			•		105
Spring Lake 732-449-8005	•		•	•	•	•			•	•		98

*County park located in Long Branch.

New Monterey Hotel and Boardwalk, Asbury Park, N. J.

A circa 1910 postcard of Asbury Park shows that narrow beaches are a longtime feature of this shoreline.

course, beach erosion is almost a universal characteristic of the entire New Jersey shoreline. South Shore's Cape May certainly shares such problems. But the North Shore's beaches seem especially vulnerable to loss of sand.

Protective concrete and rock seawalls line much of the North Shore. Sand-trapping groins projecting vertically from the shore are very common in most North Shore resorts, much more in evidence than in most of the communities in the south.

The North Shore's communities tend to vary drastically from one another in their styles, reputations, and the income level of their visitors. These contrasts among neighbors, while also common along the rest of the Jersey shore, somehow seem sharper and more readily observed here. One step over an otherwise invisible political boundary transports visitors into another world, as at the Asbury Park–Ocean Grove line.

Just as visitors will find elsewhere along the shore, one or two resorts are ancient by American standards, but many are the products of a real estate boom, led and fed by railroads, in the 1870s and 1880s.

Although the history, character, and general tone of these towns can and do change abruptly at municipal borders, the North Shore, south of Sandy Hook, is an intensely urbanized seashore. South of Sandy Hook, there is a really long, sometimes skinny, city.

The North Shore has a much higher year-round, permanent population than any point farther south, except Atlantic City and its suburbs. There are no "summer-only" towns among the North Shore resorts because of the huge metropolitan area that centers on Manhattan but extends far into northeastern New Jersey. Commuter trains serve the shore down to Bay Head. Although people do commute from South Shore resorts into the Philadelphia metropolitan sprawl, the volume of commuters is small compared with that of the North Shore. South of Bay Head, only Atlantic City enjoys regular train service, with commuting supplemented by the Atlantic City Expressway.

The North Shore offers a great variety of vacation styles, prices, and experiences. Enjoy exploring it.

Sandy Hook

Sandy Hook, part of Gateway National Recreation Area, is well named. At the northern end of the Jersey shore, a long strip of sand extends northward from the base of the Highlands. It seems to point directly at the Narrows, the channel between Staten Island and Long Island now crossed by the Verrazano Bridge. The Hudson River and New York City are thataway, Sandy Hook seems to be saying. The hook image comes from the slightly

Sandy Hook guards the southern edge of the entrance to New York Bay, which gave it its one-time military significance. The New York skyline is just visible to the north.

bowed shape of this sandy peninsula, with its northern point rounded off and hooking to the west.

Sandy Hook is the product of the northbound alongshore current, which moves sand up the coast from the general vicinity of Barnegat Inlet. In a way, Sandy Hook is another "good news, bad news" story. The good news: Sandy Hook is growing. When the original Sandy Hook Lighthouse was built in 1764, it was about five hundred feet from the northern tip. That site now is more than one and a quarter miles from the tip. The lengthening of Sandy Hook provides more beach for visitors to enjoy, and that extra beach is conveniently located for the millions who live nearby.

On the other hand, where does Sandy Hook's fresh sand come from? Stand on the seawall at Sea Bright or Monmouth Beach to the south of Sandy Hook, and look at the beach. Without expensive beach replenishment projects, there would be no beach comparable to the broad stretches of sand at, say, Wildwood. The bad news is that Sandy Hook's gain is the North Shore's loss. The most likely locations of beach sand left along the shores of some resorts from Long Branch and Monmouth Beach to Sea Bright will be found in pockets to the south of the many rock and concrete groins along this shore. Beaches here are mostly narrow and steep, at best; at worst, nonexistent. The ocean giveth and the ocean taketh away through wave and current action.

Sandy Hook has had an interesting history. The famous lighthouse dates to 1764. The eighty-five-foot-tall light was built by New York merchants in the interests of reducing shipwrecks—and reducing marine insurance losses—along the Jersey shore approaches to New York Harbor. It is the oldest still-functioning lighthouse in the Western Hemisphere. It was so critical to safeguarding shipping to and from New York that patriots tried to destroy it during the Revolution. They wanted more, not less, British shipwrecks when New York was held by the Redcoats. Sandy Hook Bay often sheltered ships that anchored near the Highlands to take advantage of "the Spout"—a spring of cool, clear water. Captain Kidd was among those filling his casks, and there are many rumors of buried treasure.

Sandy Hook had a long military history, strategically located to help defend the entrance to Lower New York Bay and Raritan Bay. A fort was planned for Sandy Hook as early as the 1690s, but it was never begun during that era. Just before the Civil War, work began on a fort, but it was not completed. Finally, Fort Hancock was built; it functioned from the 1870s till the Nike missiles that formed the fort's last defense system were removed in the 1960s. During World War II, the military tested radar devices at Sandy Hook. In 1962, the state leased the lower two miles of Sandy Hook as a state park. Then in 1972, the federal government decided that all the land attached to Fort Hancock had little military value anymore, and there was a

Massive cannon guarded the approaches to New York from the Civil War to World War I.

Nike missiles were the last generation of weapons here before the military base was trans-formed into a park.

real need for more recreational space close to New York City, and so Gateway National Recreation Area was born, administratively combining Sandy Hook with Liberty Island, Ellis Island, and various parks in Staten Island. Fort Hancock itself became part of this recreation area in 1975. The Coast Guard still maintains a station near the tip of Sandy Hook.

Sandy Hook has it all—great beaches for swimming, surfing, sailboarding, and fishing; interesting nature trails; and history. The small Sandy Hook

Ghost Stories and Superstitions

Near where the Highlands tower over the base of Sandy Hook is the Jersey shore's most famous haunted house. The Shoal Harbor Museum is housed in the 1663 Whitlock-Seabrook House, a.k.a. the "Spy House," probably the oldest house built on the Jersey shore. The famous old structure is now part of Monmouth County's Bayshore Waterfront Park. The Spy House nickname originated during the Revolution, when Americans hid in underbrush nearby to spy on British ships anchored in Sandy Hook Bay. These spies would stop at this house, then converted to an inn, for food and a few drinks between shifts on spy work. No fewer than thirty ghosts are said to hang out on occasion, a New Jersey record. For information, call 732-787-1807.

Other famous haunted houses along the shore include the Hildreth House, built at Cape May in 1722 and later moved to Rio Grande. Now a part of Winterwood Gift Shop, Hildreth House ghosts include a one-time slave, a British soldier once granted refuge in the house, and two spinster sisters who once owned the house.

Drowned sailors and passengers, victims of shipwrecks all along the shore, people hundreds of shore ghost stories. The ghosts allegedly haunt the beaches where their dead bodies washed up on shore. They are said to be particularly unhappy and unresigned to their fate when the wrecks and deaths were deliberately caused by pirates, also known as "wreckers" or "moon cussers" (cursers); they supposedly hated the light of full moons, which took away the looter's advantages. The Jersey coast was once called the Graveyard of the Sea, and every island and town has some ghost stories to tell.

Superstitious sailors over many generations have avoided killing any seabird—in particular, petrels or albatross—as they may be the spirits of drowned sailors. Many landlubbers also follow this ban on killing seabirds, so this superstition may actually encourage conservation. Not many landlubbers, though, accept the old sailor's belief that being defecated upon by a seabird is a good omen.

Museum and tours of parts of the fort complex will interest history buffs. The lighthouse, still working, is not open to visitors. Amenities include restrooms, bathhouses, and snack bars.

The Spermaceti Cove Visitors Center contains exhibits on natural habitats and local wildlife, and on the founding of the U.S. Life Saving Service, now part of the Coast Guard. The cove got its name long ago when a dead whale washed ashore there. Fort Hancock's 12-inch guns could fire seven-hundred-pound shells over seven miles. Also on display is a mammoth 20-inch Civil War–era Rodman gun.

The gun battery tunnels at the fort are especially interesting. Huge cannons were designed to pop up from underground, fire sixteen-inch-diameter shells at enemy ships, and then quickly duck down into the tunnels before the enemy could fire back at them. Ingenious. But they were only actually needed once, during World War I. A German submarine surfaced off the Hook and fired a few rounds at the fort. The fort's mammoth guns replied with enough shells to sink a fleet of battleships. The sub's fate is unknown.

Nature trails take visitors through a variety of wildlife habitats. Bird-watching is popular. Yes, the bright red fruit of the common prickly pear cactus is edible, but don't touch—you are on government land. The same for beach plums, which were a favorite American Indian dessert. By the way, the most common plant of all is poison ivy—stay on the trails and keep alert.

Lighthouses

Among the Jersey shore's most famous landmarks are its great lighthouses. The most notable include Sandy Hook Light, a national historic landmark; the Twin Lights atop the Highlands, once the most powerful light on the coast, where Marconi first demonstrated his "wireless telegraph"; Barnegat Light, known as "Old Barny"; Atlantic City's Absecon Light; and Cape May Light. These great towers long have guided ships at sea. The gently shelving beaches, shifting shallow inlets, and offshore sandbars of New Jersey's coast are deathtraps for ships, and the Jersey shore required many tall lighthouses.

The first New Jersey lighthouse, Sandy Hook Light, an octagonal, 105-foot tower, was privately financed by New York City merchants eager to protect shipping. Begun in 1761, the light has shone since 1764, except in wartime. Cape May Light was the first to be built by the federal government in 1823, followed by Navesink or Highlands Light in 1828. The Twin Lights are not identical twins; the south tower is square, and the north tower is hexagonal. Built on the Highlands, a steep cliff already high above the bay, the towers are only 70 feet tall, but their total height is 150 feet. Barnegat Light was originally built in 1834. This first version fell into the sea, a victim of erosion. The present "Old Barney" dates to 1858. Barnegat Light was especially important to navigation, as it stands exactly on the 40th parallel north of the equator. Absecon Light was built at Atlantic City's north end in 1857. By 1900, the federal government maintained fifteen lighthouses and beacons from Sandy Hook to Cape

Special advice to treasure hunters: don't. Leave your shovels at home; it's federal land. Yes, it is certain that the infamous Captain Kidd, along with a lot of other people, did land on Sandy Hook to replenish their freshwater supplies. And it is said that, in 1948, a few gold coins were found on the bayshores of Sandy Hook. But no one ever found the treasure chest supposedly buried there by Captain Kidd. By the way, the story is that the captain always buried two dead men along with the treasure, so if you're beachcombing and you come across human bones . . .

Speaking of human bones, a Revolutionary War–era atrocity happened at the base of Sandy Hook in 1782. British forces hanged a captured American captain, Joshua Huddy, on charges that he had shot an English sympathizer, Philip White. Evidence proved that Huddy was in a British prison when White was killed, but he was hanged anyway. This caused a general outrage even among the British public. It is said that Captain Huddy's ghost still roams Sandy Hook.

Constructed in 1764, Sandy Hook Lighthouse is the oldest lighthouse on the east coast. It was built with money contributed by New York merchants to guide ships safely into port.

May. One by one, most of the picturesque lighthouses have been decommissioned as navigational aids employing newer technologies have come into use. Barnegat Light went out of official service in 1930, followed by Absecon Light in 1932 and the Twin Lights in 1949.

Less famous than their taller cousins but just as picturesque are Sea Girt Lighthouse and North Wildwood's Hereford Inlet Lighthouse. These two lights look like Victorian houses to which someone added a light as an afterthought.

Most of the lighthouses listed above are open to the public. Not open to the public are several lighthouses that are still functioning and maintained by the Coast Guard, including five to the west and north of Sandy Hook, on Sandy Hook and Raritan Bays and the Hudson River, and eight more on Delaware Bay and the Delaware River west and north of Cape May Light.

For more information on the Sandy Hook Unit of the Gateway National Recreation Area, call 732-872-5970. This is a *very* popular park in season; get there early or risk being turned away due to overflowing crowds and parking lots.

⚑ Sea Bright and Monmouth Beach

It's a tossup between which is the more annoying of two serious problems here for day-trippers. Along portions of the shoreline to the south of Sandy Hook, the beaches may either suffer from erosion or be inaccessible to those not lucky enough, or rich enough, to belong to a beach club.

North Shore beaches tend to be steeper and shorter than those along the central and southern shores. Some beaches consist of a disjointed series of shark-fin-shaped crescents of sand, which has been trapped on the south side of groins. In a few cases, even these may disappear entirely at high tide, until the next round of beach nourishment projects.

Many beaches are owned by the residents of beachfront houses and are not open to the public. Actually, this is more a case of visitors not being able to get to the beaches because reaching them from public roads would require crossing private land. In New Jersey, the state owns beaches up to the mean high-tide mark. Property owners here along the beach can and do prohibit trespassing. Beach clubs similarly restrict access to the water by posting "members only" signs on their property.

All of this can be very frustrating to nonresidents and nonmembers. Don't waste your time fretting about this situation. Wide, inviting public

Sea Bright lies on a narrow ribbon of sand between the ocean and the Navesink River.

beaches await you to the north of the private beaches, on Sandy Hook, and to the south, at Long Branch's Seven Presidents Park.

Sea Bright once was famous for its Lawn Tennis and Cricket Club, which says a lot about its social pretensions. Anyone for cricket? Sea Bright does have one public beach, and its many good restaurants happily host residents and nonresidents, members and nonmembers alike. Public parking with access to public beaches is scarce, but then, anyone living in Sea Bright could easily walk to the seafront anyhow. Monmouth Beach is another beach-club type of town. Here, even a glimpse of the ocean is denied the peasants, as the wooden platforms and steps up to the top of the massive seawall also are posted private property.

Observant visitors will notice that, as would be true anywhere, land values have a strong influence upon land use. This is especially evident at seashore resorts, where the most valuable land is that within a few blocks of the beach and, to a lesser degree, the bay. In mainland beach towns, like Long Branch or Asbury Park, the types of commercial use that require a lot of space relative to their income-producing potential—like warehouses, used-car lots, or construction materials yards—are always located in inland places, far from the sound of the surf. In those resort communities located on islands—especially narrow islands like Long Beach Island—there is a strict segregation of land uses and commercial establishments. Try finding, say, a cemetery on a resort island, or a trucking terminal, or a junkyard. Relative location always is important; in beach communities, it is location relative to the sea that dictates land values and the resulting land uses.

Long Branch

Both Long Branch and Cape May lay claim to the title "Nation's Oldest Seaside Resort"—or maybe the contested title should be "New Jersey's Oldest Seaside Resort," as New Englanders have their own candidates for the oldest resort title. Not that it matters a whole lot, except perhaps to residents of Long Branch and Cape May. What is clear is that Cape May's height of popularity among the elite was from the 1850s through the 1870s, while Long Branch's heyday was after the Civil War to the early twentieth century.

At one time, Long Branch was a famous, or maybe notorious, gambling resort. Roulette, dice, and card games helped attract the "fast crowd," and President Grant enjoyed visits to the casino. Monmouth Park Racetrack sprang up nearby. Prostitution, though illegal, found a tolerant political environment here. Then, the turn of the century saw a period of public moral outrage. Gambling was outlawed in many jurisdictions, and the laws eventually even were enforced, to the dismay of many tourists and local entrepreneurs. Long Branch suffered mightily when the New

Visits by Presidents and Other Notables

The first presidential visitor to the Jersey shore was Franklin Pierce, who arrived at Cape May in 1855. Apparently he used a warship as transportation. President Ulysses S. Grant visited Cape May at least four times but then went to Long Branch, where rich friends built him a house. President Chester A. Arthur once visited Cape May via a government steamboat, and President Benjamin Harrison was given a summerhouse at Cape May Point by his good friend, the wealthy Postmaster General John Wanamaker. Harrison was given the use of a suite at the Congress Hall Hotel in Cape May for his office. He commuted by carriage from his Cape May Point residence. Before his election, Abraham Lincoln and his wife, Mary, visited Cape May.

Franklin Pierce (term, 1853–57) was the first president to vacation on the Jersey shore.

It is said that President Grant especially enjoyed the casino at Long Branch. Other Long Branch presidential guests included Hayes,

Jersey State Legislature passed antigambling laws in 1897. Long Branch once was described as "America's Monte Carlo"; as much as $10 million changed hands on bets in a single season in the mid-1880s, and at Monmouth Park races on opening day in 1870, a record $31,000 purse was offered. Those were enormous sums for the times.

The evolving antigambling era was not Long Branch's only foe. Nature, in the form of ocean waves and currents, attacked the shoreline. Ocean Avenue, once the scene of daily parades of millionaires dressed in the latest fashions, riding in fancy carriages drawn by matched teams of handsome horses, has had to be moved back from the encroaching sea no less than four times. Since the Revolution, Long Branch has lost a thousand feet of beach to the sea; the waves advanced thirty feet during one stormy night alone.

Long Branch is another beach-club town. This, in combination with high bluffs (twenty-five to thirty feet) along the much-eroded beaches, restricts public access to the sea.

〰〰〰〰〰〰〰〰〰〰〰〰〰〰〰〰〰〰〰〰〰

Garfield, Arthur, Harrison, and McKinley. Mrs. Lincoln stayed at Long Branch by herself on occasion during the Civil War years, and New Jersey resident Woodrow Wilson stayed in West Long Branch, just a Frisbee's throw from the beach. In its day, Long Branch also attracted such notables as George Pullman of Pullman Sleeping Cars, Buffalo Bill and Annie Oakley, Oscar Wilde, and actress Lillie Langtry.

Left: Abraham Lincoln (term, 1861–65) visited Cape May before his presidency. Right: President Ulysses S. Grant (term, 1869–77) and his family at their Long Branch cottage in the 1870s.

Though there are many impressive mansions here (way back in the 1880s, there were several million-dollar estates), the town of Long Branch clearly has seen better days. Much of the seafront is rock and concrete seawall, with little surviving beach.

Located on the amusement pier at Long Branch, Kids World is a free paradise for toddlers, providing everything from amusements to beach access to a petting zoo.

Seven Presidents Oceanfront Park

This county park honors the seven U.S. presidents who summered in the neighborhood. There are three public bathing beaches, complete with changing facilities and fast-food concessions. Two kiddie playgrounds and three surfing and sailboarding beaches round out the attractions. There is an admission fee in summer, but it's well worth it.

Elberon, Deal, and Allenhurst

These three communities lie between Long Branch, to the north, and Asbury Park, to the south. Elberon, essentially a suburb of Long Branch, was founded in the 1870s by promoter Lewis B. Brown—get it, L. B. Brown, Elberon. It gradually became an exclusive resort, with emphasis on "exclusive." Deal was incorporated in 1898 as another exclusive playground for the rich. An attraction was Deal Lake, which had been an ocean inlet. Real estate promoter James Bradley turned the inlet into a freshwater lake by having a three-mile dike built.

Why the Curative Sea Air Couldn't Save President Garfield

When James A. Garfield, Civil War hero and twentieth president of the United States, was wounded in 1881 by two gunshots fired by Charles Guiteau, he was brought to the Long Branch suburb of Elberon to recover. The thinking was that since Garfield had summered at Long Branch before, it might be the perfect spot for him to convalesce. The wounded president was running a fever due to massive infections, and Washington, D.C., in July was miserably hot and humid. The seashore would be cooler, and people believed that sea air was healthful.

The bedridden president arrived by train. To spare Garfield a painful transfer to a carriage, train tracks were laid directly to a seaside house owned by a friend. Three-quarters of a mile of track were completed in twenty-four hours by volunteers. But despite the healthful sea air, Garfield died on September 19, 1881, seventy-eight days after being hit with two .44-caliber bullets, one of which simply grazed him.

Of America's four presidential assassinations, two presidents, Lincoln and Kennedy, received fatal head wounds that no one could have survived, regardless of their doctors' skills. Garfield and McKinley, however, received abdominal wounds that probably could have been treated successfully with modern medicine, especially Garfield's. Large doses of antibiotics likely would have worked, had they been available.

James A. Garfield was shot in 1881, the same year he became president. His doctors sent him to the shore to recuperate.

Deal and Allenhurst have a fine collection of lovely mansions along Ocean Drive, but these impressive seafront homes mean that public access to beaches is quite limited. For casual visitors, Deal, Allenhurst, and Elberon are "look but don't touch" communities. Much of Deal's seafront is owned by a private club called the Deal Casino. If you are not a resident, you'll never gain membership. Even if you are a resident, you'd better know the right people to become a member. The newly rich need not apply. But still, this part of the shore resembles a scaled-down version of Newport, Rhode Island, and these towns make a beautiful drive.

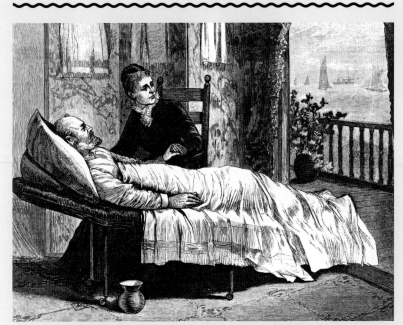

The wounded Garfield with his wife at Elberon on September 13, 1881, a few days before his death.

Many a war veteran was then walking around with a bullet in his body, but instead of leaving the bullet where it had lodged in President Garfield, his doctors probed for it endlessly with nonsterile instruments and fingers, spreading the infection, which eventually overwhelmed the president. Cool breezes of healthful sea air, it seems, can't counter poor medical practices.

It is said that at his trial, assassin Guiteau commented that Garfield's own doctors really killed him, not the bullets. That was probably true, but beside the point. Guiteau paid the ultimate price for his crime.

Large houses at Deal, which is among the wealthiest communities on the Jersey shore.

Asbury Park

While many New Jersey seashore towns were founded purely as land spec-ulation—create a town, advertise it, sell lots, get rich—others were prod-ucts of the religious camp-meeting enthusiasm of the 1860s through the 1880s. Of course, the camp-meeting communities managed to put a few dollars in the pockets of the faithful, too. Asbury Park was the perfect com-bination of the two motives.

When nearby Ocean Grove was founded in 1869, the community was tightly controlled in terms of personal behavior. Strict standards were enforced by the Camp Meeting Association, which owned all real estate and leased land rather than sold it. If your behavior didn't measure up, your lease was up. According to Harold Wilson in *The Story of the Jersey Shore*, the Camp Meeting leaders didn't want "anyone offensive [read: party types] next to your cottage." Now that "God's square mile" was safe from lowlifes, like card players, the Camp Meeting Association worried about its more distant neighbors.

When a five-hundred-acre tract just north of Ocean Grove came on the market, James Bradley, a wealthy industrialist and a Methodist, bought it so as to keep beer-drinking types from profaning the Sabbath on the doorsteps of Ocean Grove. Bradley named his planned resort after the Methodist bishop Francis Asbury and prohibited alcohol and gambling. Apparently the word about no alcoholic beverages didn't reach everyone, and Asbury Park grew up to be very different from Ocean Grove. And grow up it did, for Asbury Park, assessed at $16,000 in 1870 when Bradley purchased the land, was valued at $2 million by 1889.

The near-opposing social and religious values emerging in Asbury Park and Ocean Grove led to tensions between the residents and governments of the two towns. In Ocean Grove, the sanctity of the Sabbath was interpreted rigidly. Not only was vehicular traffic on Sundays prohibited, but newspapers could not be sold in Ocean Grove on Sunday. To discourage having bootlegged newspapers fall into the hands of Ocean Grove's less religious folks, Asbury Park's government agreed not to allow the selling of newspapers within one block of the Ocean Grove border. Apparently, if you were willing to walk farther than that for your paper, you'd earned the right to read it. But when Ocean Grove demanded that trains not be allowed to stop on Sundays at the train station shared by Asbury Park and Ocean Grove, Asbury Park's residents rebelled; this was just too much. The town of Asbury Park petitioned the state's Public Utilities Commission to require Sunday train service in the public interest. The commission agreed; Ocean Grove lost the court appeal.

But ironically, Ocean Grove won in the long run. It never lost its small-town, clean and upright, very appealing ambience. Asbury Park fell on hard times by the close of the twentieth century. Could cocktails in them-

Asbury Park's middle-class elegance is evident in this boardwalk scene from 1909.

Disasters as Tourist Attractions

Many Americans seem to take a strong interest in gruesome accidents. Famous disasters fascinate—as long as they happened to someone else, that is. Car commuters are familiar with "gaper" delays—traffic jams caused by drivers' slowing down to gawk at smashed vehicles and smashed people pushed to the side of the road and awaiting wreckers and ambulances.

Victorian-era entertainment at seashore resorts often featured paintings, sceno-graphs (revolving circular paintings), dioramas, or theatrical reenactments of classic or contemporary disasters, complete with sound effects and "wonderful electrical and mechanical effects." Usually advertised as "educational," popular subjects included the Johnstown Flood, Custer's Last Stand, and the sinking of the *Titanic*. Also featured, in due course, were notable train wrecks, the sinking of the *Lusitania*, and various land and naval battles.

The New Jersey coast itself has been the locale of many famous shipwrecks, producing genuine disaster scenes, some of which intrigued tourists and generated profits. As quoted in journalist Hal Burton's book on the *Morro Castle*, an 1884 editorial in the Asbury Park *Daily Spray* declared: "We need a first-class shipwreck . . . to make Asbury Park a famous winter resort. The [unlucky ship] should strike head-on and we could accommodate her all winter." Half a century later, Asbury Park got its macabre tourist attraction in the form of the *Morro Castle* disaster.

selves be some sort of urban curse, leading to decay? Nah, it must be more complicated than that.

Asbury Park had enjoyed a spectacular rise from 1870 to the 1950s. Just as Atlantic City had surpassed the older Cape May on the South Shore, Asbury Park had overshadowed venerable Long Branch after 1900. Asbury had become the North Shore's biggest town and busiest convention center as Long Branch faded following the end of legal (or tolerated) gambling.

But by the late 1960s, Asbury Park was in trouble. Familiar urban ills—an aging housing stock, too little reinvestment in maintaining and modernizing its supporting infrastructure, and suburban malls drawing customers away from its large, formerly prosperous downtown—led to a near-fatal image decay. Middle-class visitors stopped coming.

Then an unlikely hero initiated a change in Asbury Park's public image, and none too soon. A talented composer-musician named Bruce Springsteen almost single-handedly popularized the "Jersey Sound." Rock and roll!

On Friday night, September 7, 1934, the *Morro Castle* was returning to New York from a cruise to Havana, Cuba. The fast, modern liner caught on fire, most likely due to arson, and was soon engulfed in flames. By early the next morning, three miles off Sea Girt, it was a powerless, drifting hulk. Both the dead and the living began to wash up on the beaches. When the wreck broke away from its tow, the ship beached just two hundred feet off Asbury Park. What may be New Jersey's worst traffic jam ever resulted, with the lines of cars reaching back to the Holland Tunnel, as curious or perhaps slightly ghoulish crowds headed for the resort to view the smoldering ship from the comfort of the boardwalk.

Perhaps the Depression-era crowds were secretly pleased that folks who could afford a cruise to Havana were not immune to bad luck. Local businesses had their best day ever, and the city actually considered claiming the ship as salvage and making her a permanent attraction. Special trains brought the curious from New York and Philadelphia.

But the carnival atmosphere soon faded. From a high of 150,000 tourists on Monday, September 10, the crowds tapered off to a handful after the end of the month. When the wreck finally was towed off the beach on March 14, 1935, Asbury Park was happy to see it go, as its novelty had worn off and the cargo of cowhides had rotted, producing an eye-watering stench. Picture postcards of the wreck, however, continued to be sold long after the ill-fated ship was scrap.

The Boss's first album was titled *Greetings from Asbury Park* (1973); the album cover featured a classic postcard of that title, and a legend was born. Asbury Park's image became more that of a funky blue-collar music capital, a Jersey shore version of Detroit's Motown fame. The Stone Pony, scene of Springsteen's early appearances, is still in business. Rumor has it that the Boss still drops in on occasion.

Asbury Park seems to be in the early stages of revitalization, and with good reason. After all, the

Bruce Springsteen in Asbury Park in 1979 by Joel Bernstein.

The renovation of Asbury Park's classic hotel, the Berkeley-Carteret, is one sign of urban renewal. To the left is a statue of James Bradley, the real estate promoter who helped create Asbury Park, Ocean Grove, and Bradley Beach.

beach is still there, and the location relative to New York hasn't changed. They're not making any new beaches, and Asbury Park eventually will recover from the bad old days of the end of the twentieth century. Local rumor has it that country music superstar Johnny Cash has invested in real estate development here. The classic art deco Berkeley-Carteret Hotel has been attractively renovated and updated. This hotel, incidentally, was named for the two Colonial "proprietors" of New Jersey, Lord John Berkeley and Sir George Carteret.

 Ocean Grove

Ocean Grove is a unique little community that is well worth at least a brief look, even for those used to quite different resort atmospheres. This jewel of the Jersey shore is a neat, little Victorian seaside town, known to its founders as "God's square mile." It is the best known and best preserved of a string of camp-meeting towns along the Jersey shore, and it's well worth a visit from any other North Shore resort.

Camp meetings originally served both the religious and social needs of families scattered on frontier farms in the early nineteenth century. Isolation was a problem for those early frontier-farming folks. Neighbors might be far away in terms of horse and wagon trips over primitive dirt roads. The

nearest church might be such a long, hard ride as to make weekly atten-
dance an impossibility. One answer was camp meetings, especially favored
by Methodists. The whole family would pack up and camp out for a week
or so, together with other like-minded people. There would be several outdoor services every day, with guest preachers, Bible study groups, picnics,
and games. Farm families would squeeze into a week all of the year's
churchgoing and socializing, then go home.

In the 1870s, there was a "great revival" movement to reorganize camp
meetings as a kind of religious vacation retreat, now attracting mostly
urbanites. For the more Puritan-minded, camp meetings were a socially
acceptable excuse for having a really great vacation, and seashore locations were popular. Ocean Grove, Ocean City, Asbury Park, Seaside Park,
Cape May Point, Atlantic Highlands, Avon by the Sea, and Belmar all had
some element of religious camp meetings in their founding. Ocean Grove
was the only such community, however, to remain uprightly religious and
sedate in function and appearance.

In keeping with the "camp" theme, early camp meetings were summer-
only tent communities. Gradually, tents were replaced by wooden cottages,
often uninsulated and unheated. Intended strictly for summer use, these
often were cheaply constructed, with low ceilings and small rooms. Later
they were expanded and upgraded, or replaced by more substantial houses
suitable for year-round occupancy.

*The famous tents on permanent foundations have been a feature of Ocean Grove life for
more than a century.*

Ocean Grove, circa 1906, has long been a popular, if sedate, resort.

Conservative Ocean Grove retains about one hundred tent-houses—tents erected on permanent wooden platforms with attached wooden kitchen-bath-storage units. In all early camp meetings, the central and most important building was the tabernacle or religious meeting facility.

With its tent-houses, Victorian cottages, and magnificent Great Auditorium, Ocean Grove is a time capsule from 1890. Ocean Grove's main avenue shopping district has such nostalgic small-town charm that it could have been airlifted to Disney World as the model for its "Main Street." Behavior was strictly regulated, perhaps to emphasize the contrast with the then wide-open, notorious resorts like Long Branch, Cape May, and Atlantic City. In those towns, booze flowed freely and gambling and prostitution were openly tolerated, attracting free-spending, rather rowdy crowds.

In Ocean Grove, nightlife featured dramatic sermons by famous preachers, along with Bible study groups. Liquor was forbidden (it still is), and the Sabbath was kept holy—and quiet—by an ordinance prohibiting *any* vehicular traffic on Sundays. Chains were stretched across the entrance gates. There is a story that President Ulysses S. Grant once set off on a Sunday visit to his sister, who owned an Ocean Grove cottage. His carriage was stopped at the border, and the guards explained politely that even the president had to leave the carriage at the gate and walk. The president walked,

The cozy porches of the summer cottages at Ocean Grove seem to reflect the enjoyment of tranquil summers of long ago.

The Great Auditorium hosts many secular, as well as religious, programs.

graciously. Ocean Grove is paradise for fans of quaint Victorian bed-and-breakfast houses.

This custom of sealing off Ocean Grove from its less holy neighbors on Sundays did not end until a New Jersey Supreme Court ruling in 1974 terminated the Camp Meeting Association's governmental powers. Although cars were now allowed on Sundays, many of the old traditions persist. If

An Answer to Their Prayers

Both Cape May and Long Branch, in their mid-nineteenth-century hey-days, earned reputations as flashy, let-the-good-times-roll, anything-goes towns. High-stakes gambling, heavy drinking, and the presence of many "ladies of the evening" gave them a Las Vegas–like aura of glamorous misbehavior. Atlantic City, too, had earned a naughty reputation by the 1890s. In reaction, more staid and sober middle-class Americans dreamed of churchgoing, clean-living resorts where the faithful could mix Sunday school rules with sand and surf.

Ocean City, founded in 1879 by three Methodist ministers, originally forbade certain activities on the Sabbath, such as sea bathing, driving a horse and buggy, and traveling to the mainland by boat. Those restrictions lapsed years ago, but it is still illegal to sell alcohol at any time, anywhere in the municipality, and it remained illegal to sell anything but food on Sundays until 1986, after state courts challenged the so-called "blue laws."

Ocean Grove, founded in 1870, once was a private club that prohibited liquor, theatrical shows and other public entertainment, tobacco, dancing, and card playing. And watch your mouth, too. Swearing was illegal, even in boats on the lake, although no one ever figured out how to enforce that rule. Vehicles were refused entrance on Sundays, even in emergencies. Many of Ocean Grove's more extreme restrictions were ended by law in 1974, but it remains a dry town with quiet habits and ambience.

An interesting thing happened on the way to the twenty-first century. The wide-open, sin-tolerant towns like Atlantic City and Asbury Park experienced serious declines in reputation and real estate values by the 1970s, while the more moralistic towns like Ocean Grove and Ocean City retained their middle-class ambience and high real estate values. Maybe there is something to these religious values and high standards of public morality.

A frontyard angel is representative of the spirit of Ocean Grove.

you prefer peace and quiet on vacation, Ocean Grove is for you. If you are the nightclub type, try Atlantic City, Seaside Heights, or—closer to Ocean Grove—Asbury Park, Belmar, or Manasquan.

At Ocean Grove, interesting sites include the Great Auditorium (1894), which seats seven thousand and has near-perfect acoustics and the largest auditorium-type pipe organ in the world. A giant electric American flag above the altar can be made to "wave" electronically. In addition to Sunday services and guest preachers, many nonreligious musical programs are offered, including a Mozart festival, popular stars, and doo-wop shows. Organ concerts are held Wednesdays and Saturdays.

Also visit Centennial Cottage, a fully restored, typical summer cottage of a hundred years ago. There is an admission fee. For information, call 732-774-1869.

For general information on Ocean Grove, call the Chamber of Commerce, 800-388-GROVE or, in New Jersey, 732-774-1391. Ocean Grove is so compact, it is the perfect place for walking tours; maps are available at the Chamber of Commerce.

Bradley Beach, Avon by the Sea, and Belmar

Driving along the North Shore usually leaves an impression of one long city. Only the names of individual towns on welcome signs provide any distinction to the long succession of hotels, motels, condos, and summer homes. But that is the usual experience; in contrast, the North Shore communities of Bradley Beach, Avon by the Sea, and Belmar are separated from one another by lakes, parks, and the Shark River Inlet.

Bradley Beach is named for James A. Bradley, who also founded Asbury Park. In fact, there is a statue of Bradley in Asbury Park, near the Berkeley-Carteret Hotel. That the local hero is not a political or military figure, but a real estate developer, tells us a lot about the Jersey shore. In contrast to Asbury Park, Bradley Beach is a quiet, middle-class, family resort. Neighboring Ocean Grove must find Bradley Beach a congenial neighbor. Avon by the Sea is another peaceful, mostly permanent and seasonal home community.

Belmar, to the south of Avon by the Sea, is across the Shark River Inlet. The Belmar Marina is home to a fleet of party boats. The term "party boats" as used along the Jersey shore does not refer to wild partying. Also known as "head boats," party boats take individuals and small parties of fishermen (yes, mostly men) out for a full or half day of fishing. They charge by the head, per trip. Belmar is also an important commercial fishing port. Commercial fishing facilities (wharves, processing plants, storage and repair areas) along the Jersey shore are under a lot of economic pressure. River or bay frontage often is worth more to developers than to commercial fishing enterprises, with their relatively modest profits. Waterfront condos pay better than fish.

In keeping with the Shark River name, shark fishing is very popular. Dusky, blue, brown, mako, hammerhead, tiger, and thresher sharks have all been caught in Jersey waters, even an occasional great white. Sportfishing for sharks has become so popular that some express fears that they may be overfished. Sharks are top predators—that is, they have no enemies other than people and other sharks. They reproduce slowly, as, before being actively hunted by people, they had few worries once reaching maturity. Belmar is also a beach town, and the beach is fairly wide, thanks to the long jetties protecting Shark River Inlet. These jetties trap sand that otherwise would be carried northward by the alongshore current.

Spring Lake and Sea Girt

The social atmosphere changes visibly from Belmar southward to the definitely upper-middle-class resort of Spring Lake. The actual Spring Lake and Lake Como help create a distinctively beautiful physical environment. Known locally as the "Irish Riviera," Spring Lake does in fact seem like an upper-crust suburb that would have one heck of a time every St. Patrick's Day. The town has a small, country town image, with a charming little business district and truly lovely homes. The grand Essex and Sussex Hotel, used as a setting in several movies, is now a condo. The boardwalk is a lovely place to jog, stroll, or people watch, but it doesn't have the action of some more popular resorts. Spring Lake is more the kind of place where feeding the ducks and swans on the lake is as exciting as it gets. It is a quiet, uniquely beautiful town, well worth a look even for those not staying there.

A small museum operated by the Spring Lake Historical Society is located in the Municipal Building. It is open only a few days a week. For hours, call the Chamber of Commerce at 732-449-0577. Along with some grand old hotels, Spring Lake has a variety of bed-and-breakfasts in interesting old homes.

In many ways a near clone of its neighbor to the north, Sea Girt is just as attractive and peaceful. The beach has no public facilities, and parking there is severely restricted. This suggests that the local attitude is, if you can't walk to the beach from home, forget it. The state of New Jersey bought 165 acres of oceanfront land at Sea Girt early in the twentieth century. This is presently used as a National Guard training site and the State Police Academy, where both state and municipal police are trained.

Sex on the Beach

Gender separation when bathing, an early-nineteenth-century phe-nomenon, produced a curious combination of prudishness and nude bathing. When future resorts were still isolated villages, and high natu-ral dunes screened bathers from view of the hotels, gentlemen custom-arily bathed in the nude—"nature's garb," as it was known. Women, however, were usually swathed in heavy woolen costumes that covered them as completely as their normal clothing. As the century progressed, men, too, became encumbered by bathing suits that covered the torso, thighs, and upper arms. Nevertheless, local boys continued to bathe nude at secluded spots and in the off season right up into the 1920s.

Mixed bathing was generally frowned upon in the early years of the nineteenth century, though little was done officially to prevent it. Up until the Civil War, it was customary for hotels and boardinghouses to post notices of bathing times: Before 6 A.M., gentlemen could bathe "in natural abandon," and women were prohibited from the vicinity. Female bathers had the beach to themselves from 6 to 7 A.M., 11 to noon, and 4:30 to 5:30 P.M. White flags flew from poles along the dunes

Beachwear of the Victorian era.

By the Roaring Twenties, beachwear became less inhibited.

during ladies' hours, and red flags signaled men only. Married men were allowed to accompany their wives during "white flag" times.

"Sea bathing" in these days was not the same thing as swimming. Few adults ventured into the water above their knees; jumping up and down in the surf was about it. This was a good thing, too, as the bathing costumes of the day constrained arm and leg movement and weighed heavily when saturated.

In some areas, the "cover-up" mentality lasted a surprisingly long time. As recently as the late 1940s, many resorts required males over the age of ten or twelve to wear tank tops on the beach.

An interesting progression has taken place in bathing suits and beachwear. In the earliest years of sea bathing, many bathers simply used cast-off street clothes—especially those men who chose not to bathe naked. Women's beach and surf costumes were modeled on streetwear, if not actually recycled street costumes. After more than a century of specialized swimwear, roughly from the Civil War through the 1960s, cast-off street attire has reappeared at the beach. Cut-off jeans, walking shorts past their prime, and T-shirts now are worn side by side with more traditional beachwear. Very brief bikinis, first popular in the 1960s, now are acceptable and unremarkable. Unlike many European resorts, however, topless and nude beaches have not yet appeared on New Jersey strands. But we can hope.

The opulent Essex and Sussex Hotel—now a condo—at Spring Lake is typical of the grand hotels that served wealthy vacationers nearly a century ago.

This state-owned land once included the governor's official summer home. The state had purchased the New Jersey building at the 1906 Louisiana Purchase Exposition in St. Louis and moved it to Sea Girt. The large, Colonial-style mansion ceased being New Jersey's "summer capital" in 1942, when Gov. Charles Edison closed it as a wartime austerity measure. It was never reopened.

Manasquan and Brielle

Manasquan, once known as Squan Village, has a fairly long history as a resort for these parts. While the strip of resorts between Bradley Beach and Sea Girt owed their existence to the extension of the railroad south from Long Branch in 1875, Manasquan earlier hosted the owners of small pleasure craft, thanks to Manasquan Inlet. Typical of this seashore region, the inlet was nearly closed by sand on several occasions. As early as 1879, the federal government spent $39,000 to clear and maintain the inlet. Manasquan Inlet today is New Jersey's northern entry to the Intracoastal Waterway, which continues all the way to Florida.

According to popular New Jersey author John Cunningham, *Manasquan* is derived from a Native American word, a real tongue twister: *Manatah-squawhan*. This was alleged to mean "stream of the island for squaws"—a

Gifts of the Sea

Although the deliberate luring of ships into shallow water by "wreckers" is a thing of the past, and the many legends of pirate treasure chests have never produced an actual, historically verified treasure, the ocean's waves and sandbars do occasionally provide an unexpected gift to seashore residents in the form of jettisoned cargo. And by the way, "jetsam" is material that floats as a result of a deliberate tossing overboard; "flotsam" is material that was accidentally lost, from either a ship or a waterside facility.

Atlantic City residents long remembered the March 30, 1903, grounding of United Fruit Lines' *Brighton*. As the story is told in Ed Davis's *Atlantic City Diary,* the ship ran aground in a storm near the inlet end of Pacific Avenue. To lighten the load and refloat the ship, crew tossed overboard twenty-six thousand bunches of bananas and four hundred bags of coconuts. Eager locals waded into the surf to get their share, and bananas were on everyone's table for weeks. Banana cream pie, anyone? The *Brighton* did float off the sandbar and continued her voyage to New York.

In 1946, about two thousand mysterious bottles washed ashore in Ventnor. The labels had washed off, but Ventnor residents discovered that the contents looked and smelled like shampoo, and so used the contents.

Perhaps even more welcome gifts were the liquor bottles, full and still capped, that regularly appeared in the surf along the entire shoreline during Prohibition days. Schooners and small freighters from the Caribbean, Bermuda, or Canada regularly patrolled the coast just beyond the territorial limits of Coast Guard control. At night, local boats swarmed around these supply ships to buy illegal alcohol. What with accidental capsizes and difficulties of transferring cargo at night between ships rocking and rolling in the waves, many a bottle fell into the sea, and beachcombing became a profitable and enjoyable hobby.

It is said that the long, narrow, shallow-draft speedboats called cigarettes (for their general shape, not their cargo) originated in the Prohibition era. Often powered by pairs of automobile or even aircraft engines, these smuggler favorites easily outran Coast Guard vessels.

place where wives were parked in safety while their men went off hunting and fishing. It's a nice thought, if now politically incorrect.

Brielle is a pleasant residential area located on the Manasquan River behind Manasquan. While Manasquan has both an ocean beach and an inlet beach, a favorite of surf fishers, Brielle is more famous for its charter and party fishing boats.

Nearby Attractions

Turkey Swamp County Park

This Monmouth County park, located in Freehold, makes a good day trip from the North Jersey shore resorts, offering nature trails, picnic areas, restrooms, sport fields, fishing, and boating (bring your own boat). Perhaps most important for budget-minded campers are reasonably priced pull-through campsites with water and electric hookups. Thirty-two sites are available on a first-come, first-served basis; another thirty-two are reserved (two-night minimum, prepaid). For information, call 732-842-4000. Reserve well in advance for summer camping. The park is free, except camping fees.

Cheesequake State Park

This is a delightful island of natural environments—forest, fields, marshes, white cedar swamp—in a heavily urban-suburbanized area, located off State Route 34 or the Garden State Parkway, Exit 120. Visitors enjoy more than thirteen hundred acres with nature trails, a nature center, campgrounds, swimming, fishing, basketball, crabbing, and in winter, cross-country skiing. There is an entrance fee in summer, and a fee for camping. The campground has a bathhouse and restrooms, but campsites do not have water or electricity. For information, call 732-566-2126.

Double Trouble State Park

What a great name! This free park is located off U.S. Route 9 in Berkeley Township, Ocean County. The park has five thousand acres of Pinelands habitats along Cedar Creek and offers hiking, bird-watching, biking, horseback riding, picnicking, and canoeing and fishing. A historic logging and saw milling village in the Pinelands has fourteen original structures. September and October offer a chance to see cranberries being harvested. There are no facilities. For information, call 732-341-6662.

Garden State Arts Center, Holmdel

Would you like to enjoy opera, ballet, symphony orchestras, jazz bands, or top-flight entertainers under a gigantic concrete umbrella with an uncanny resemblance to a huge flying saucer? The Garden State Arts Center, a.k.a. PNC Bank Arts Center, just off Exit 116 of the Garden State Parkway, offers all that and more. An open-sided amphitheater, the Arts Center has a capacity of 17,500, with 7,000 theater-style seats in the pavilion area and the rest in lawn spaces, where you may sprawl out under the stars on your own blanket.

Nearly fifty concerts are presented each summer. This highly accessible venue for superstar entertainers sells out quickly, so make your reservations early. Past performers include Liza Minnelli, Bill Cosby, Itzhak Perlman, Harry Belafonte, Rodney Dangerfield, Steve Martin, Tom Jones, the Boston Pops, the London Symphony—you get the picture. A series of ethnic heritage festivals is held annually, celebrating the artistic heritage (including cuisine) of the Polish, Irish, Germans, Scots, Scandinavians, Russians, Jews, Italians, Ukrainians, Slovaks, and Hungarians, who make up the ethnic mosaic that is New Jersey. During Christmas season, this is the location of the state's largest drive-through holiday light display. There are occasional free events for children, seniors, and the disabled. For information, call 732-335-0400.

Deep Cut Gardens

About a hundred acres of exotic trees and plants, including some spectacular specimens, can be admired in Monmouth County Park, which features walking paths, greenhouses, and gift shops. The "Deep Cut" is a small stream. The park is free, easily accessible from North Shore resorts, and has restrooms. For information, call 732-842-4000.

Maybe these lovely gardens should be called Godfather Park. One-time organized crime boss Vito Genovese spent a lot of money creating spectacular gardens on his estate. Local legend has it that he built a swimming pool next to a replica of the volcano Mount Vesuvius (of Pompeii fame) that could light up and emit smoke at the press of a button. Sorry, both pool and volcano are gone.

Longstreet Farm

Inside Holmdel Park, a large Monmouth County park with hiking trails, playing fields, a fishing and skating pond, and picnic areas, is Longstreet Farm—a living-history exhibit of farm life as it was in the 1890s. Here you can try to milk a cow (not as easy as it looks), weed the garden, or better yet, watch others do farm chores. Call 732-946-3758.

Allaire Village and Park

Allaire Village, located in Allaire State Park, off Exit 98 of the Garden State Parkway, was an early iron-making center. The furnaces, fired by charcoal produced in the surrounding pine forests, processed bog iron ores; the remains of the "great blast furnace" are impressive. Jersey bog iron furnaces could not compete when Pennsylvania coal and iron ores came into production in the 1840s, and so Allaire, like other Pinelands furnaces, went cold.

The village charges no admission fee, is open year-round, and has a visitors center, gift shop, restrooms, and snack bar. The park (732-938-2371; fee in summer only) has picnic tables, a nature center, fishing, swimming, restrooms, bathouse, and the New Jersey Museum of Transportation.

Pine Creek Railroad

Steam train enthusiasts will really enjoy the narrow-gauge Pine Creek railroad, next to Allaire Village in Allaire Park, which uses original locomotives and cars from as far away as Newfoundland and Hawaii. Short rides are available for a fee in antique cars pulled by either vintage steam or contemporary diesel locomotives. This is an absolute must for railroad buffs and kids. An annual highlight, in June, is a reenactment of the Civil War's Great Locomotive Chase. In 1862, Union soldiers commandeered the locomotive *General* at Marietta, Georgia, and began a breakneck ride through the South. Confederates gave chase in the locomotive *Texas,* eventually catching up with the *General.* Both locomotives had been made in Paterson, New Jersey. A 1956 movie, *The Great Locomotive Chase,* was based on this true incident. Call 732-938-5524.

Monmouth Battleground State Park

This park, at 347 Freehold-Englishtown Road in Freehold, off U.S. Route 9, preserves much of one of the most critical battlefields of the American Revolution. This was one of the few times that the poorly equipped, relatively less well-trained American Army met the British Army in a classic head-to-head confrontation on the field of battle. This was the only battle in which the two opposing commanders-in-chief, George Washington and, at the time, British general Henry Clinton, met in combat. Although the battle was almost a draw, the British retreated first and lost at least a hundred men more than the Americans. The Americans gained confidence because they had stood up to England's best. The fifteen-hundred-acre park has two picnic areas, hiking trails, and a playground.

Other than George Washington, whose courageous leadership reversed a near defeat at the hands of the unaggressive Gen. Charles Lee (later court-martialed and relieved of command), the hero of the day was Molly Pitcher. Molly was a real person, Mrs. Mary Hays, who fetched water by the pitcher for parched American soldiers. The day was miserably hot, and thirty-seven Americans and fifty-nine British soldiers died of sunstroke. When her husband, an artilleryman, was wounded in battle, Molly took his place at his cannon and earned her place in history. History buffs can still visit Molly Pitcher's well. General Washington rewarded Molly's bravery by making her an honorary officer. For information, call 732-462-9616.

Monmouth Museum

Located on the Brookdale Community College campus on Newman Springs Road off the Garden State Parkway, Exit 109, in Lincroft, the museum features revolving exhibits designed around significant ideas and concepts, such as coping with land use planning problems as urban-suburban areas grow, an especially relevant topic in high-population-density New Jersey. An admission fee is charged. For information, call 732-747-2266.

Monmouth County Historical Association Museum

Located in downtown Freehold, this charming museum features Emmanuel Leutz's great painting of George Washington's triumphant victory at the Battle of Monmouth. Artist Leutz also painted the famous and inspiring picture of Washington Crossing the Delaware, a detail of which is reproduced on the New Jersey quarter. For information, call 732-462-1466.

Fort Monmouth Army Communications-Electronics Museum

This highly specialized museum, located about two miles from Long Branch at Eatontown, on State Route 35, depicts both the history of Fort Monmouth, once the U.S. Army Signal Corps Communications School, and the development of military communications technology and electronic equipment. Some communications gear from foreign armies is also on display. Admission is free. Open Monday through Thursday; inquire at Main Gate for directions. For information, call 732-532-1682.

Monmouth Park Racetrack

One of two traditional, nonharness horse race tracks at the shore (the other is Atlantic City Racetrack), Monmouth Park is located in Oceanport near Long Branch. Racing here dates back to 1870, when Long Branch was a gambling mecca for the rich and famous. Located just off State Route 36 (Garden State Parkway Exit 105), Monmouth Park offers tours as well as exciting horse races in season. For information, call 732-222-5100.

Freehold Raceway

If you're interested in harness racing, where jockeys ride behind in tiny two-wheeled, rather flimsy-looking carts called sulkies instead of astride the horses, check out this raceway, located at U.S. Route 9 and State Route 33 in Freehold. Freehold can be reached just off U.S. Route 9, south of Freehold; it is about fourteen miles from Long Branch. Dining is available in the stadium. For information, call 732-462-3800.

Lakehurst and the End of the Airship Era

History-minded disaster buffs will enjoy a half-day trip to Lakehurst, readily accessible from North Shore or Central Shore resorts (get off the Garden State Parkway at Exit 82, and head west on State Route 37). There are no tours at present, but huge hangars, easily visible from the road, still exist as a reminder of Lakehurst U.S. Naval Air Station's brief role as an international airship port.

This is where a famous disaster—the explosion and burning of the German dirigible *Hindenburg* on May 6, 1937—effectively ended interest in airships as passenger carriers. Lakehurst was the East Coast home of the U.S. Navy's airships, which were used for reconnaissance and carried no passengers. Lakehurst had lots of flat, open space and was not too far from New York (fifty-five miles, as the airship flies, midtown to Lakehurst), and the presence of a tall mooring mast and crews skilled in docking the sometimes unwieldy mammoth airships naturally attracted the German airships as well.

Compared with present-day airliners, the great airships were very slow but very comfortable. Before the hydrogen-filled *Hindenburg* was destroyed in a spectacular blaze that killed thirty-six people, airships had provided a level of luxurious comfort that even first-class air passengers today would enjoy.

As historian Kevin Hudson noted, *Hindenburg*'s thirty-four double cabins carried up to sixty-eight passengers, ensuring individual attention. There were three bars, open all day and most of the night, as well as a smoking room, a small library, a dining room with specially made chinaware and silverware, a writing room, and an observation lounge, featuring a grand piano. A surviving menu card for lunch lists honeydew melon au citron, Hungarian goulash, cold asparagus vinaigrette, éclairs, and coffee. Transatlantic flights took as little as forty-three hours. This too-brief era of leisurely, luxurious airship travel ended in New Jersey's Pinelands close by the North Shore.

The North Shore's Other Shore—the Bayshore

The ocean shoreline of the North Shore ends with Sandy Hook. However, the coastline of Sandy Hook Bay and Raritan Bay, to the west, is another shore in both the physical and recreation senses. In the past, Highlands, Atlantic Highlands, Leonardo, Ideal Beach, Keansburg, Union Beach, Keyport, Cliffwood Beach, and Raritan Bay Beach all had resort activities. The Bayshore communities have had to cope with two crucial changes, however, which led to a long decline in their resort businesses.

Water quality has been a problem. The natural cleansing effect of the ocean's tides and currents, diluting and carrying away pollutants, doesn't function as well in the partly enclosed bay waters as it does along the open ocean coasts. The many factories and refineries around Raritan Bay and along the channels separating Staten Island from New Jersey have concentrated pollution in the bay waters. Beaches on the Bayshore are narrow or absent. Large quantities of flotsam make the beaches less desirable, and the coarse, rather orange color of most beach material lacks the appeal of the finer, beige-white sands of nearby ocean beaches.

Although water quality is improving, swimming, fishing, and shellfishing are restricted in Raritan Bay until the state's ongoing battles against pollution are finally won. Sandy Hook Bay is somewhat less polluted than Raritan Bay, but the shellfishing grounds are still condemned, and it is not advisable to eat finfish caught in the bay, wiping out the once-thriving sportfishing industry. Boating remains an important attraction, with many marinas along these shores.

With the opening of the Garden State Parkway in 1954, residents of North Jersey could travel to ocean beaches in the same time it used to take them to get to Bayshore beaches. Most visitors to the Bayshore towns today are day-trippers, as there are relatively few overnight accommodations. There are, however, many good restaurants in places like Highlands and Atlantic Highlands.

Historic sites like Twin Lights attract increasing numbers of tourists. In 1729, the New York Merchant's Exchange erected a semaphore tower at what is now the Twin Lights. The semaphore relayed messages from incoming ships about their cargoes. The Twin Lights State Historic Site at Highlands is a small museum in an 1862 structure, which replaced an 1828 light. The two towers were built at the same time, but the south tower is square and the north tower octagonal. At night, the two lights, one flashing and the other fixed, provided a distinguishing characteristic from other lights, thus aiding navigation. The lights are located atop a two-hundred-foot bluff above Sandy Hook Bay, and the north tower may be climbed for a fantastic view of Sandy Hook, New York Bay, and Manhattan. This elevation, directly on the coast and close to New York City, was why the Italian inventor Guglielmo Marconi chose the site to experiment with his great invention, the wireless telegraph, a major leap forward in communications technology, from 1895 to 1899. As a result, the Twin Lights became the nation's first wireless telegraph station operating on a regular, commercial basis. The free Twin Lights museum contains examples of New Jersey small craft designs, lifesaving equipment, and a replica of Marconi's successful wireless apparatus, as well as a small book and gift shop and restrooms. For information, call 732-872-1814.

Nearby the Twin Lights is 266-foot Mount Mitchell, the terminus of Atlantic Highlands' Scenic Drive. The view is impressive; on a clear day, the Empire State Building in Manhattan is visible. Though people from Colorado or California might fall over laughing at the thought of a 266-foot-tall "mountain," this *is* the highest point directly on the East Coast south of Maine.

Keansburg Amusement Park opened in 1904, making it New Jersey's first amusement park and among the country's thirty oldest parks. This elderly ancestor of such family fun paradises as Disneyland and Disney World has a vintage feel, although it is well maintained. Summer hours are 9 A.M. to about

The Twin Lights of the Navesink Highlands have long been landmarks for seashore-bound New Yorkers. The south tower is shown here.

midnight. For information, call 800-805-4FUN or 732-495-1400. Keansburg's (and the Bayshore's) largest amusement enterprise includes Runaway Rapids Waterpark, which features a water slide that runs *uphill*. Until the 1930s, steamboats from Manhattan took fun lovers to Keansburg for either daytime family fun at the park or nighttime adult fun at the many bars and nightclubs.

Belford, the third-largest commercial fishing port in New Jersey, is a good place to photograph the fishing fleet and docks. If you're going to cook your own dinner, the seafood co-op there will sell you the freshest fish at good prices. Other attractions are the State Marina at Leonardo and the marinas in Keyport. Once a busy shipping port and steamboat building center, Keyport's days as a steamboat port were ended by a late-season hurricane in 1950, which wrecked the docks. Steamboat building began around the Civil War era. By 1917, the town had started building amphibious airplanes, an industry that lasted until the 1930s. All of this interesting history is documented in the Steamboat Dock Museum, located at the waterfront end of Broad Street. The museum is free, but hours are quite limited. Call ahead for hours, 732-264-2102.

Ferries to and from Manhattan

The ferries are back—faster than ever, and commuter-oriented this time rather than aimed at vacationers. But they're back. The New York Fast Ferry and the Seastreak Fast Ferry connect Highlands, Keyport, and Atlantic Highlands with Manhattan. The New York Fast Ferry leaves from Sandy Hook Bay Marina or the Clam Hut in Highlands; both New Jersey termini have service to East 34th Street or Pier 11, Wall Street. This ferry advertises cheaper round-trips at off-peak hours; consider reversing the usual commute and visiting Manhattan from North Jersey's "other shore" with no traffic or parking problems. The views alone should be worth it. Call 800-NYF-NYFF for information.

Also providing fast ferry service is Seastreak America, operating from Highlands and 2 First Avenue in Atlantic Highlands. Call 800-BOATRIDE for details, including weekend departures.

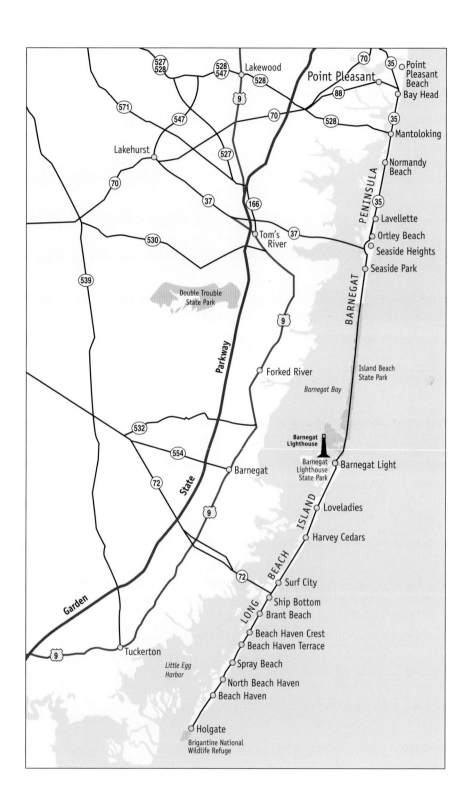

5

The Central Shore

New Jersey's Central Shore is the region between Manasquan Inlet and Barnegat Inlet. The Central Shore divides neatly into two parts on a physical basis: the Barnegat Peninsula (Manasquan Inlet to Island Beach State Park and Barnegat Inlet) and Long Beach Island.

THE BARNEGAT PENINSULA

North of Manasquan Inlet, the North Shore is a mainland shore, along which narrow barrier beaches have almost blocked the mouths of small rivers such as the Navesink, Shrewsbury, and Shark. Southward from Manasquan Inlet, the long barrier beach that extends from Mantoloking to the Barnegat Inlet is a peninsula. (Okay, technically, the Intracoastal Waterway Canal connecting Manasquan Inlet and Silver Bay, the upper part of Barnegat Bay, makes it an island.) The Barnegat Peninsula section of the Central Shore includes the towns of Point Pleasant Beach, Bay Head, Mantoloking, Normandy Beach, Ocean Beach, Lavallette, Ortley Beach, Seaside Heights, Seaside Park, and South Seaside Park, at the entrance to Island Beach State Park.

From Point Pleasant Beach southward, the beaches tend to be broad and very attractive compared with the relatively narrow and less gently shelving beaches more typical of the North Shore.

The Central Shore region includes all Ocean County resorts, from Point Pleasant Beach southward to Beach Haven Inlet.

Central Shore Beach Facility Profiles

Facility Phone Number	Accommodations	Amusements	Bathhouses	Beach Fee	Boardwalk	Fishing	Lifeguard	Picnicking	Rafting	Surfing	Tennis Courts	Garden State Parkway Exit
Barnegat Light 609-494-7211	•		•	•		•	•	•		A	•	63
Bay Head 732-892-0636	•		•								•	98 S/90 N
Beach Haven 800-292-6372	•	•	•	•		•	•			A	•	63
Beach Haven Crest 609-494-7211	•		•		•	•				A		63
Beach Haven Gardens 609-494-7211	•		•		•	•				A		63
Beach Haven Park 609-494-7211	•		•		•	•				A		63
Beach Haven Terrace 609-494-7211	•		•		•	•				A		63
Berkeley Twp. 732-269-4456	•	•		•	•	A	•	•	•	A	•	80/82
Brant Beach 609-494-7211	•			•	•	A	•	•	•	A	•	63
Brick Twp. 732-262-1075	•			•	•	A	•	•	•	•		90 N/91 S
Brighton Beach 609-494-7211			•		•	•				A		63
Harvey Cedars 609-494-7211			•		•	•				A	•	63
Holgate 609-494-7211	•		•		•	•				A	•	63
Island Beach State Park 732-793-0506		•	•		•	•			•	A		82
Lavallette 732-793-7477	•		•	•	•	•	•	•	•	•	•	82 N/98 S
Loveladies 609-494-7211			•		•	•				A	•	63
Mantoloking 732-899-6600			•		•					•		98 S/90 N
Normandy Beach 609-341-1000			•									82
North Beach 609-494-7211			•		•	•				A		63

Facility Phone Number	Accommodations	Amusements	Bathhouses	Beach Fee	Boardwalk	Fishing	Lifeguard	Picnicking	Rafting	Surfing	Tennis Courts	Garden State Parkway Exit
North Beach Haven 609-494-7211			•		•	•			A			63
Ortley Beach 732-341-1000	•		•	•	A	•	•	•	•			82
Peahala Park 609-494-7211			•		•	•			A	•		63
Point Pleasant Beach 732-899-2424	•	•	•	•	•	•	•	•		•	•	98 S/90 N
Seaside Heights 800-SEASHORE	•	•	•	•	•	A	•		A	•		82
Seaside Park 732-793-0234	•	•	•	•	•	•	•	•	•	•	•	82
Ship Bottom 609-494-7211	•		•		•	•	•		A			63
Spray Beach 609-494-7211	•		•		•	•			A			63
Surf City 609-494-7211	•		•		•	•			A	•		63

A = After hours

Point Pleasant Beach

All of the seafront towns in the Central Shore region lie within Ocean County, New Jersey's fastest-growing county by far. You'll soon know why as you tour this beautiful shoreline, and then realize that most of the rest of the county lies in the relatively empty woods of the Pinelands. Ocean County's population is mostly in sight of salt water. Point Pleasant Beach has a reputation for the width of its beach and the variety and quality of its seafood restaurants. Party boats and commercial fishing boats make this one of the Jersey shore's busiest fishing spots. Nearby, in Point Pleasant off West Lake Avenue, is the New Jersey Museum of Boating, which displays locally built boats, scale models, drawings, and photos. For information, call 732-295-2072.

Point Pleasant Beach is home to a commercial fishing fleet and likes to boast that it is the seafood capital of New Jersey. It's *a* capital, not *the* capital, as many other seashore communities land a lot of fish and shellfish, caught by both commercial and sportfishermen.

Partly thanks to the sand-trapping jetties built to protect Manasquan Inlet from closing in with sand buildup, the physical qualities of the beaches here are superior to most North Shore beaches. A local "urban myth" is that English author Robert Louis Stevenson visited this area in the late nineteenth century and was there inspired to write his classic *Treasure Island.* A small island in the Manasquan River was informally renamed Treasure Island to commemorate Stevenson's visit.

Jenkinson's Boardwalk amusement complex features an aquarium open year-round. This major attraction, at 300 Ocean Avenue in Point Pleasant Beach, features a touch tank where sea creatures can be picked up for a good close look, as well as sea exhibits featuring sharks, alligators, penguins, seals, and coral reefs. For information, call 732-899-1202.

 ## Bay Head and Mantoloking

Bay Head's beach is lined with multimillion-dollar mansions, all in a New England, vintage seaside style. Think Cape Cod. The town's social class and attitude toward day-trippers can be summed up by describing its losing court battle to restrict the use of its beaches to local residents only. The beach is owned by the Bay Head Improvement Association, which granted membership and beach badges only to Bay Head residents. When those less fortunate nonresidents wished to purchase beach badges, they were refused. A court finally decided that beach badges must be sold to out-of-towners as well. But they're not cheap and not easy to obtain. You get the picture.

Mantoloking, like Bay Head, features fabulously expensive housing and equally fabulous and numerous No Parking signs. This very private town offers few services to short-term visitors. Huge seafront mansions form a "millionaire's row" that effectively blocks public access to beaches. People like Katharine Hepburn and Richard Nixon used to summer here. Not together.

 ## Normandy, Ocean, Chadwick, Lavallette, and Ortley Beaches

Just as Bay Head and Mantoloking fall into a natural grouping of splendid estates, these little towns share a characteristic of tiny cottages on postage-stamp-size lots. Here, the presence and recreational opportunities of the bay become stronger and more obvious. Like Bay Head and Mantoloking to the north, Normandy, Ocean, Chadwick, Lavallette, and Ortley Beaches are pretty much seasonal residential communities, but with lower price tags for houses.

📐 Seaside Heights

Now here is a boardwalk! Seaside Heights is as different from the more sedate summer cottage communities to the north as it is possible to be: noise, glitter, neon, games of chance, pizza, and amusement rides. Seaside Heights is fun—rather frantic and crowded fun, but classic New Jersey boardwalk fun. Head for the Casino Pier if this is your first immersion experience in a seaside fun factory. This very large pier offers thirty-five rides, including New Jersey's only "sky ride" on the beach, carnival-style games, and a wide variety of food stands. Also on the pier is the Water Works, including a fifty-four-foot-high freefall water slide (you could locate this with your eyes closed; just home in on the screams of delight and terror), tube rides, lazy river, and children's water play area.

Seaside Heights is like "Wildwood North," full of exuberant activities and happy crowds. Unlike some in Bay Head or Mantoloking, no one here is pretending they're on Martha's Vineyard or some similar exclusive and expensively quiet retreat. The latest in thrill rides share space with more traditional ones, including a beautiful vintage carousel, a historic Dentzel-Looff creation that is more than ninety years old.

This is a relative newcomer among Jersey shore towns. Only in 1911 did a highway penetrate this far south from Point Pleasant. Just two years later, a long bridge connected the area with Toms River across the bay.

Cedar Point, Toms River, N. J.

Made in Germany. Imported & Published by Chas. R. Berrien, Toms River, N. J.

Until the 1870s, Ocean County's shoreline was almost vacant, and the county seat and largest town, Toms River, shown here circa 1906, was a tiny, fading port on the bay.

The Intracoastal Waterway

Many residents and visitors to the New Jersey shore confront the Atlantic Intracoastal Waterway while in a car rather than enjoy it in a boat. In summer, especially, traffic jams occur where backroads drawbridges must be raised to accommodate the masts of sailboats using the waterway or accessing it from an inland stream. Many a driver has sat frustrated as a pleasure boat sails serenely through, the summer sailors waving cheerfully to the hundreds of trapped motorists looking on. The traffic problem is created because the largely north-south-trending waterway intersects the east-west roads that lead from the mainland to the barrier beaches. The newest bridges solve this problem by arching high above sailing mast heights.

The Atlantic Intracoastal Waterway is twelve hundred miles long, from Boston to Florida. It is exposed to the wind, waves, and currents of the open ocean in only two stretches, from Boston to Rhode Island, and for a thirty-seven-mile-long section of the Jersey coast. The great bulk of the waterway lies behind islands and sandbars, which provide sheltered waters for small craft from New Jersey to Florida.

From New York Bay, past Sandy Hook to Manasquan Inlet, boats must travel in open ocean. From Manasquan Inlet to the Delaware Bay end of the Cape May Canal, the Intracoastal lives up to its name, following a series of river estuaries, back bays, and connecting canals behind the protecting beaches. The channel has an official or target depth of at least twelve feet, but shifting currents can, at least temporarily, make this an unrealized goal. The U.S. Army Corps of Engineers is more or less continuously dredging the waterway. Although the Gulf Intracoastal Waterway, from Texas to Florida, carries a lot of commercial barge traffic, pleasure boats have the Atlantic Intracoastal much to themselves. Small craft typically take about ten days to cruise its full length.

One reason Seaside Heights lacks an early history is that the town's site was underwater until 1812. In that year, storm waves closed and filled in Cranberry Inlet, which used to be a busy channel between Barnegat Bay and the ocean. Ships moving to or from Toms River used Cranberry Inlet until nature closed it, forcing Toms River shipping to take a twelve-mile detour south to Barnegat Inlet.

Along with its traditional boardwalk rides and thrills, Seaside Heights offers several great water slides, a varied nightlife, and countless special events, festivals, and seasonal celebrations. Contact county, regional, or town visitors bureaus (see Information Sources on page 233) in advance

Seaside Heights, above, and neighboring Seaside Park are the liveliest amusement centers on the Barnegat Peninsula section of the Central Shore.

about events you'd like to experience. Spring brings the Leprechaun Contest (dress your tot in green) and St. Patrick's Day Parade, Palm Sunday Egg Hunt, Easter Promenade, and Mother's Day celebration. Summer offers the Father's Day celebration, kite flying, arts and crafts festivals, Christian Family Week, Ocean Cruisers car show, and Barnegat Bay Crab Race, in which winners and losers alike end up in the pot. Evidently having failed to pay attention in Sunday school class, Seaside Heights has chosen to celebrate Mardi Gras (which elsewhere comes just before Ash Wednesday) the week after Labor Day. But it's the idea that counts, not the calendar. The Mardi Gras spirit of outlandish costumes, with many in drag, familiar to most through the New Orleans drinking fest version, is in full swing. Fall features a vintage auto show, seafood festival, Clownfest weekend, and the Italian Street Festival–Columbus Day Parade.

🚩 Seaside Park

Neighboring Seaside Park is yet another religious camp meeting in its origins. This time, it was the Baptists, not the more active Methodists, who founded a resort free (for a while, at least) of the curse of demon rum. Seaside Park got a rail connection to the mainland in 1881, when a rail bridge to Toms River was completed. From Seaside Park, the rails continued

Saving Lives along the Shore

Particularly in the first half of the nineteenth century, New Jersey's coastline was a death trap for ships and sailors. A sandbar ran along most of the Jersey shore, varying in distance offshore from three hundred to eight hundred yards and covered by as little as two feet of water at low tide. It was largely an unmarked shore; most lighthouses and beacons were yet to be built. There was a busy traffic of ships bound to or from the great ports of New York or Philadelphia. Many great ships came to grief on the sandbars and beaches from Sandy Hook to Cape May. Over two hundred major shipwrecks on Jersey beaches were recorded between 1800 and 1900. Fall and winter storms along the coast were especially dangerous, and the loss of life was appalling.

In 1848, a former governor of New Jersey, newly elected to Congress, persuaded the federal government to appropriate $10,000 to fund eight lifeboat stations between Sandy Hook and Little Egg Harbor. The following year, six more stations were built between Little Egg Harbor and Cape May. One of the original lifesaving stations, originally at Sandy Hook, is on display at the Twin Lights.

When a wrecked ship was spotted from shore, a lifeboat would be launched to rescue stranded crew and passengers. In really rough weather, an ingenious "life car" was used. A specially adapted cannon would fire a grappling hook to the ship, which would be fastened securely to the doomed vessel. An enclosed iron life car, shaped like a large, hollow torpedo, would be sent out to the ship on the connecting cable and bring the shipwreck victims back to shore one by one.

The value of these lifesaving stations, the first ever funded by Washington, was proven in 1850. The sailing vessel *Ayrshire,* with 201 English and Irish immigrants aboard, was stranded off Absecon Island (the future site of Atlantic City) in a bad storm. All but one was rescued from the roaring surf by the courageous men of the local lifesaving station.

northward to join the existing New York and Long Branch Railroad. The fact that the railroad never did turn southward toward Barnegat Inlet helps explain why the southern end of the Barnegat Peninsula remained undeveloped, allowing the state to establish Island Beach State Park.

Seaside Park has a boardwalk featuring the Funtown Amusement Pier. This attraction includes the tallest thrill ride in New Jersey, the 225-foot Tower of Fear. For the slightly less fearless but still adventurous, there is a

Metal lifesaving cars were suspended from steel cables and shot out to stranded ships by special guns. The cars then carried endangered sailors and passengers safely back to shore.

In only two years, 1848 to 1850, fourteen stations had been built about ten miles apart. By 1872, twenty-eight stations had been erected up and down the coast, an average of five miles apart. In 1915, the Lifesaving Service became part of the Coast Guard; by that time, superior technology had reduced the number of wrecks.

The Coast Guard today continues the proud tradition of saving people from shipwrecks, while vacationing swimmers in distress off the beaches are rescued by municipal lifeguards (see page 40). That the federal taxpayers got their money's worth by funding the old Lifesaving Service is illustrated by these amazing facts: Just between November 1871 and June 1877, 1,411 people were rescued along the Jersey shore, while only 12 lives were lost.

120-foot high Ferris wheel, along with about thirty-five other rides and attractions, including kiddie rides, carnival-style games, and go-cart racing.

South Seaside Park is notable for having a few streets, labeled "lanes," lined with some of the smallest, most closely spaced cottages this side of a dollhouse museum. About the size of a closet in the master bedroom of a mansion in Deal or Allenhurst, these tiny cottages have no lawns or front yards, but front directly on the narrow lanes. They are so close side-

A classic, Wildwood-style honky-tonk boardwalk at Seaside Park.

The rows of tiny, boxlike summer cottages at South Seaside Park stand in sharp contrast to neighboring Island Beach State Park.

by-side that by local tradition, beer cans frequently are passed hand-to-hand from one house to another through adjacent windows. Located just a few blocks from the wide-open spaces of Island Beach State Park, the rows of identical cottages in such close juxtaposition look like a caricature of look-alike, cookie-cutter suburbia or an illustration from a cautionary tale about inadequate planning and zoning.

Island Beach State Park

To reach Island Beach State Park, just keep driving south from Seaside Park. This is one of the state of New Jersey's greatest gifts to its citizens—eleven whole miles of pristine, natural barrier beach. Out-of-state visitors are welcome, too, but they should vow never to tell another cynical joke about New Jersey. To beach fans, this is just about paradise. This is what most of the rest of the Jersey shore looked like before boardwalks, water slides, pizza stands, and motels.

This wonderful park features swimming, boating, scuba diving, surf fishing, crabbing, clamming, and just about anything it's legal to do on a magnificent beach. From October 15 to April 15, you can ride a horse on the beach; bring your own horse, and keep off the dunes. The park offers many opportunities to combine recreational activities, such as canoeing or kayaking, with educational and interpretive opportunities. Island Beach has a national reputation for successfully blending conservation with a high level of public access and recreational use of the land and resources. Some areas are closely restricted to protect wildlife, and the Sedge Islands on the southern bayside recently were designated as the state's first marine conservation zone, intended to protect this fine example of the elaborate web of life in tidal marshes.

Island Beach once was separated from Seaside Park and points north by Cranberry Inlet, now filled in by natural wave and current actions. The

The entire Jersey shore once looked like this wildlife area in Island Beach State Park.

~~~~~~~~~~~~~~~~~~~~~~~~~~~~~~

Jersey Jaws

While wading or swimming along New Jersey's coast, what are your chances of being attacked by a shark? Many Americans assume incorrectly that shark attacks are a hazard of tropical waters only.

Armed with our highly developed brains and technologies, people are, in effect, the ultimate "apex" predators on the planet. The thought that *we* could become prey is chilling and deeply disturbing. Many species of sharks are known to attack humans, the most fearsome being the great white. The possibility, however remote, of being eaten alive induces a gut-wrenching fascination with the great whites in particular.

New Jersey author Peter Benchley, whose 1974 bestseller was the basis for one of Hollywood's enduring classics, *Jaws*, set his story on an imaginary island off the New England or New York coastline, not in tropical waters. The shark lore in both book and movie is quite accurate in most respects, except for the somewhat exaggerated size of the villain. As *Jaws* educated us, sharks are common off northeastern U.S. shores, and fatal attacks have occurred as far north as Nova Scotia's Cape Breton Island. In his book *Close to Shore,* Michael Cappuzzo informs us that many great white "pups" are found off Montauk Point, Long Island. This suggests that great whites are far from rare in nearby waters.

Should you stay out of the water at New Jersey beaches? Considering the huge numbers of New Jersey bathers, the odds favor shark-free enjoyment of the water. Whole decades pass without any reported attacks. For the entire twentieth century, the numbers of documented shark attacks along northeastern shores are as follows: Connecticut, two; Delaware, four; Virginia, five; Massachusetts, seven; New York, twelve; New Jersey, twenty-eight.

The number of attacks in New Jersey is small in comparison with those off Florida or California. The number of shark attacks per year, worldwide, appears to be increasing, though. The record high to date was seventy-two attacks in 1995; this included thirty-four in the United States, five in Australia, four in Brazil, and three each in South Africa and the Bahamas.

In his fascinating 2001 book, *Twelve Days of Terror,* New Jersey author Richard Fernicola retells and analyzes the story of the twelve days in July 1916 when four people were killed by sharks in New Jersey waters and a fifth was seriously injured. First to be attacked was a young Philadelphian at Beach Haven. He had made two mistakes: He was wearing a black bathing suit, which likely caused a shark to think he was a seal, a favorite shark prey, and he was accompanied by a dog, whose irregular thrashing is known to attract sharks. This victim died in only three and

A plastic shark on a bait store near Cape May reminds everyone that sharks are both prey and predator all along the coast.

a half feet of water. Five days later, a hotel bellboy was killed while swimming off Spring Lake's segregated "servant's beach." Six days following this second fatal attack, a shark killed two and severely injured a third in the Matawan River, a brackish tidal creek draining into Raritan Bay. The seashore's tourist industry lost an estimated $16 million (in 2001 dollars) as shark panic frightened away visitors. Were these deaths and maiming caused by one shark or as many as five? What species of shark was involved? Dr. Fernicola uses both his medical expertise and knowledge of shark behavior in an attempt to solve these mysteries. His surmises may shock; I won't give away his conclusions, but think *Jaws*.

One last thought. Most shark experts assert that the single most important reason for the worldwide increase in shark attacks is the increasing number of people venturing into the ocean for fun. More potential prey equals more opportunities for sharks. On the other hand, 1916 aside, only one other shark attack, nonfatal, has been recorded in New Jersey in recent years. Enjoy the water.

state park includes about three thousand acres, which have had an interesting history. Several private owners tried to develop resort communities, but with little success. The Great Depression of the 1930s killed the development dreams of the last private owner. The War Department took over the property during World War II, evicting the few residents in order to conduct top-secret research and development of rockets. By 1945, army engineers and scientists had successfully launched supersonic rockets with a nine-mile range.

This beautiful state park protects beaches in their pristine natural state, without board-walks, piers, or any attempts to alter the natural processes of waves and currents.

In 1953, the state acquired the property to ensure that Island Beach would remain a natural beauty spot forever. The park was open by 1956 and has been popular ever since. There are two bathing beaches with clean, modern restrooms and bathhouses. Picnicking on the beach is permitted, and open fires are allowed in areas safely distant from dune vegetation. Snack bars are open in summer. The park's twenty-four hundred or so parking spaces fill up early on summer days, so get there really early. There is a fee for parking. Call 732-795-0506 for information on special permits and restrictions for scuba diving, dune buggy driving on special trails, and fishing.

The park also has nature trails and an interpretive center, and bird-watching is popular and rewarding. Island Beach is home to New Jersey's largest osprey colony. Twenty-six active osprey nests atop man-made platforms produced forty fledglings in 2001, and a peregrine falcon tower had the first successful breeding nest east of the Mississippi in fifty years. More than two hundred species of birds can be found here, including wading birds, shorebirds, waterfowl, and migrating songbirds. There is a resident colony of red foxes, which often beg for food along the roadside—please don't feed them. As always in New Jersey, watch out for poison ivy.

The park features many handicapped-accessible nature trails, interpretive centers, and fishing areas. Wheelchairs with wide, soft wheels designed for beach use are available at the two beach-access bathhouses.

〰〰〰〰〰〰〰〰〰〰〰〰〰〰〰〰〰〰〰〰

Whale-Watching

Many of New Jersey's shore towns offer visitors an opportunity to go to sea for an hour, a day, or a half day of whale-watching. Americans' attitude toward whales has come a long way since Colonial days. Whereas once New Jerseyans made a living killing whales, now some owners of sightseeing or sportfishing boats offer whale-watching trips. People are fascinated by the enormous, intelligent, and very threatened creatures.

American Indians used whales for food. When whales were stranded on or near the beach (which still happens on occasion), locals took full advantage of this accidental arrival of lots of good meat. They soon advanced to "shore whaling." Spotters kept watch for spouting whales close to shore. When one was observed, the Indians launched canoes and attacked the whales with bows and arrows and crude lances. The many small wounds eventually caused enough blood loss to kill the whale. Basically, the poor animal was harassed to death. Whalers worked only in winter, when whales were most likely to surface off the Jersey shore.

Early Europeans used the same approach, but with slightly superior weapons. Once the whale was dead, it was towed onto the beach and processed for whale oil, used mostly in oil lamps. Americans of European background had no taste for the meat.

Whaling was very profitable in the 1690s. A 250-ton whale yielded over thirty-five hundred gallons of whale oil, which together with whalebone, was worth from $1,000 to $1,500—a fortune at that time.

It is likely that the first non-Indians who came to the seashore were whalers. Early Cape May was a whaling town. The first landowner on Long Beach Island was a New England whaler. Harvey Cedars originally was Harvey's Whaling Quarters. By about 1870, so many whales had been killed that their scarcity ended the industry on the Jersey shore. Today Americans are forbidden to kill the threatened animals, and we hunt them with binoculars and cameras instead of harpoons.

Nearby Attractions

Toms River

At Water Street and Hooper Avenue in Toms River, across Barnegat Bay, is the Toms River Seaport Museum, with a collection of more than twenty small vessels, including a sneakbox, a Hankins rowing skiff, and a Brockway lifesaving surf rowboat. Boats are built and restored here, and there are special seminars and presentations. For information, call 732-349-9209. Also of interest is the Ocean County Historical Society Museum, housed in a large Victorian mansion at 26 Hadley Avenue. Exhibits range from Native American artifacts through the Revolutionary War period to a display on Lakehurst Naval Air Station. For information, call 732-341-1880.

Cattus Island

One of the county's largest parks is Cattus Island, at 1170 Cattus Island Boulevard. This park is perfect for nature hikes and bird-watching, and has an environmental center with a variety of exhibits and programs. For information, call 732-270-6960.

LONG BEACH ISLAND

The name says it all. Long Beach Island is long—at least nineteen miles in length, about three times the average length of the islands to the south, in Atlantic and Cape May Counties. Nowhere is it wider than one mile; in many places it narrows to a half mile. The island is one long series of beaches—some of New Jersey's best, keeping in mind that New Jersey's beaches include some of America's finest.

With no boardwalks, relatively few nightspots, and one amusement center, Long Beach Island is not the place to look for glamour and bright lights. There are plenty of good restaurants, but the island is mostly seasonal residential. One road bridge, State Route 72, connects the mainland with the island. It terminates at Ship Bottom, where you can turn left toward Barnegat Light or right toward Beach Haven. In either direction, you'll encounter beautiful beaches, some more accessible than others.

Although a few hardy, determined souls traveled by stage from Philadelphia to Tuckerton, then hired a boat to take them across Little Egg Harbor to the island as early as 1765, Long Beach Island remained isolated from mass tourism until 1872. In that year, a new railroad spur from Tuckerton extended to a bayside dock, where a steamboat waited to ferry visitors to the new resort of Beach Haven. By 1885, the railroad had crossed the bay and was extended the length of the island, serving what was by now a string of fast-growing little towns. Finally, in 1914, the construction of the road bridge made it possible to drive to the island.

The familiar health claims advanced for clean salt air get a special spin on Long Beach Island, which early claimed to be a kind of national refuge for hay fever sufferers. At least in theory, the island is so distant from mainland sources of pesky pollens as to be free of hay fever allergens.

The whole island has a compact, small-town feel, perhaps because open skies over water lie to both left and right as you cruise up or down the island's spine, and there seem to be no buildings over three stories in height. This central artery is officially labeled Long Beach Boulevard, Bay Avenue, or Central Avenue, depending on which jurisdiction it travels through, but locals just call it "the Boulevard on L.B.I."

While the shorter, wider offshore islands to the south are composed of one, two, three, or four separate municipalities, there are more than a dozen very small communities on Long Beach Island. From north to south, the main ones are Barnegat Light, Loveladies, Harvey Cedars, North Beach, Surf

〰〰〰〰〰〰〰〰〰〰〰〰〰〰〰〰〰〰

Wrecking for Fun and Profit

There's a dark side to the early days of life on the Jersey shore. "Wreckers," sometimes called pirates, were shore men who made a living by salvaging goods and materials from shipwrecks. This went on when few people lived on or near the beaches, and at a time when lighthouses and other navigational aids were scarce or absent.

Most of the coast's wreckers were honest enough recyclers, supplementing a tough living as farmers or fishermen. Ships' timbers became buildings, furniture, or firewood, and rescued cargoes were resold. But problems arose when the wreckers became more concerned with securing merchandise than with assisting floundering crewmen or passengers.

On occasion, the wreckers actually caused wrecks. On dark winter nights when strong currents were running, an unscrupulous wrecker might tie a lantern to a donkey's tail and lead it slowly along the beach. The swinging light would be mistaken by ship's navigators as the running lights of another vessel under way, causing them to fatally miscalculate the shoreline's location, and luring the ship onto the beach or offshore sandbars.

Occasionally the cargo was a pleasant surprise. When the British brig *Delight* was stranded off Peck's Beach in 1779, she was claimed as a prize of war by rebel Americans. They sold her cargo, which turned out to be rum and sugar from Jamaica. It was reported that sixty-six barrels of rum aboard mysteriously disappeared from the inventory between the time the ship was first boarded and the auctioning of the cargo.

City, Ship Bottom, Brant Beach, Beach Haven Crest, Beach Haven Terrace, Beach Haven Gardens, North Beach Haven, Beach Haven, and Holgate. Only the tax assessor and the beach tag enforcers know, or care, where one town ends and another begins, unless, of course, one needs to call the cops. No one town really dominates the island, although Beach Haven is the largest. Altogether, the island towns have a winter population of less than twelve thousand; the summer season has ten times that.

In terms of municipalities or local governments, there are only six separate jurisdictions on Long Beach Island. These include the municipalities of Barnegat Light, Beach Haven, Harvey Cedars, Ship Bottom, and Surf City, as well as Long Beach Township, which includes the communities of Beach Haven Crest, Beach Haven Gardens, Beach Haven Inlet, Beach Haven Park, Beach Haven Terrace, Brant Beach, Brighton Beach, the Dunes, Haven Beach, Holgate, Loveladies, North Beach, North Beach Haven, Peahala Park, and Spray Beach. For most visitors, this is completely useless

Barnegat Lighthouse, or "Old Barney," has stood sentinel at one of the Jersey shore's most dangerous inlets since 1859. The lighthouse was rescued from certain destruction by local citizens who built protective wave barriers of junked cars when the light was abandoned by the federal government.

information—except in case of an emergency. To call the police in any of those many parts of Long Beach Township, call the township at 609-494-3322. Dial 911 from anywhere on the island for fire, first aid, or an ambulance. Remember that beach badges are good only in the municipality in which they were purchased.

There are some interesting stories behind some of Long Beach Island's place names. Ship Bottom was named after a local legend. It seems that one of the many shipwrecks along the coast was beached upside down. Local "wreckers" who had come to salvage the wooden vessel heard a human voice coming from inside the hull. When they cut an opening, a beautiful young woman, speaking only an unrecognized foreign tongue, climbed out—the only survivor of the wreck. Loveladies is neither a command nor a wish; it was named after a certain Captain Lovelady. Harvey Cedars was a whaling station once operated by Dan Harvey. Surf City also started life as a whaling station. Evidently, Long Beach Island's whalers were a persistent lot, not giving up the business until there were no more whales to kill, around the 1830s. Surf City's original name was Great Swamp, somehow lacking in tourist appeal.

Not only is there a bewildering array of place names for such a small island, but these communities manage to represent most of the great variety of types of Jersey seashore towns. In Loveladies and Harvey Cedars, most of the beach is private property with no public access. Loveladies' "Golden Mile" has many houses in the $1 million to $2 million range, with real estate ads referring to "access to exclusive beach" and "deeded access to bay."

Long Beach Island's star attraction and symbol is Barnegat Lighthouse, at the northern tip of the island. "Old Barney," as it is affectionately known, was built in 1859 to replace an 1834 light, which fell into the eroding waves in 1856. That earlier light, only forty feet tall, had a constant, rather than rotating or flashing, light, which meant that sailors at sea could confuse the light with that of another ship.

The second lighthouse was built right. At 172 feet, Old Barney was the tallest structure on the Jersey coast for a long time. Its light was the most powerful on the entire East Coast—it could be seen for thirty miles at sea. This lighthouse was designed and built under the command of Gen. George Meade, who later won the Civil War turning point battle of Gettysburg. He built it to last, with brick walls ten feet thick at the base, tapering to eighteen inches thick at the top. It is double-walled, with air space in between to reduce moisture rot. In 1927, the lighthouse was replaced by a lightship anchored eight miles offshore. Old Barney later came close to toppling into the sea. When built in 1859, it was 900 feet from the waves. Only seven years later, the shoreline had advanced 450 feet, and by 1927, waves were practically lapping at its foundations. When federal interest in saving the nonfunctioning lighthouse seemed unenthusiastic, local admirers of the grand old light dumped junked cars in front of it, forming a makeshift breakwater that actually saved the structure until the government built

Long Beach Island Museum, housed in an old church, is a delightful attraction at Beach Haven.

proper jetties and a dike to slow erosion. In 2002, yet another rock and concrete seawall was built to save Old Barney from the sea.

Now the property of the state, Old Barney is open to the public daily from Memorial Day through Labor Day, and weekends in May, September, and October. The athletic and ambitious can climb the 217 steps to the top for a spectacular view. The lighthouse has an admission fee, but the surrounding state park, New Jersey's smallest at thirty-six acres, is free. For information, call 609-494-2016.

What is there to do on Long Beach Island, besides go to the beach? The lovely beaches are the number-one attraction, but there are plenty of other activities. Go fishing; just go to Barnegat Light's bayside for good choices in "head boats." Rent bikes or ride your own; the terrain is bike-friendly, with the nearest hill probably forty miles away. Take a walking tour of Beach Haven's Victorian district. Take a boat ride across the bay to Tuckerton Seaport on one of the *Black Whale* cruises from the docks at Beach Haven's bayside at Centre Avenue (609-492-0333). Or take a speedboat to Trump Marina Casino in Atlantic City from the *Black Whale* dock. How about a bay cruise or sunset cruise from either Beach Haven or Barnegat Light? For the young and the brave, go parasailing from Bay Haven Marina.

Indoors, you can take an art class for all ages in painting, sculpture, ceramics, jewelry, or crafts at the Long Beach Island Foundation of the Arts and Sciences in Loveladies (609-494-1241, ext. 300). Also check out the two small but worthwhile museums on the island. Barnegat Light Museum is at 5th Street and Central Avenue in the town of Barnegat Light. Exhibits include the original lens from Old Barney's light. The museum (609-494-8578) is open daily in July and August, weekends only in June and September. There is no fee, but donations are solicited. Near the opposite end of the island in Beach Haven is the Long Beach Island Museum, on Beach Avenue at Engelside. Beach Haven was founded as a Quaker summer retreat. The town's second-oldest religious structure, an Episcopal church, now houses the museum, open daily in summer (a week before Memorial Day to a week after Labor Day). The aptly named museum (609-492-0700) exhibits artifacts and pictures from the whole island, not just Beach Haven. An admission fee is charged.

⬊ Barnegat Light

The little community of Barnegat Light at the northern tip of Long Beach Island is the fishing capital of southern Ocean County. It's a famed center of "head boats"—so much a head for a day or half day of ocean fishing. Most Barnegat Light head boats can be found along Bayview Avenue

~~~~~~~~~~~~~~~~~~~~~~~~~~~~~~~~~~~~

Crabbing for Fun and Food

Crabbing requires little skill and simple equipment. Boat rental establishments on either side of the bay will supply nets, bait, and string along with the rental rowboat. Blue-claw crabs are scavengers; they'll eat anything in the animal kingdom. The art and science of crabbing consists of waiting for a crab (often, several at a time) to grab and hold on to your bait, dangled in front of them on a string. Crabs are attracted by the smell of rotting meat, so the older and smellier the bait—cut-up chunks of anything handy from the water—the better.

After letting the bait rest on the shallow bottom for a while, slowly and steadily draw it up toward the surface. As the bait becomes visible, slide your handheld net under the bait to catch the crabs. Be quick with the net; crabs quickly let go of the bait as they approach the surface and see the net. Jersey blue-points or blue-claws are pretty crafty. Among crabs of the world, Jersey crabs have high IQs (at least higher than, say, cucumbers), but enough will be suckered by your smooth, slow raising of the bait to fill your basket. Boat rentals include a short stick nailed across the bottom of a longer stick. Do not keep crabs that measure, across the shell points, less than the length of the short stick (four and a half inches, hardshell). Also toss back any females carrying eggs attached to their bottom shell. There is no closed season, and the recreational limit is one bushel.

The traditional way to prepare and serve crabs is to cook them in rapidly boiling, spiced water, and serve on layers of newspaper spread on the table. Buy lots of paper towels along with Crab Boil spice, always available in local groceries. It is messy, but fun. Bon appetit!

between 19th and 6th Streets. Interestingly, this town is also a fine-arts center, with a collection of quaint arts and crafts shops, known as Viking Village, on the bay at 19th Street.

Barnegat Inlet is guarded by the state's most photographed lighthouse. The inlet is notoriously rough sailing—*Barnegat* is Dutch for "inlet (or channel) of breakers"—but it is a busy one for sport and commercial fishing boats. About eighty years ago, the town of Barnegat Light was the object of a Viking invasion. Not the kind of slash, grab, and burn invasion of Europe's Middle Ages, but a peaceful arrival of Scandinavian fishermen and their families, looking for good fishing. They found it.

It is estimated that 961,000 sportfishermen fished in New Jersey's ocean waters in 2000. More than half of the six million plus fishing trips to the shore were to off-shore ocean waters out to three miles, with the balance to rivers and bays. New Jersey anglers brought home more black sea bass, blue-fish, summer flounder, tautog, weakfish, and winter flounder than were landed in any other Atlantic seaboard state. Conservation measures place minimum length restrictions and numbers of fish limits on sportfishers; these regulations change every year. If you want to fish while visiting

The Graying of the Shore

As all of us paying into Social Security, wondering if we'll ever collect ours, know, the percentage of people over sixty-five keeps increasing. This "graying of America" is especially noticeable at the New Jersey shore.

In 1950, 8 percent of Americans were past their sixty-fifth birthday. By 1990, this percentage had increased to 12.5 percent. The state of New Jersey is slightly grayer than the national average, at 13.4 percent. By 2050, one in five Americans will be sixty-five or over.

Between 1900 and 1990, America's population multiplied by three. During those decades, the number of Americans over sixty-five increased ten times.

Meanwhile, at the seashore and in nearby mainland communities, the proportion of those over sixty-five is much higher than the averages for the state and the nation. Ocean County is over 23 percent "gray," and Cape May County is second oldest, on average, at 20 percent. Of course, these county data include many retirees living in inland locations as well as seashore residents. It comes down to money. Everyone might want to retire at the shore, but everyone can't afford it. If you can see the ocean from your windows, you are rich. If you can hear the surf but not actually see it, you're a little less wealthy. If getting to the beach takes more than twenty minutes by car, you really need to clip those supermarket coupons. But the shore clearly is the big attraction for retirees, whether they can smell salt water at home or not.

What's going on? First, these retirees almost certainly have happy memories of the shore. No longer tied to another location by a job, many choose a retirement location in or near the resort they've been visiting for a lifetime. Often their vacation cottage or condo becomes their full-time residence on retirement. The clean air, recreational opportunities (plenty of time for fishing), and slower pace of seashore towns (after Labor Day, anyhow) all count.

Among the best reasons for retiring to the shore, or at least close by, is that the seashore is a grandchild magnet. Grandparents know that grandchildren and children will willingly visit the old folks at the shore. So bring your bikinis and surfboards, and come on down!

Barnegat Light is an important center for head boats, providing day or half-day fishing trips.

Barnegat Light, call the New Jersey Division of Fish and Game, 609-748-2020, for up-to-date regulations.

In addition to fishing, crabbing and clamming long supported the area's preresort population. Mainland bayside towns like Tuckerton, Barnegat, and Waretown made Barnegat Bay and Little Egg Harbor crabs and clams famous treats for New Yorkers and Philadelphians. If you're vacationing at Barnegat Light in late summer or early fall, crabbing is a great family activity that also provides the makings of a fine meal.

Beach Haven and Holgate

Beach Haven long has been the largest tourist center on Long Beach Island, featuring a charming little historic district downtown and the island's sole amusement center, Fantasy Island Amusement Park, which breaks shore tradition by not being on the seafront. The Fantasy Island complex is near the bay, possibly because Beach Haven has no boardwalk.

Maybe it's the bayside location, but Fantasy Island has one feature that will cause universal rejoicing: ample free parking. Adjacent to Fantasy Island is a large complex of nautically themed shops offering leisure wear, gifts, and souvenirs. Bay Village and Schooners Wharf feature a variety of

Garveys, Sneakboxes, and Sea Bright Skiffs

With small boats, as with any other product of human design, solving different problems—particularly problems handed to people by different physical environments—often produces new designs. At the least, older designs are altered to fit the local circumstances.

Basic jobs involving boats at the New Jersey shore include fishing, crabbing, clamming, and duck hunting. Traditional boat types didn't always work well in the intertwined land-and-water realm of marshes threaded by narrow channels; shallow bays; and pounding surf. New Jersey seashore boatbuilders are credited with developing three types of small craft: garveys, sneakboxes, and Sea Bright skiffs.

Shipbuilding is a traditional craft along the shore and back bays. An obvious need for boats, and boat repairs, is combined there with the local availability of Atlantic white cedar in the swamps of the Pinelands. This cedar is light but strong wood, very slow to rot.

Garveys are unglamorous little boats usually with both ends squared off. In fact, there is no "front" or "back," no pointed bow at all. Their occupants often have to reverse course in the shallow, marshy waters where they are used for clamming. They can float in six inches of water, and their flat bottoms make it easier for clammers to stand up safely to handle their awkward rakes and tongs. Some adaptations of this design have a pointed bow and small cabin.

Sneakboxes need as little as four inches of water. Designed to slip quietly into marsh fringes and shady riverbanks, they are the duck hunter's favorite. Sit in the bottom rather than on a seat, cover the boat with some grasses and cattails, and ducks don't notice you, at least in theory.

Skif is an old German word for a light rowboat, so modern skiffs are descendants of an old style. Jersey shore fishermen had a special problem, though, if they needed to launch a small boat into the breakers from the beach rather than into the quieter waters of a bay or channel. So they invented Sea Bright skiffs.

A flat-bottomed, shallow draft garvey, a design that originated on the Jersey shore, provides a stable platform for taking clams with long-handled rakes or tongs.

These boats will float in a foot of water and have upward-curving bows that keep them from swamping while being pushed out into the breakers. Most Jersey shore visitors have seen Sea Bright skiffs—they are the familiar lifeboats on the beach.

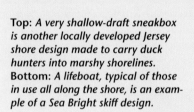

Top: A very shallow-draft sneakbox is another locally developed Jersey shore design made to carry duck hunters into marshy shorelines. Bottom: A lifeboat, typical of those in use all along the shore, is an example of a Sea Bright skiff design.

food and bars with live entertainment, along with plenty of shops and boutiques in an architecturally interesting, compact, and enjoyable setting.

The Victorian ambience of Beach Haven can best be savored by staying at a small bed-and-breakfast or guesthouse establishment. Beach Haven ranks with Ocean Grove, Cape May, and Spring Lake in having successfully restrained growth to keep the atmosphere of a small town. Beach Haven's first growth spurt, from 1890 to 1893, has left many lovely Victorian cottages, though they do not make up as large a uniform district as in Cape May.

Below Beach Haven, at the southern tip of Long Beach Island, is a two-and-a-half-mile-long stretch of barrier beach and fringing salt marsh, preserved from development as the Holgate National Wildlife Refuge. The public is encouraged to observe but not touch the wide variety of birds. Dune buggies and four-wheel-drive all-terrain vehicles are allowed on the beach here with the appropriate permits, obtainable at Long Beach Township's offices. Stay off the dunes, and avoid disturbing any bird nests. The refuge is not equipped with either restrooms or a visitors center. Administratively, Holgate is part of the Forsythe National Wildlife Refuge, headquartered at the Brigantine unit, off U.S. Route 9 South at Oceanville. For information, call 609-652-1665.

Breaking with tradition, Beach Haven's family amusements and leisure shopping district are on the bayside rather than on the oceanfront.

Although Beach Haven's Victorian district is not as extensive or well known as those in Ocean Grove or Cape May, it is the largest on Long Beach Island.

The fact that charming little Beach Haven is the "big city" for the whole island should be a clue that life on the island is slow-paced, very relaxing, and free of the kind of raucous boardwalks and nightspots found in, say, Wildwood or Seaside Heights. Even though some of them include "city" in their names, the Long Beach Island communities really are more like tiny villages in winter.

Nearby Attractions

Tuckerton Seaport

Tuckerton once was such an important seaport and shipbuilding center that George Washington named it the country's third official port of entry during the Revolution. It was an important port for privateers, officially sanctioned and patriotic pirates, during the Revolution and the War of 1812. There are ambitious plans to re-create the Colonial seaport atmosphere as a tourist site, expanding on the nucleus of the Barnegat Bay Decoy and Baymen's Museum (609-296-8868, www.tuckertonseaport.org). From Long Beach Island, take State Route 72 west across the bridge, then turn left (south) on the Old Shore Road, U.S. Route 9. The museum, on a forty-acre site, provides a good overview of the bay region's past economy and culture. Highly recommended.

The main museum is housed in a replica of the Tucker's Island Lighthouse, which fell into the sea in 1927. There are exhibits on the region's whaling industry, pirates, pioneering resorts, and the early lifesaving service, as well as a large display of duck decoys. (Look carefully at the group of ducks floating in the river near the museum—they all are realistic decoys!) You can watch master decoy carvers at work, learn how to rake for clams, learn how the locally invented "sneakbox" boats were built, and watch local white cedar and oak trees milled into boatbuilding materials. There are also a seafood restaurant, visitors center, and gift shop. The seaport can be reached by boat from Beach Haven; call the seaport or *Black Whale* dock, 609-492-0333. Or bring your own boat to the seaport; free dockage is included with your admission ticket.

U.S. Route 9

In this part of New Jersey, U.S. 9 mostly follows the Old Shore Road, a Colonial road that followed an Indian trail. You'll know it's an old road when you notice the many historic buildings crowding up to the side of the road (road widening has absorbed their front yards) and the picturesque villages and towns along the route. Route 9 is a long antiques row, with antiques and collectibles shops lined along the road like loosely strung beads. You'll find many one-of-a-kind bargains and souvenirs of the shore's past.

The Pinelands

Located on the mainland behind the shore resorts, from Delaware Bay to the latitude of Manasquan Inlet, is a huge ecological preserve and recreation area known as the Pinelands National Reserve, the country's first national reserve. At 1.1 million acres, it accounts for 14 percent of the state of New Jersey and is only a little smaller than Rhode Island. Not exactly a park, the reserve imposes strict controls on any further development. In this most densely populated of states, the Pinelands Reserve is an almost empty area of pine and oak forest, yet it is only an hour and a quarter's drive from Times Square. There are several state parks within the Pinelands. Ocean County's Bass River State Park, off Exit 52 of the Garden State Parkway, offers camping, swimming, boating, fishing, hiking, horseback riding, and picnicking, with amenities such as restrooms, hot showers, laundry, and a snack bar. There are fees for camping, horse rental, and summer season admission. For information, call 609-296-1114.

Other Pinelands region state parks, most with visitors centers, camping, fishing, swimming, boating, and other activities, include Belleplain Forest, in Cape May County; Lebanon State Forest and Penn Forest, in Burlington County; and Wharton State Forest, off U.S. Route 206 in Burlington, Camden, and Atlantic Counties. For details on any of these recreation opportunities, contact the New Jersey Division of Travel and Tourism, 20 W. State Street, P.O. Box 820, Trenton, NJ 08625, telephone 609-777-0885 or 800-VISITNJ; or the New Jersey Division of Parks and Forestry, 501 E. State Street, P.O. Box 404, Trenton, NJ 08625, telephone 609-984-0370 or 800-537-7397. State welcome centers are located in service areas along the New Jersey Turnpike, Garden State Parkway, and Atlantic City Expressway. Hours vary; call 609-292-2470.

Camping, at either a state park or a private campground, is a great way to enjoy the peace and serenity of the Pinelands. More than twenty-five thousand campsites across the state could host upward of one hundred thousand campers at one time. For more information on camping, call the New Jersey Campground Association at 800-2CAMPNJ.

The joys of camping include having deer, raccoons, rabbits, chipmunks, and birds as your close neighbors. Aside from watching out for rattlesnakes and moccasins, the most serious problem with local wildlife in the Pinelands used to be the probability of chipmunks invading your camp to steal marshmallows. Recently, though, bears have been reappearing in South Jersey after more than a century's absence. Not that any campers should panic; bears are a fact of life for campers and hikers in the backcountry of most states, and confrontations with bears are still rare, but be aware.

Some environmentalists long have advocated the deliberate reintroduction of black bears (many of which are actually brown), but the state has taken no such controversial action. But now the bears seem to be taking reintroduction into their own paws. They are walking south and east from the mountains of northwest New Jersey, where the bear population has climbed to an estimated nineteen hundred. This density has led to bear migrations as well as more contacts with humans. Younger bears apparently are being driven out of areas already well populated by older dominant males defending their territories. It must be a tough choice—fight it out with an aggressive mature bear or cross the New Jersey Turnpike (apparently through culverts or on smaller road bridges, so that dead bears have shown up in traffic lanes only rarely).

Canoeing is a good way to enjoy and explore the Pinelands. The Batsto, Mullica, Oswego, and Wading Rivers in the heart of the Pines are all suitable rivers for canoeing; the Wading River is the best. Because these little rivers flow rather sluggishly across a coastal plain, they offer a leisurely trip through tranquil oak and pine woods. No whitewater hereabouts. The most excitement possible is the

uncommon event of a nonpoisonous but aggressive black snake dropping into your canoe from overhanging tree branches. But with any luck, the only problem will be negotiating occasional tight turns or very shallow parts.

You will have a choice of canoe rentals in the vicinity of Chatsworth, Egg Harbor, or Vincentown—just ask around and follow the signs. Chatsworth is a tiny but interesting community. The canoe rentals for the Wading River are on County Route 563, between Chatsworth and Jenkins, a community that manages to be smaller than Chatsworth and still exist. For a fee, Mick's (609-726-1380) or Pine Barrens Canoe Rental (609-726-1515) will drive you to a put-in point, pick you up at the end of the route, and drive you back to your car.

Chatsworth

Chatsworth has long been the unofficial "capital of the Pines." Although it's a very small community, many places in the Pinelands are even smaller. In keeping with the "capital" image, the Buzbys, father and son, each were known as the "king of the Pineys," thanks to their operation of Chatsworth General Store, the only grocery–gas station–informal meeting place for many miles.

The old general store, dating to 1895 and located in an 1865 building, is now a book, arts, and crafts store specializing in Pinelands history, arts, and culture. At State Routes 563 and 532 (609-894-4415), it's a must-visit for students of Pinelands history, folklore, and environment.

Six Flags Great Adventure Amusement Park

When you've "done" the thrill rides available at Asbury Park or Seaside Park and still hanker for more, Six Flags Great Adventure is for you. Easily reached via the Garden State Parkway to I-195, Exit 16, Six Flags Great Adventure has everything a large amusement park should have—all the traditional rides, a super roller coaster, a gigantic Ferris wheel, a water park, and a drive-through safari park. All in all, there are more than a hundred rides and attractions, including a dozen coasters. Hurricane Harbor is a forty-five-acre water park featuring twenty slides and a million-gallon wave pool. The safari park is the largest this side of Africa. There, about fifteen hundred wild animals live in fenced-off but still very open compounds arranged along a five-mile drive. This is a very interesting experience. It is a kind of reverse zoo, where the animals have freedom—within extensive fenced areas designed to separate large predators from potential prey—and people stay in their cars with the windows closed. No convertibles, for obvious reasons. No vinyl tops either—the monkeys like to rip them off. Monkeys have been known to playfully use car hoods as restrooms—they seem to enjoy the discomfort of their observers. At least your kids won't forget their wild animal safari. Of course, you don't have to use your own car—take the tram. The park is open every day in summer. For information, call 732-928-1821.

New Egypt Speedway

The New Egypt Speedway, on County Route 539 off County Route 528, about twenty miles west of Lakewood, has a half-mile clay track for big-block modified sports cars, super stocks, and street stocks racing from April through October. There is a supervised playground facility for kiddies. For information, call 609-758-1900.

Lakewood

Lakewood, a multiethnic community reached via State Route 88 west from Point Pleasant, or Garden State Parkway Exit 88 to State Route 70 west to U.S. Route 9 north, has several interesting alternatives to the beach. The beautifully restored, 1,042-seat Strand Theater at 400 Clifton Avenue (732-367-7789), now on the National Register of Historic Places, showcases top-name entertainers and national tours. Firstenergy Park, at 2 Stadium Way (732-902-7000), is the home of the Lakewood Blue Claws, a Class A affiliate of the Philadelphia Phillies. Minor league ball is a lot of fun without the traffic jams, hassle, and high costs of attending major league games—and you probably are watching future major league stars play. The Lakewood Incline, at 485 Locust Street (732-901-7900), is an indoor park for boards, bikes, and blades.

Popcorn Park Zoo

This zoo, first opened in 1977, has a unique goal: taking care of animals that, for one reason or another, need a good home. This includes specimens of local wildlife that were orphaned and unable to look after themselves, injured animals that needed a safe place to recuperate, and one-time wildlife pets discarded by their owners and lacking survival skills to fend for themselves. Some local and exotic wildlife were rescued from abusive or uncaring owners, while some aging former circus or carnival performers, no longer able to run through their tricks, were donated to this refuge as a "retirement home" alternative to being put down. Animals on view include monkeys, lions, bears, tigers, elephants, and deer. This is a worthwhile experience, combining a good zoo with the heartwarming knowledge that these animals are surely better off here than any alternative. You can almost see the animals smiling. On Humane Way (isn't that a great name!) in Forked River, telephone 609-693-1900. You will be happy to donate.

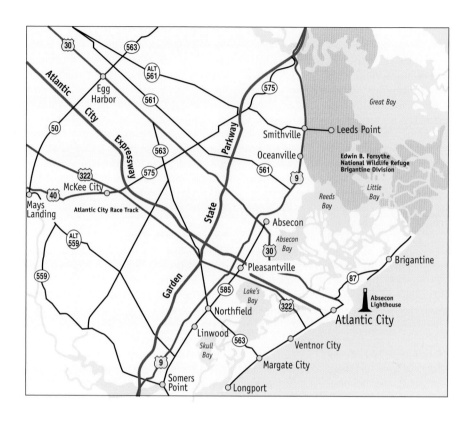

Atlantic City and Its Neighbors: Beach Facility Profiles

Facility Phone Number	Accommodations	Amusements	Bathhouses	Beach Fee	Boardwalk	Fishing	Lifeguard	Picnicking	Rafting	Surfing	Tennis Courts	Garden State Parkway Exit
Atlantic City 609-348-7100	•	•			•	•	•	•	•		•	•	36, 40/38 S, 38 N
Brigantine 609-266-7600	•			•		•	•	•	•		•	•	40 S, 36/38 N
Longport 609-822-6503				•		•	•				•	•	36 S, 29 N
Margate 609-822-2605				•			•				•	•	36 S, 36/29 N
Ventnor 609-823-7900	•			•	•	•	•	•	•		•	•	36 S, 36/29 N

6

Atlantic City and Its Neighbors

Everything about Atlantic City seems to be described in superlatives—first, biggest, grandest, and most. If Americans from parts of the United States other than New Jersey and its neighboring states could name only one Jersey shore resort, the odds are overwhelming that it would be Atlantic City. If citizens of other countries could name but one seashore resort in the United States, Atlantic City most likely would be it. While Atlantic City is not America's, or New Jersey's, first or oldest resort, it is the first city by the sea to be "created" by a railroad. It is the largest and most famous of all of New Jersey's seashore cities and the only true metropolitan center, with a string of seashore suburbs—Brigantine, Ventnor, Margate, and Longport—as well as a series of mainland suburbs, Absecon, Pleasantville, Northfield, Linwood, and Oceanville. Atlantic City is the central star of an urban "solar system" all its own. This chapter will focus first on Atlantic City, then its seashore neighbors, then on nearby and mainland attractions. More than any other resort, Atlantic City epitomizes the New Jersey seashore experience.

Atlantic City

The central question about Atlantic City's spectacular renaissance through the agency of legalized gambling is, why Atlantic City? Why was Atlantic City the first jurisdiction in the United States to break Nevada's long monopoly on legalized gambling? The answer lies in Atlantic City's his-

This shore region includes all Atlantic County resorts, from Brigantine to Longport.

tory, and in political solutions to economic problems. Politics—lots of politics—are involved.

The old Atlantic City, "B.C." (Before Casinos), was a resort that was past its prime. From the onset of the nation's Great Depression in the 1930s, through to the 1970s, Atlantic City experienced a long, slow, rather gentle and genteel decline. Crowds still came, but for shorter stays. They enjoyed themselves, but they seemed to spend less. The average age of visitors increased; many came to revisit memories of happier days, for them, and for the grand but fading resort.

On the Boardwalk in Atlantic City

In Atlantic City, the Boardwalk always is spelled with a capital "B." It is an official "street" on the city map. Atlantic City likes to claim that it built the world's first boardwalk in 1870. The idea was a practical one—to save beachfront strollers from the inconvenience of walking in shoes across the soft sand. Not incidentally, the wooden promenade also saved hotel carpets from the gritty, often sticky, sand tracked in by beachgoers.

Atlantic City's first effort, opened on June 26, 1870, was only ten feet wide and eighteen inches above the sand. It was designed as a seasonal convenience; it could be disassembled in twelve-foot sections for winter storage. The idea often is credited to the fortuitously named Alexander Boardman, a conductor on the Camden and Atlantic Railroad.

A second boardwalk soon was built; it was twenty feet wide and elevated on pilings. Following severe hurricane damage in 1889, a yet larger boardwalk was authorized, twenty-four feet wide and built atop steel pilings. It was then four miles long. By 1896, it was forty feet wide. The present reincarnation is sixty feet wide and six miles long. It is the longest and best known of many imitators. (The sixty-foot-wide standard was first established in 1902.)

But was Atlantic City's Boardwalk really the first? Cape May claims that an 1868 effort there actually was an expansion of an even earlier version, known locally as "Flirtation Walk." Such short plank walks were, in fact, common along the Jersey shore—so common that no one thought to publicize them or think them novel.

There is no dispute, however, that Atlantic City's Boardwalk was the first to parallel the seafront, as a promenade lined with shops and restaurants, rather than be built at a right angle to the sea, providing access across the dunes.

Gambling on Renewal

By the 1970s, Atlantic City's citizens sensed some trouble ahead. Approximately 120 years after Atlantic City was founded on an offshore sandbar, the city's economy and reputation were fading. The once glamorous, fabled "Queen of the Jersey Shore," as it immodestly proclaimed itself, looked backward to its glory days rather than forward. In his landmark 1975 study of Atlantic City, *By the Beautiful Sea*, Charles Funnell concluded, "Ultimately, changing modes of transportation practically destroyed the resort's ability

The Boardwalk is Atlantic City's main contribution to seaside resort tradition and architecture. This postcard image is from circa 1910.

to attract patronage across class lines, threatened the physical appearance of the city, and sapped the illusion-creating potential the town once so vigorously exploited. Atlantic City did not 'fall'—it was abandoned. It persevered in formulas which had been highly successful, but though a large part of its patronage continued to respond eagerly to what it offered, an important minority left it behind, to return no more."

Basically, by the 1970s, the people of New Jersey felt sorry for Atlantic City and its citizens. It had been such a great place in memory; now it needed help. If Atlantic City couldn't help itself—and evidently it couldn't—how could the state help the old resort once again rise to success?

The road to renewal first needed an answer to what went wrong. For one thing, owners and operators of hotels, restaurants, and entertainment businesses had failed to keep up with changing tastes. Aging buildings weren't kept fresh and up-to-date. New facilities just were not being built. The places that attracted, accommodated, and entertained visitors had become shabby and old-fashioned.

Early Success

In Atlantic City's early days, all the facilities were new, and new equals desirable for American tourists. The early success of Atlantic City is illustrated by the size and plushness of its hotels. For example, the United States Hotel, which occupied an entire city block and had rooms for six hundred guests, was described in an 1878 account by T. F. Rose as "large, airy, comfortable, carpeted, and furnished in walnut, with gas in every room." He continued, "in every respect [it] will compare with a first class city hotel. There are also attractive billiard rooms, ten pin alleys, and shooting galleries and daily morning, afternoon, and evening open air concerts are given by a celebrated orchestra." Host to President Grant in 1874, the hotel had been one of the most successful ventures of the railroad company. By 1894, it had been torn down, an example of the energetic drive to keep-up-to-date. New resorts are characterized by intensive real estate speculation and rapid construction of new, plush accommodations, restaurants, and transport facilities of the latest design. The reputation of such a resort, carefully nourished by enthusiastic public relations efforts, is at its height. It is an "in" place with a magnetic appeal to the trend followers.

As leisure time and disposable income were democratized, successively lower income groups arrived to sample Atlantic City's well-publicized delights. This trend is closely related to the progressive lowering of the cost in time and money of traveling to the resort.

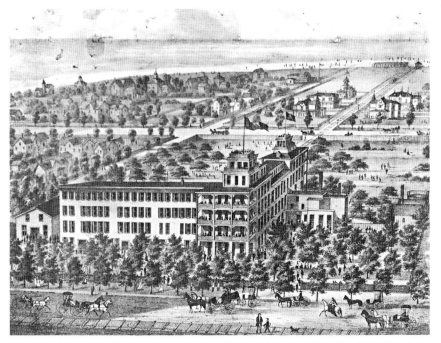

The United States Hotel, a luxurious new structure in this image from circa 1878, was torn down in 1894 in a frantic rush to keep the resort up-to-date.

Fun on a crowded Atlantic City beach in the 1890s.

The Good Old Days

The late 1800s through early 1900s were Atlantic City's glory years. There seemed to be a perfect fit between what the tourists wanted and what the city provided. As writers in the late 1800s loved to say, Atlantic City was "Philadelphia's Phun Phactory."

Success was documented in the two figures that count in resorts: numbers of visitors and numbers of dollars. In 1894, when the city's permanent inhabitants numbered about eighteen thousand, the throng of visitors topped one hundred thousand a day in late August. By the early 1900s, Atlantic City was said to "harvest" $180 million annually from its visitors—an astonishing figure, considering the buying power of a dollar then.

The grand resort's total reliance on its visitors encouraged Atlantic City locals to make every effort to please, even if it meant bending the laws a bit. The state of New Jersey long had a Sunday closing provision in its liquor laws. But many thirsty Philadelphians, in town for only a day, wanted a Sunday drink or two. What was a humanitarian bartender brimming with goodwill to do? Most Atlantic City citizens, mindful of the shortness of the season and the need to "harvest" as many tourist dollars as quickly as possible, favored either liberalized laws or ignoring laws. Local grand juries were notorious in their reluctance to indict their own for minor infractions

Front View of Main Entrance and Balcony, Blenheim Hotel, Atlantic City, N. J.

The ornate Blenheim Hotel in 1918, built of prestressed concrete, was typical of the early-twentieth-century Boardwalk skyline.

Amusement Piers

Steeplechase and Steel Piers from Hotel Chalfonte, Atlantic City, N. J.

By the early twentieth century, Atlantic City boasted multiple amusement piers.

Amusement piers seem to have originated on the south coast of England early in the nineteenth century. They reached their full potential along the New Jersey coast in the late nineteenth and early twentieth centuries. Some fine examples survive at places like Atlantic City and Wildwood.

The original purpose of piers was straightforward enough—to provide a landing stage for ships, especially where shallow water inshore meant connecting a deepwater berth with land. Piers originally intended as landing stages soon took on other functions, however. People enjoyed the novelty of walking above the waves, and they strolled the piers even when not embarking or disembarking. Enterprising merchants set up stalls on the piers to sell candy and souvenirs to the crowds. Piers started charging admission, and soon piers were built as attractions in themselves, with little or nothing to do with boat landings. It occurred to entrepreneurs that building amusement piers out over the sea in effect created additional profitable space along crowded seafronts. They need only purchase a seafront lot to gain access to free space above the waves.

(continued on page 164)

(continued from page 163)

No. 280. Young's Million-Dollar Pier
Atlantic City, N. J.

Young's Pier, one of the first built of concrete, cost a million dollars to construct.

England's Margate, in 1815, was the first to charge admission to piers. Brighton, England's Chain Pier may have been the first to add band concerts, novelty shops, and refreshment stands, in 1823.

In 1878, a pier was built at Long Branch, designed to handle ships, but it was soon festooned with merchants' booths. Cape May's Iron Pier, constructed in 1884, boasted a music auditorium and a huge dance floor. Atlantic City built a pier in 1882; it lasted only one season, destroyed by storm waves. Fire is second only to storms as hazards to piers, which frequently must be rebuilt. More piers appeared at Atlantic City in 1884, 1891, 1898, 1899, 1902, 1906, and 1910.

Typical amusement piers offered "games of skill" that rewarded winners with plush teddy bears and similar carnival-type prizes. As late as the 1940s, pier arcades had rows of hand-cranked kinetoscopes, a crude predecessor of movies, in which a series of still photos was flipped rapidly before the eyes to give the illusion of movement. Modern arcades still feature games with prizes, along with video games.

The larger piers, such as Atlantic City's classic Steel Pier (since rebuilt on a smaller scale), once boasted large ballrooms with nationally famous bands, vaudeville shows with top stars, movies, game arcades, and the world-renowned diving horses.

like selling alcohol on Sundays. The local police, too, were said to experience temporary blindness in the neighborhood of saloons doing a roaring Sunday business.

The city's open tolerance of prostitution and mildly (by today's standards) pornographic revues and exhibits added to its already slightly tarnished reputation. As the fictional Godfather would have said, Atlantic City was simply giving people what they wanted. And as local newspapers truthfully pointed out, the owners of "low" bars and brothels were, like their customers, mostly Philadelphians.

Not that there was any shortage of good, clean fun. The notion of charging beach fees hadn't occurred to anyone. (Atlantic City still has free beaches, now a rarity in the state.) Sand and surf provided a free and ever-fascinating playground for all. Legitimate theater was of Broadway quality; indeed, Atlantic City became a popular "tryout" town for Broadway-bound shows. Mechanical amusements were the best anywhere. Beach and Boardwalk, then as now, were paradise for people-watchers. Fresh seafood was inexpensive.

Some of the guests managed to drop nothing at all into the local cash registers. They wore bathing suits under their street clothes and brought picnic lunches from home in shoeboxes. This led to the local derogatory term, "shoebies" for those cheapskates who spent nothing beyond train fare.

All in all, a good time was had by everyone. And for decades, people kept coming back.

By the early twentieth century, virtually all Americans could afford at least a day trip to Atlantic City if they lived close enough. And as Charles Funnell has written, Atlantic City had become so typical a resort that Teddy Roosevelt remarked, "A man would not be a good American citizen if he did not know of Atlantic City." But there were problems ahead.

The Period of Decline

By World War I, most of Atlantic City's resplendent and extravagant seafront hotels had been built; few more on the truly grandiose scale would be added. The railroad was still fulfilling its dominant role, although motorists were beginning to clog the highways in summer. The costs of reaching Atlantic City were decreasing. The railroad, whose speed made day trips feasible, was carrying progressively lower-income groups to Atlantic City. Entertainment facilities increasingly reflected their tastes and incomes. This shift in emphasis toward working-class tastes was both a cause and a consequence of the upper middle class's declining loyalty to Atlantic City.

The mechanical amusements, cheap vaudeville theaters, and garish entertainments that so thrilled the working classes helped drive away the upper middle class from the ornate hotels and high-class restaurants. Also, richer folks had more time and money to explore newer resorts that were farther away. Tourism is an industry in which fashion and the search for the new and different play an important role.

The fact that Atlantic City's fortunes were tied to trains was both good and bad. Trains had created and built Atlantic City. But the last excursion trains were phased out after World War II, leaving Atlantic City with only minimal, commuter-oriented train service. The two replacements for trains in vacation travel—limited-access, high-speed highways and jet airplanes—both favored other resorts. Atlantic City was the loser under these new rules. Although Atlantic City's Bader Field, one of the first municipal airports in the nation, is convenient to downtown, the air age has not greatly benefited the resort. Other than convention trade, few visitors arrived by air until after the casinos were built. The time in the air from most of the neighboring cities of the northeastern Megalopolis to other resorts, such as those of southern Florida, is not all that much greater than that to Atlantic City. Also, economical operation of fast jets on a regularly scheduled basis requires terminals at the largest cities within the region. Short-haul service to Atlantic City has not been all that successful, although it has continued and may have a bright future.

The individual mobility of automobile vacations led to a quite different style of vacation from that of the old railroad resorts. Whether for a day or

Atlantic City's densely built-up, narrow streets of 1916 were more suited to pedestrians and trolleys than the floods of cars to come.

P4216   Hotel Dennis and Casino. Atlantic City. N. J.

Much of the old Atlantic City skyline, as in this early 1920s view, was ruthlessly destroyed by the 1960s, a contrast to Cape May's successful preservation efforts.

a month, the Victorian vacationer was tied to that one city, perhaps even to a particular hotel, and his dollars were spent mostly within the confines of that resort. Private automobiles had two major effects upon tourism, neither of which really benefited Atlantic City. Vacationers arriving in cars wanted to be able to park their cars conveniently and, preferably, free of charge. Crowded, densely built-up Atlantic City was friendly to pedestrians, but not cars. By the auto age, most of the city's buildable land was occupied by multistory structures packed tightly together. The narrow streets of an earlier era could not accommodate both heavier traffic and curb parking on both sides. Relatively few new, large motels were constructed in a city where many hotel rooms were empty even in peak season. Cost-conscious vacationers could stay "offshore" (on the mainland) at cut-rate motels constructed along the highways and drive daily to the beaches, crowding Atlantic City's beaches and streets, but leaving little money behind. The much-sought-after middle-class "family trade" increasingly preferred the smaller, less crowded, less expensive towns along the coast. The new highways that brought vacationers to Atlantic City also helped them reach other resorts or commute into Atlantic City from less expensive locations. Highway improvements further increased the distance that day-trippers could travel from home to resort to home in one day.

Commonly in aging resorts, the natural amenities that led to the founding of the resort now are of deteriorated quality, with environmental pollution a serious problem. Declining resorts often attempt to modify

Picture Postcards

Picture postcards long have been the most popular souvenirs. They're cheap, colorful reminders of fun days and a wonderful way to brag about your travels to friends and relatives.

Sending picture postcards quickly became a fad from the last years of the nineteenth century into the first decades of the twentieth. The U.S. Post Office first issued plain postcards in 1873. The idea of picture postcards, however, seems to be an import from Europe. The very first picture postcards suppposedly were printed in Austria in 1869. German printers made them popular by the 1880s. The first picture postcards in the United States were sold at the 1893 Chicago World's Fair. Shortly after, a German-American printer in Atlantic City was publishing views of that resort, and the fad was under way. By 1898, a major New York printing house was in the postcard business, issuing black-and-white scenes of that city.

The first picture postcards were well suited to people in a hurry or people who didn't like to write. Until 1907, the entire reverse side of picture postcards was reserved for the address. The sender could only sign his or her name or squeeze a few words beneath the photo (a strip intentionally left blank by some printers) or in a convenient stretch of

Watching the Bathers from the Boardwalk-Atlantic City.

Prior to 1907, when the Post Office permitted a split reverse side—half for the address, half for the message—messages were written only in the blank space under the photo or in a convenient patch of sky.

Beach Scene, Atlantic City, N. J.

A typical hand-tinted color postcard published in Germany, the leader in color printing techniques at the time.

sky in the photo. Since 1907, the reverse side has been split between message and address. Postcards became so popular that in 1908, the U.S. Post Office delivered over 667 million cards.

Businesses often used postcards featuring views of their store or factory as direct-mail advertisements. Both Atlantic City and Asbury Park soon had boardwalk stores selling only postcards; many Americans began collecting the cards. Prior to World War I, many cards were still printed in Germany, which led the world in color printing technologies at the time. In *Greetings from New Jersey,* postcard historian Helen-Chantal Pike points out that in an era when few homes had telephones, twice-a-day mail deliveries meant that penny postcards served to keep people in touch with one another; social affairs and invitations were sent by postcard. Wish you were here!

their appeal to vacationers. The resort may choose to emphasize its historical and cultural uniqueness over its less-than-first-rate physical location. In other words, while superior climates, lower costs, easier access, more modern and glamorous facilities, and less crowded beaches all may characterize other, newer resorts, some unique quality of the older resort must be emphasized to lure tourists.

Mechanical Amusements

Mechanical amusements, those staples of amusement parks and many seashore boardwalks, have been around longer than you might realize. The three basic rides—the merry-go-round, the Ferris wheel, and the roller coaster—were all popular by the 1890s.

Amusement rides are a natural outgrowth of nineteenth-century Americans' fascination with machines. Many people worked with machines at their daily jobs. They probably rode to work in electric streetcars and traveled to the seashore by steamboat or steam railroad.

Roller coasters were like bumpier, faster, mildly scary trolley rides. The first crude roller coasters were called toboggan slides, switchbacks, or scenic railways. These first appeared at the shore in 1889, but there is on record a contraption with an inclined plane and rolling carriages built in Paris in 1817. These ancestors of roller coasters had become, by the end of the nineteenth century, like dwarfed railcars, offering the illusion of speed spiced with (mostly imaginary) danger. Maybe their greatest attraction was that their cramped seats forced young men and women to sit very close and be thrown into each other's arms on sharp turns.

The official debut of the Ferris wheel was at the 1893 Chicago World's Fair, when steel construction engineer George Ferris designed a 250-foot wheel carrying thirty-six glass-enclosed cabs or cars, each with a capacity of sixty riders. While Ferris's mammoth wheel popularized the ride, it is likely, though not well documented, that Atlantic City saw the first such amusement ride as early as 1872. Local boy William Somers definitely built one on the Boardwalk in 1891. Somers had built these wheels at Asbury Park and Coney Island before Ferris planned his giant wheel for Chicago. Somers sued Ferris over copyright infringement and won, but Ferris died before paying Somers.

Merry-go-rounds, powered by human or animal muscles, seem to date back to late-eighteenth-century western Europe. Atlantic City's first successful merry-go-round, in 1876, was powered by a horse. This type of ride was introduced from Germany, which had a merry-go-round factory as early as the 1840s.

On the rebuilt Steel Pier, traditional amusements still entertain.

Casinos Yes! captures the local enthusiasm for legalized gaming. The referendum on legalizing casinos in Atlantic City was approved in November 1976.

A notable example of capitalizing upon the historic landscape is Cape May's largely successful preservation of its Victorian townscape. Cape May's stock of 1850s through 1890s architecture helps draw visitors to an otherwise out-of-the-way site with relatively narrow beaches.

By the 1970s, though the remaining great hotels of the turn of the century through the 1920s were flamboyant and varied, Atlantic City's architecture was not quite old enough yet to draw the full interest of the preservationists and nostalgia buffs who have made a pet of Cape May. Too, the demolition of some old hotels had left great gaps in Atlantic City's oceanfront skyline. While Cape May's small-town Victoriana is charming, Atlantic City simply could not become another, larger Cape May. So just what could Atlantic City do to regain its status as a world-class resort?

The Legalization of Gambling

Atlantic City was beginning to show its age. No major new hotels had been built for decades. The all-too-short tourist season left many locals on the unemployment rolls for about eight months a year. The problems of Atlantic City spurred a variety of efforts to revitalize the city by the 1960s. A new high-speed toll highway, the Atlantic City Expressway, was built between Philadelphia's New Jersey suburbs and the aging resort. A new state college was built on the mainland nearby. There was talk of improving rail service by extending a suburban high-speed commuter railway from Philadelphia all the way to Atlantic City. Local business and political leaders had been discussing the possibility of legalized gambling as an economic stimulus. Major hotel owners were split on the controversial proposal. The Quaker owners of the Chalfonte-Haddon Hall Hotel, for example, strongly opposed legalizing casinos.

A referendum on gambling casinos appeared on the November 1974 ballot, but it was resoundingly defeated, three to two. The 1974 proposal, however, while supposedly designed to help Atlantic City, would have made casinos a matter of local option anywhere in the state. Clearly, the possibility of a casino in everyone's hometown was unpopular. In 1976, the ballot proposal was restricted to legalized casinos in Atlantic City only. This time, state revenues from casinos were to be devoted to property tax and utility bill relief for the elderly poor—a maneuver that attracted many votes. The campaign of the "Committee to Rebuild Atlantic City" succeeded. The first casino opened in 1978. Ironically, it was the Chalfonte-Haddon Hall property, under its new owner, Resorts International.

But would casinos thrive by the sea? Would the new industry bring prosperity to the old resort? New Jersey's governor helped open the first casino, Resorts International, on the Memorial Day weekend of 1978. It was a winner—an instant hit. Local legend has it that this pioneer casino took in so much money in those first days that the counting room couldn't handle the volume of cash. It is said that supermarket bags of bills accumulated on the floor until the accounting staff caught up. According to Michael Hawkins

Atlantic City's first casino, Resorts International, opened in May 1978. It was a great success.

in "The Atlantic City Experience," Resorts' seven-month-long first year of operations earned a gross income of $156 million, representing a 200 percent return on equity.

Here's a snapshot of the casino industry in Atlantic City nine years after Resorts International first opened its doors to the crowds lined up there. According to Don Russell, in "Atlantic City's Bet on Gambling," on an average day in 1987, 110,000 visitors and nonresident workers joined the city's 37,000 residents. More than 82,000 people visited the city's twelve casinos, with 1,452 charter buses arriving in town. Gamblers dropped over 46 million quarters in slot machines, and gross winnings, or how much the casinos took in, amounted to about $6.5 million.

Less than two years after the first casino opened, seven more appeared and the Boardwalk was transformed by a building boom.

Atlantic City had become America's most popular resort destination, with more than 35 million visitor-days per year; in comparison, Walt Disney World sees about 18 million visitor-days per year. Wages in the hotel and casino industry topped $700 million a year, and more than 46,000 people were now employed in an industry that did not exist until 1978. Between 1976, the year in which the casino referendum was approved by New Jersey voters, and 1984, per capita income in the United States doubled, but Atlantic City's grew by 134 percent. In 1987, Atlantic City had ten times as many visitors as it had in 1976. The state's 8 percent tax on gross revenues of casinos already had transferred more than $1 billion to the state treasury. Indirect taxes—sales taxes and the city's luxury tax paid by casino patrons—generated another $20 million per year.

The visible effects of the casino industry on Atlantic City can be compared to a growing snowball, or maybe it was more like an avalanche filmed in slow motion. At first, little seemed to be happening, at least for the better.

In her book about Resorts International, author Gigi Mahon described the scene in the summer of 1977—a year after voter approval of legalized gambling in Atlantic City, but a year before opening day: "Up at the Chalfonte-Haddon Hall, a handful of construction men labored through the heat, a renovation under way. But for that, the facades of the old hotels remained as they had for years, sagging, gray, like the faces of the people

〰〰〰〰〰〰〰〰〰〰〰〰〰〰〰〰

The Legend of Saltwater Taffy

Saltwater taffy is a soft, chewy confection that has become a popular treat and souvenir gift from the Jersey shore. If Atlantic City can be said to export anything besides happy memories and sunburns, saltwater taffy would head the list.

Legend has it that taffy maker and vendor David Bradley's candy stand on the beach was flooded in 1883 by a high tide, soaking his stock. He turned catastrophe into an advertising slogan, calling his candy "saltwater taffy." Thus, a star was born.

Although the taffy, available in a variety of flavors, does contain salt, as does most candy, there is no seawater in saltwater taffy. Once produced by more than four hundred candy makers, the popular taffy's top two makers, Fralinger's and James', are based in Atlantic City, which remains synonymous with the treat. At the height of the taffy's popularity, about 1940, visitors mailed over three million pounds to friends in one season, in addition to on-the-spot consumption.

In June 1985, Fralinger's Original Salt Water Taffy celebrated its hundredth anniversary with a special taffy pull on the Boardwalk. More than 250 people carefully stretched out the pliable candy to produce the longest single piece of taffy ever— at five hundred feet, ten inches, a world record that was enshrined in the Guinness Book. Anyone, incidentally, can use the name saltwater taffy; no one ever thought to copyright it.

---

who sat on the Boardwalk day after day. It was the same Atlantic City, long ago duchess of resorts, now an arthritic and dowdy dowager trying desperately to cling to her past. A bag of worn-out bricks on splintered pilings."

Did the legalization of gambling work? In a word, yes. Casino revenues from 1978 to the present brought a total of $60 billion into New Jersey's treasury. The legalization of casinos in Atlantic City has created almost 50,000 jobs directly in the casino industry, and an estimated additional 50,000 jobs in industries within New Jersey that supply and service the casinos. And this creation of 100,000 jobs in the state did not cost the state a dime. In contrast, other states and local governments have spent millions in their efforts to attract new jobs into their economies.

Gambling on the Future, Gambling in the Future

Atlantic City's present and future depend on Americans' attitudes toward gambling. Today the industry prefers to use the term *gaming*, which they believe sounds classier and has fewer negative connotations than *gambling*.

Fading glory: Most old hotels could not readily be adapted to modern casino standards, and so most were demolished.

The old glitz was replaced by the new glitz of Taj Mahal and other thematic casinos.

Over our country's history, we Americans have changed our attitudes several times about permitting, encouraging, or criminalizing gambling. Popular ambivalence toward gambling characterized Americans long before New Jersey's 1976 referendum, and it continues to this day.

Colonial America openly tolerated lotteries. Such upright citizens as Benjamin Franklin printed lottery tickets, which were sold to support good causes, much as chances today are sold on new cars to raise money for vol-

How Much Is Park Place?

First-time visitors to Atlantic City often come to realize that the street names, though not the actual streets, somehow seem familiar. Then the realization comes that the popular Parker Brothers game of Monopoly is based on Atlantic City. Not only the names of the streets, but the relative value of real estate reflects Atlantic City's reality.

Players around the world know that Boardwalk is the most expensive property to purchase or rent, and the cheapest are Baltic Avenue and Mediterranean Avenue. As visitors to the resort quickly realize, the single most important influence on real estate values is proximity to the seafront. In all seaside towns, ocean views command the highest prices; we'd all like oceanfront rooms. Properties tend to get cheaper the farther from the ocean they are, except for bayfront locations, which may be valued higher than interior locations but still lower than the seafront.

The creator of Monopoly was Charles Darrow, a Philadelphian. A frequent vacationer to Atlantic City, Darrow adopted his favorite resort's geography of street names and real estate prices for his game. Today the game is marketed in twenty-six countries and is available in eighty languages.

The next time you cringe when landing on your opponent's Boardwalk property equipped with a hotel (rent: $2,000), remember that the comparative real estate values are pretty accurate. The cheapest location with hotel, Mediterranean Avenue, rents for only $250, or $2 with no buildings. Drive by the real Mediterranean Avenue, or any other Atlantic City Monopoly location, and you'll see that Monopoly remains a generally good guide to real estate prices today. Trivia question: Which of the game's property locations is not in Atlantic City? It's Marvin Gardens, in neighboring Ventnor.

unteer fire departments. Many a Colonial college and church were built with lottery proceeds.

Atlantic City was not the first case in which legalized gambling was used to revitalize a depressed economy, nor was it the last. Nevada was particularly hard hit during the Great Depression, and the state decided to legalize all forms of gambling. Thus the modern gambling industry was born. Until 1978, when New Jersey's first casino opened, Nevada enjoyed a national monopoly on legal gambling. Still, at least the western half of the country was closer to Nevada than to Atlantic City. But because of its success, Atlantic City served as a role model for depressed regions elsewhere. Gam-

The spaces on the game of Monopoly are named for avenues in Atlantic City.

bling was introduced to many reservations of Native Americans, the poorest of the census-tabulated minorities; on riverboats, to bring money to depressed old industrial cities; and to Mississippi, America's poorest state.

By 1984, seventeen states and the District of Columbia had legal, government-run lotteries; these lotteries had total sales approaching $7 billion. Today, forty-eight states, with the exception of Utah and Hawaii, have some form of state-sponsored gaming—lotteries, off-track betting, casinos, or a combination of these.

Lotteries, and now casinos, are seen as a painless form of voluntary taxation. Legalized casino gambling is most attractive to states when most of the gamblers are from out of state. In this way, most of the gambling losses are "exported"; after all, revenues from gambling are based entirely on net losses by gamblers. As long as legal casinos serve largely out-of-state gamblers, they contribute to real economic growth within the state.

Expansion of the casino industry in Atlantic City has not been one of continuous growth at a steady pace. The early success of Resorts International produced a boom between 1978 and 1981, in which the number of casinos jumped from one to nine, casino square footage increased by almost eight times, casino employees went from 3,226 to almost 28,000, and rooms in casino hotels went from 724 to 4,781. The annual increase in casino gross revenue, or "winnings," remained in the double digits until 1985.

Between 1981 and 2002, only three more casinos opened, and growth rates slowed noticeably. The increase rate of the gross "win" stayed below 10 percent a year after 1984. During the 1990s, the number of casino employees fluctuated between about 44,000 and 49,000. However, both casino floor areas and number of hotel rooms were higher by 2001 than they had been in 1991. Casino floor area, which since 1993 has included simulcast horseracing rooms, has increased by just under 60 percent, to more than a million square feet. What is even more impressive is the growth in casino hotel rooms, from 9,419 in 1991 to 11,466 by 2001.

The increase in the number of hotel rooms is significant because it points to a new trend that few had predicted. Atlantic City has clearly been moving from a day-trip resort to a destination resort, in which vacationers stay longer and to which they travel increasing distances. The 22 percent increase in hotel rooms from 1991 to 2001 is a respectable achievement, and one trend that will continue. The Casino Control Commission, in its annual report for 2001, predicted another 3,200 rooms by the summer of 2004.

Since the 2001 figure of 11,466 rooms was reported, Harrah's has built another 452-room addition; Resorts is adding another 459-room tower; Tropicana is adding 502 rooms; and Showboat is adding 544 rooms. Atlantic City's thirteenth casino, the opulent Borgata, in the Marina District, opened in the summer of 2003, contributing another 2,002 rooms. The Sheraton Atlantic, a new, noncasino hotel next to the $268 million Convention Center, has 502 rooms. A Boardwalk noncasino hotel, Atlantic Palace, has 302 units, many of them two-bedroom suites.

Atlantic City seems poised for another period of fast growth despite the minuscule increase in wins reported for 2001—a year of deepening recession, falling stock markets, and the tragedy of September 11, which considerably slowed the entire tourism and travel industry. Actually, the disasters of September 11, which had a strong negative impact on air travel, may have helped Atlantic City in the long run by increasing tourism at resorts that can be easily reached by road and rail, rather than relying heavily on air travel.

Today the revitalized Atlantic City draws more visitors than any other single locale in the United States, except Las Vegas. Of these, about seven million were overnight guests. At 94 percent occupancy year-round, Atlantic City has a much higher occupancy rate for hotels than the U.S. average. Casinos pay 70 percent of all property taxes collected in Atlantic City.

And gaming industry insiders predict that Atlantic City will be home to seventeen casinos by 2008. Atlantic City will continue to reign as the Queen of the Jersey Shore as it moves to more closely resemble its original model, Las Vegas.

The Casinos

Before the first casino opened in Atlantic City, the size of the legalized gambling market was unknown. The fact that a huge, formerly unserved market existed in the Northeast was the reason for the success of Atlantic City's first casino, Resorts International. Resorts' seven-month-long first year generated a gross income of $156 million. In its first full month of operation, Resorts' "win" was $16 million.

As the market grew, and more and more casinos opened, they began to develop marketing strategies to differentiate themselves and establish unique identities.

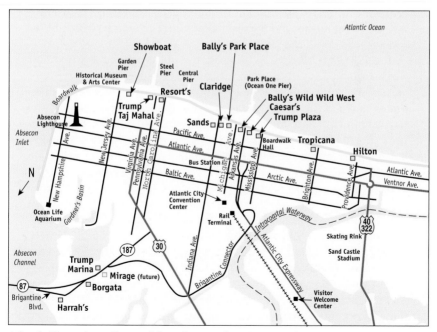

Atlantic City casinos. Plans call for a fourteenth casino near the Borgata on the bayside, although vacant land is also available on the Boardwalk northeast of Showboat.

According to gambling expert James Smith, in "The Premium-Grind," Nevada's casinos generally fall into one of two categories: premium or grind joints. Premium casinos strive for an upscale image. Lavishly decorated, they emphasize table games with fairly high minimum wagers. Premium casinos rely heavily on "high rollers" who may stay several days and gamble large sums. For their select clientele, premium casinos are happy to provide complimentary luxury suites, preferred seating at shows featuring big-name entertainment, and any other services that will keep the high rollers coming back. These wealthy players routinely risk many thousands of dollars. They typically stay for days, not hours, and expect elegance and impeccable service. They play table games in which they hope experience

The Jersey Shore at the Movies

A very specialized job in the movie industry is that of location scout. Few movies now are filmed entirely on sound stages or studio "back lots"—false-front sets of big-city street scenes, phony suburban developments, or exotic-looking "foreign" locales. Shooting on location adds realism and cuts set construction costs. Why build a replica when the real place can be used? State and city film commissions happily cooperate in "one-stop shopping" for permits, permissions, crowd control, traffic rerouting, and the like, to give local economies a little boost and perhaps polish the local image.

The 1981 film *Atlantic City,* directed by Louis Malle and starring Burt Lancaster and Susan Sarandon, probably is the best-known film shot mostly on location at the Jersey shore. It dramatized the transition from a down-at-the-heels, fading resort to the new era of casinos. The classic Knife and Fork Inn was the scene of a meal shared by the two stars. *The King of Marvin Gardens* (1972), starring Jack Nicholson and Bruce Dern, emphasized Atlantic City's fading glamour in the precasino era. Other seashore locales in notable movies include West Long Branch's Monmouth College, whose 130-room, French-style Shadow Lawn mansion, once used as a summer White House by President Woodrow Wilson, became Daddy Warbucks's estate in the 1982 musical *Annie,* starring Albert Finney, Aileen Quinn, and Carol Burnett. Woody Allen's *Stardust Memories* (1980) was filmed in both Spring Lake and Ocean Grove. Woody was so grateful, in fact, for the fine cooperation of Ocean Grove's residents that he paid to have the famed Great Auditorium's neon cross restored. Scenes for *Ragtime,* a 1981 film starring James Cagney, were filmed at Spring Lake's classic Hotel Essex and Sussex (now a condo). Spring Lake also provided background for scenes in *The Subject Was Roses* (1968), with Patricia Neal.

Skyline of Atlantic City at night.

and familiarity with the rules will count in their favor. Premium houses' showrooms feature top-name entertainment. (It is said that the late Frank Sinatra was the champion draw for high rollers.)

In contrast, "grind houses"—also known as "sawdust joints," as opposed to "carpet," or premium, casinos—prosper on a high volume of gamblers who bet less, a lot less, than the high rollers. Grind houses typically feature many slot machines and have relatively fewer table games. They rely on large numbers of low rollers who wager modestly but as a group are highly profitable. Senior citizens arriving by chartered buses, prepared to lose little more than the $10 rolls of quarters that are part of their day-trip packages, are the main patrons of the grind houses. Food is often served buffet style, most patrons do not stay overnight, and the showrooms feature revues rather than renowned stars. Whereas premium houses offer tickets to boxing matches and other special events to their high-rolling clientele, grind houses offer their clients meal coupons, chances to win cars, and discounted revue tickets. Many patrons of grind houses have too little experience to confidently play table games where skill counts; instead, they prefer the no-skill slot machines.

Atlantic City seems to have pioneered a hybrid premium-grind operation, says Smith, basically trying to combine both types of customer appeals. Contrasts among Atlantic City's casinos in 2001 are neither obvious nor consistent. They all cater to some degree to the whole spectrum of gamblers, aiming at as broad a market segment as possible. Economic survival requires satisfying all varieties of gamblers. The ratios of slots to table games does vary from casino to casino, but all seek to please everyone, from high rollers arriving in private planes from the Far East to senior citizens stepping off chartered buses to eagerly cash in their bonus coupons for $10 rolls of quarters.

To create distinctive identities, Atlantic City's casinos employ themes that are shaped and expressed by architecture, interior decoration, costumes of dealers and other employees, and the names of lounges, showrooms, and restaurants. Some of the most obvious examples include Showboat's New Orleans Mardi Gras, Taj Mahal's Oriental–Arabian nights fantasy, Bally's Wild, Wild West, and Caesars' Imperial Roman theme. Gambler or not, it can be fun to visit a variety of casinos to identify and enjoy their themes, however overstated or understated they may be.

Atlantic City's casinos now are open twenty-four hours a day, every day. For gamblers, there are slot machines, blackjack, poker, craps tables, roulette, baccarat, "Big 6" wheels, and keno. Betting on simulcast horseracing takes place in rooms separate from the casino floor. Top-name entertainment is an everyday fact of life in the casinos' showrooms. Besides show business superstars, many casinos offer Broadway-quality revues. Check the ads in the Philadelphia, New York, and Atlantic City newspapers, especially the Sunday editions. Considering the quality of entertainment offered, ticket prices are reasonable. All casino hotels provide huge parking garages; there is a

Bally's Wild, Wild West, another casino in a fantasy environment.

state-mandated uniform $3 parking fee, which is earmarked for urban revitalization projects in Atlantic City. Many casinos will give you a voucher for free parking if you join their frequent patrons club.

The Casinos in Detail

Most casinos suggest contacting Ticketmaster at 800-736-1420 or www.ticket master.com, or visiting a Ticketmaster outlet.

Resorts Atlantic City (Resorts International), 1133 Boardwalk (North Carolina Avenue and the Boardwalk), 609-344-6000 or 800-GET-RICH; reservations, 800-336-6378; box office, 800-322-SHOW. Main showroom, Superstar Theater; also, Rendezvous Lounge, Carousel Cabaret; seven restaurants; 686 rooms. This was Atlantic City's first casino, and one of the largest. Classic older hotel, with decorative art deco touches. Resorts purchased and rebuilt the famous old Steel Pier, across the Boardwalk from the casino, then sold it to the Taj Mahal.

Caesars Atlantic City, 2100 Pacific Avenue (located at Arkansas Avenue and the Boardwalk), 800-524-2867; reservations, 800-443-0104; box office, 800-677-7469. Fabulously decorated in Roman style (check out the togas on the waiters), this casino is second in glitz only to Caesars Las Vegas. Main showroom, Circus Maximus Theater; eight restaurants; 645 rooms.

Bally's Park Place, Park Place and the Boardwalk, 800-225-5977; reservations, 800-225-5977; box office and show information, 800-772-7777. Atlantic City's third casino, Bally's is one of the smaller hotels, with 510 rooms and four restaurants. Main showroom, Bally's Park Cabaret, is a rather intimate showroom that showcases solo acts. Technically an extension of Bally's Park Place (at least to the Casino Control Commission), Bally's Wild, Wild West is a wonderfully phony Wild West mining town themed casino, which is well worth a look whether you are a gambler or not.

Sands Hotel and Casino, Indiana Avenue and Brighton Park (fronting on the Boardwalk; once known as the Brighton), 609-441-4000; reservations, 800-257-8580; box office and show information, 609-441-4100. Main showroom, Copa Room; food court; two other plush restaurants; 501 rooms. One of the smaller casinos, Sands welcomes you with one of the broadest selections of quality fast food anywhere.

Harrah's Atlantic City (Harrah's Marina), 777 Harrah's Boulevard (Brigantine Boulevard), 609-441-5000; reservations and box office, 800-242-7724. Located on Absecon Inlet, across from the Farley State Marina, Harrah's was the first to break the tradition of first-class hotels always being on the Boardwalk. More than one hundred boat slips are available to customers bringing their own yachts. Lacking a yacht, you could take a water taxi from other resorts; check service schedules locally, as some water serv-

Some of Atlantic City's largest casino hotels are located back on the bay in the Marina District.

ices have folded due to erratic demand. Main showroom, Broadway by the Bay Theater; three restaurants. Especially notable: Harrah's provides a kids' supervised "fun center," where customers can leave the kids safely playing video games.

Atlantic City Hilton Casino Resort (formerly Golden Nugget), Boston Avenue and the Boardwalk, 609-340-7100; reservations, 800-257-8677; box office, 800-843-4726. Main showroom, Opera House; three restaurants; 804 units, most with ocean view. Completely redecorated since its Golden Nugget days. Known locally as perhaps the most elegant casino.

The Claridge, Park Place and the Boardwalk, 609-340-3400; reservations, 800-257-8585; box office, 800-752-7469. Today the Claridge actually boasts that it is the city's smallest casino, offering a cozier atmosphere and more individualized services. Main showroom, Palace Theater; four restaurants; 504 units. Older, completely renovated hotel in classic Atlantic City style, the Claridge, which opened as a casino-hotel in July 1981, was Atlantic City's last big, ornate hotel when first opened in 1930.

Tropicana Casino and Resort, between Brighton and Iowa Avenues and the Boardwalk, toward the southwestern end of the Boardwalk, 609-340-4000; reservations, 800-257-6227; show information, 800-526-2935. Main showroom, Showroom; seven restaurants; two lounges; 1,624 units. The Tropicana reigned briefly as Atlantic City's, and the state of New Jersey's, largest hotel resort.

Trump Plaza Casino, on the Boardwalk at Mississippi Avenue, 609-441-6000; reservations, 800-677-7378; show information, 800-759-8786. Next to the old Convention Hall, this is the Boardwalk's tallest hotel, at thirty-nine stories. Main showroom, Trump's Theater; seven restaurants; six lounges; 614 units.

Trump Marina, 1 Castle Boulevard (Brigantine Boulevard), 609-441-2000; reservations, 800-365-8786; show information, 800-777-8477. Located at Huron Avenue on the bayside, this is another exception to the typical Boardwalk location, like nearby Harrah's. This is the second of Donald Trump's Atlantic City casinos; the third is Trump Taj Mahal. Trump Marina has splendid views of both Brigantine Wildlife Refuge and the Boardwalk skyline. Main showroom, King's Court Theater.

Trump Taj Mahal, on the Boardwalk at Virginia Avenue, 800-825-8786; box office, 609-449-1000. Taj Mahal obviously is named after India's world-famous white marble mosque and mausoleum. Atlantic City's "Taj," as it is known, features the most exotic (some would say, most garish) architecture among the casinos, a sort of cross between the original Taj Mahal and traditional Boardwalk glitz. It's one of those "you love it or you hate it" creations. Connected to the famed Steel Pier. Main showroom, Mark G. Etess Arena.

Showboat Casino and Hotel, a neighbor of the Taj Mahal, on Delaware Avenue near the northeast end of the Boardwalk, 609-343-4000; reserva-

A gilded elephant is part of the exotic architectural theme of the Boardwalk Taj Mahal Casino.

A detailed reproduction of a French Quarter street scene is part of Showboat Casino's Mardi Gras theme. The structure actually is a parking garage.

tions and box office, 800-621-0200. Known for its exuberant New Orleans–style ambience, the Showboat is a favorite with Philadelphia-area day-trippers. A must-see-to-be-believed even if you don't gamble.

Borgata Hotel Casino and Spa, on the bay at 1 Borgata Way, off Brigantine Boulevard; information, 609-317-1000; reservations, 866-My-Borgata. This 2,002-room property, encased in a dazzling gold tower, is Atlantic City's newest casino, the first in thirteen years. It cost $1.1 billion and features eleven restaurants and a huge spa. This is the first of several planned "mega resorts" in the Las Vegas tradition.

Atlantic City's Noncasino Attractions

From Million Dollar Pier to Park Place. The old Million Dollar Pier was first opened in 1906 by John Young, who built and popularized the fabled pier. It offered popular vaudeville shows along with mechanical amusements. On Young's Million Dollar Pier, you could take a "nickel trolley ride on the ocean"; witness hourly "net hauls," in which John Young himself would identify marine life as it spilled out of the huge net suspended from the pier; or gawk at "Captain" Young's lavish Moorish-style mansion, built on the pier.

In 1983, the refurbished old pier was reopened as Ocean One—essentially a modern suburban mall surrounded not by parking lots, but by the ocean and beach. Home to 130 shops, restaurants, and snack bars, Ocean One was handicapped by one tiny omission—adequate parking.

Now, in the grand tradition of amusement piers, plans are to give the old pier a $113 million refit as Park Place—a redevelopment using the Monopoly game as its theme. In addition to retaining the shopping mall functions of Ocean One, Park Place will feature a new entertainment complex. The Monopoly-based Waterworks will have a water, light, and music show as the new pier's main attraction. And a three-thousand-space parking garage will be constructed on nearby property. The Park Place entertainment-retailing center, with over a quarter of a million square feet of retail space, is planned to open in the summer of 2004, another fine example of non-casino investment that will considerably enliven the venerable Boardwalk.

The Ocean Life Center. This beautiful new aquarium is located at historic Gardner's Basin, at the foot of Rhode Island Avenue and New Hampshire Avenue in the north end. Exhibits include giant loggerhead sea turtles, an octopus, and a 750-gallon touch tank, a children's delight, where visitors are encouraged to touch and pick up a variety of marine life, including primitive-looking horseshoe crabs. Open 10 A.M. to 5 P.M. daily; an admission fee is charged. For information, call 609-348-2880. Nearby are a re-created fishing village, seafood restaurants, and opportunities to go fishing or sightseeing aboard a variety of boats.

Atlantic City Historical Museum. This intimate little museum is located on the Garden Pier at New Jersey Avenue and the Boardwalk, just northeast of the Showboat Casino. Featured are antique souvenirs, vintage photographs, and Atlantic City memorabilia, including Miss America materials. Visit this charming museum early on in your stay in Atlantic City. The best introduction to the city's history is a continuously playing video presentation, *Boardwalk Ballyhoo*. You will enjoy the unique experience of watching this entertaining and informative documentary while

Ocean One, the future Park Place shopping and entertainment complex built on a pier.

Ocean Life, located at historic Gardner's Basin, is one of Atlantic City's noncasino attractions.

glancing out a picture window at the ocean, beach, Boardwalk, and modern skyline of the "Queen of the Jersey Shore." Admission and parking are free. For information, call 609-347-5839.

Brigantine

Brigantine had a hotel as early as 1857, only a few years after the founding of Atlantic City. However, development and population growth both were slow until a rail trestle to the island was completed in 1897. This rail connection lasted only six years; a storm in 1903 destroyed the trestle, and it was never rebuilt. It wasn't until 1924 that a highway bridge was constructed.

Brigantine's special attraction is its neighboring wildlife refuge. The Brigantine Unit of the Edwin B. Forsythe National Wildlife Refuge is located off Route 9 south in Oceanville. The refuge encompasses over twenty thousand acres of marshes—salt, brackish, and freshwater—as well as some sand beaches and forest area. This is an important stop on the Atlantic Flyway, and thousands of migrating birds stop here to rest and eat in the spring and fall. For the birds, this is a strategically located motel and fast-food stop. Because of the great variety of natural environments, an astounding array of migratory and nonmigratory birds can be observed. This is paradise for bird-watchers, and even those not particularly interested in adding new bird sightings to their lists surely will be thrilled by glimpses of bald and golden eagles, snowy owls, and more varieties of ducks and geese than you've ever dreamed of.

The view of nearby Atlantic City's spectacular skyline from the observation tower alone is worth the trip. There is an eight-mile paved road loop, as well as several hiking trails. The friendly naturalist rangers know all about the wildlife. In late spring, horseshoe crabs, looking like primitive, ugly science fiction creatures, swim ashore to spawn. Deer, rabbits, and raccoons are likely to appear, with occasional glimpses of foxes. Be warned: Since no insecticides are sprayed in the refuge, use a good insect repellent, or stay inside your car with the window closed in summer. It probably is just a local legend that the voracious Jersey "skeeters" have been seen carrying off small children, but do take insect repellent in warm weather. Oh, and watch out for poison ivy, too. There's a fee per car. Picnicking is permitted, and there are restrooms. For information, call 609-652-1665.

Brigantine is also home to the Marine Mammal Stranding Center Museum, on Brigantine Boulevard. This is an emergency first-aid and rescue station for whales, dolphins, seals, and even nonmammals such as sea turtles, sharks, and exotic or endangered fish. The center's motto is "Rescue, Rehabilitate, Release, Educate," and it does all of these very well. It has responded to over two thousand calls to help stranded sea creatures, ranging from a five-pound Kemp's Ridley sea turtle to a twenty-five-ton humpback whale, both endangered species. The center holds both state and federal permits to work with protected and rare animals and is frequently called out of state to assist in rescues. The museum has a large aquarium displaying fish, along with photos of the many successful rescues. Open every day in summer. Admission is free; donations are accepted. For information, call 609-266-0538. A visit is highly recommended.

The Brigantine Historical Museum, also on Brigantine Boulevard, is open weekends in season. Here relics of Brigantine's past are displayed. "Old" Brigantine, the northeast end of the island, isn't there anymore. Photos and relics of the now-underwater resort are in the museum. Brigantine used to extend to 51st Street; now it ends at 14th Street. Local legend says Captain Kidd buried treasure on Brigantine Island in 1698. Hope it wasn't on the northeast part. Admission is free; donations are accepted. For information, call 609-266-9339.

Ventor, Margate, and Longport

The neighboring towns of Ventnor, Margate, and Longport are all located on Absecon Island, southwest of Atlantic City. They, like Brigantine on a separate island northeast of Atlantic City, have more single-family resi-

Beached Elephant?

No, you are not hallucinating. No, you have not been in the casinos too long, and what you are seeing is not the by-product of alcohol or another controlled substance. If you are standing at 9200 Atlantic Avenue in Margate, New Jersey, you really are seeing a six-story-high elephant—a sixty-five-foot-high former real estate office, one-time tavern, sometime hotel, eventually a private home, and now a museum and National Historic Landmark that was built to look like an enormous elephant.

Lucy, who didn't get her name until she was six years old, was built in 1881. She was designed to attract attention, and she has done a good job of that. James Lafferty, a real estate developer, needed an attraction to lure potential customers to his land in South Atlantic City, as Margate was then known. The problem was that the entire Jersey shore seemed to be for sale, as new resorts by the dozen were being advertised. There was a lot of competition in the real estate business, and Lafferty thought that a giant elephant might tempt the tourists. He had Lucy built for $38,000; her frame is wood and her skin is hammered tin. She was a hit. Lafferty actually patented the idea, and architectural plans, for giant, elephant-shaped buildings. Two more were built: the smaller Light of Asia

Lucy the Elephant, formerly a hotel, is now a popular walk-through museum and National Historic Landmark.

〰〰〰〰〰〰〰〰〰〰〰〰〰〰〰〰

A view of Margate from Lucy's back.

in Cape May (1884 to 1900), torn down as a money loser, and Elephantine Colossus at Coney Island, nearly twice as big as Lucy (1884 to 1896), but destroyed in a fire.

Lucy lived on, but she began to deteriorate in the salt air. She was saved from decay or destruction in 1970 by the Save Lucy Committee, which reopened her for tours at a new site in 1974. With her old age, Lucy requires constant maintenance, which is paid for by ticket and souvenir sales. Could you look yourself in the face if you didn't take an opportunity to visit America's only surviving walk-through wood and tin elephant? For information, phone 609-823-6473 or e-mail infor@lucytheelephant.org. P.S. The view from Lucy's howdah (look it up) is great.

dences than Atlantic City, although each has some motels and condos along the seafront.

At first Atlantic City's southward expansion down Absecon Island was hampered by the "dry inlet"—a shallow channel across the island at what is now Jackson Avenue. Tidal flows flooded this inlet, eventually filling it in, and a railroad was built down to Longport by 1884.

At the southernmost extreme of Atlantic City's seashore suburbs, Longport Historical Museum documents the century and a quarter of Longport's existence. It will be of special interest to fans of local history and late Victorian resorts. Located on Atlantic Avenue, the town's main street, the museum is open on Saturdays in season. Admission is free; donations are accepted. For information, call 609-823-1115.

Nearby Attractions

Shopping in the South Shore and Atlantic City Regions

If you've browsed all the Boardwalk boutiques and still crave more shopping, try the South Shore and Atlantic City's regional mall—Hamilton Mall. From Atlantic City, take the Atlantic City Expressway to Exit 12 or the Black Horse Pike (State Route 40 and U.S. Route 322); from other shore points, take the Garden State Parkway to Exit 38A, which is the Atlantic City Expressway, then Exit 12 off the Expressway. This huge mall features three major department stores—Sears, Macy's, and J.C. Penney—plus 140 other stores and restaurants, and offers free use of children's strollers and wheelchairs. For information, call 609-646-8326.

Storybook Land

This twenty-acre children's fantasy of classic stories come to life, kiddie amusement rides, and costumed fairy-tale figures is a longtime favorite. It also has snack and beverage service and a picnic area. Open mid-March through December 30, with many seasonal specials such as Easter Bunny weekends, October hayrides, and Santa Claus Christmas fantasy. The park may close in inclement weather. It's located on the Black Horse Pike (State Route 40 and U.S. Route 322), ten miles west of Atlantic City. From Atlantic City, head west on Routes 40 and 322; from other shore points, take Garden State Parkway to Exit 36 (from the south) or Exit 37 (from the north), then head west on Routes 40 and 322. For information, call 609-646-0103.

Noyes Museum

Fred and Ethel Noyes were restaurant operators whose justly famous Smithville Inn, just up the road a few miles, still operates. The Noyeses decided to decorate their large, popular restaurant with local antiques—objects that were the tools and products of forestry, farming, and fishing industries of an earlier era in South Jersey life. Soon their acquisitions overflowed the restaurant, and they began collecting whole buildings moved onto their Smithville Village. Old farm buildings and craftsmen's shops doubled as gift and antique shops. The very best of their finds are now housed in the modern museum they built, including a collection of American folk art, bird decoys, locally produced craftwork, and fine art. There are rotating exhibits, concerts, and craft markets, a restaurant, and a museum shop.

The museum is located on Lily Lake Road, off U.S. Route 9 in Oceanville, about eight miles north of Atlantic City, as the gull flies, and two miles south of Smithville. There's an admission fee. For information, call 609-652-8848.

Balic Winery

The Balic Winery, located two miles west of Mays Landing on U.S. Route 40, is a small, rather old-fashioned, family-owned winery where the grapes are still harvested by hand. There are no regularly scheduled tours, but you can arrange tours in advance by calling 609-625-2166. There is a wine-tasting room and a wide selection of dinner, dessert, and fruit wines.

Renault Winery

The Renault Winery is located in Egg Harbor City just off U.S. Route 30, about nine miles east of the interchange with the Garden State Parkway. Look for the giant wine bottle on Route 30. There is a fee, but hey, it includes wine tasting!

A surprise for those who thought that California and New York State had a monopoly on quality American wines, this is the oldest continuously operating winery in the United States, established in the late 1850s. Winemaker Louis Renault found South Jersey soils and climate to be good for wine grapes. By the nation's hundredth birthday celebration in nearby Philadelphia, his award-winning wines had made Renault famous, and the largest American producer of champagne.

How did the winery survive Prohibition? It stopped making wine but introduced Renault's wine tonic, sold only in drugstores as a patent medicine. It was advertised as a potion to restore youth and relieve backaches. Many backache sufferers found that this tonic, which was forty-four proof, indeed helped soothe aching backs. Or at least, they no longer cared about their backs.

The winery offers tours of the winemaking and bottling processes. The "hospitality house" provides samples, with a retail outlet next door. There is also a very good restaurant, a wineglass museum, and a popular banqueting and catering hall. Don't leave without sampling the blueberry champagne; Renault is the only producer of this, a perfect souvenir of blueberry-producing New Jersey. For information or restaurant reservations, call 609-965-2111.

Wharton State Forest, Batsto Village, and Atsion Recreation Center

At more than 110,000 acres, Wharton State Forest is the largest state-owned property in New Jersey, located roughly thirty miles from Atlantic City off County Route 542. From shore resorts, take the Garden State Parkway to Exit 50, then U.S. Route 9 north to 542 west. The administrative offices, where camping permits are available, are located at historic Batsto Village, which sits at the southern edge of Wharton State Forest. Access to the grounds is free; there are fees for parking and for Batsto Mansion tours. The grounds are open daily from dawn to dusk during the summer season and on weekends and holidays. Restrooms, a museum, and a gift shop are located in the visitors center. Craft demonstrations are held from April through October.

The patriots probably would not have won the American Revolution without the many iron furnaces to produce cannonballs in the Jersey Pinelands. Batsto was one of the largest iron furnaces, using bog ores and charcoal fuel processed from the pine and oak trees. As Pennsylvania's coal and iron ores gradually forced Jersey's Pinelands furnaces out of business, Batsto diversified into glassmaking and timbering. The last private owner, Joseph Wharton, even considered piping the clean, almost sterile water from under the pines to Philadelphia and Camden to sell as drinking water. (Have you ever tasted Philadelphia's water? He would have made a fortune.) But the state of New Jersey passed a law forbidding the export of water, and the Wharton tract of approximately ninety-six thousand acres was available to be purchased by the state in 1954 for $3 million.

Start your tour at the visitors center, then stroll about the restored village to learn more about the site's history and environment. In addition to the mansion, there are farm buildings, a sawmill, gristmill, and post office—the oldest in the United States that still operates in its original location. More than fifty miles of nature trails range through the surrounding Wharton State Forest. For information, call 609-561-3262.

Atsion Recreation Center, about ten miles northwest of Batsto Village on U.S. Route 206 (north of Hammonton), offers swimming, canoeing, hiking, and fishing from Memorial Day through Labor Day. There are restrooms, picnic tables, grills, and a concession stand. Lakefront cabins are available for rent; camping permits are available at the camping office. For information, call 609-268-0444.

Historic Smithville

The Towne of Historic Smithville and the Village Greene is a large complex of restaurants and shoppes located about fifteen minutes north of Atlantic City on U.S. Route 9. Take Exit 48 off the Garden State Parkway or U.S. Route 9 north from the White Horse Pike (U.S. Route 30). The Historic Smithville Inn, which dates back to 1787, became the focus of a re-created village when previous longtime owners, Fred and Ethel Noyes, began to collect and restore historic buildings and relocate them near the inn. The Noyeses' taste for collecting also led to their equally famous cultural legacy to New Jersey, the nearby (but unaffiliated) Noyes Museum.

The "towne" and "greene" might suggest to some that this is a classic Ye Olde Tourist Trappe, but the whole thing is done so well that this is a very popular attraction, with seasonal crowds, long lines, and the need for reservations. No one will ever starve to death here. In addition to the very highly rated inn, there's a total of eight more eateries, ranging from a tavern to a bakery to a hot dog stand to an ice cream parlor. There are more than fifty "shoppes," offering everything from antiques and diamonds through a whole range of collectibles to quality clothing, furniture, and crafts. Other features are a train ride, paddleboat rides, a puppet theater, and a live-entertainment show barn. The Towne is just as popular for Christmas shopping as it is in summer. For information, call 609-652-7777 or 609-748-6160, or visit www.smithvillenj.com.

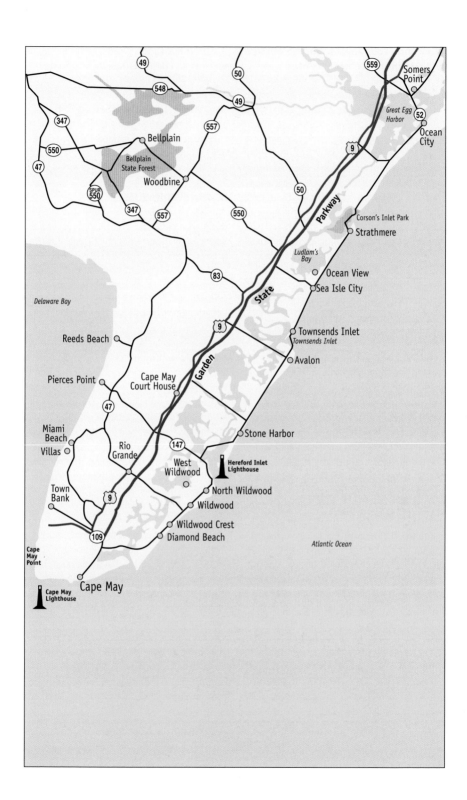

7

The South Shore

The South Shore region includes all of the seashore resorts south of Absecon Island, the locale of Atlantic City, Ventnor, Margate, and Longport. These resorts include, from north to south, Ocean City, Strathmere, Sea Isle City, Avalon, Stone Harbor, the Wildwoods, Cape May, and Cape May Point.

This relatively compact seaside region features a series of islands—classic barrier beaches—that are much wider than is typical for New Jersey barrier islands (Sea Isle City is an exception). Cape May is part of the mainland, but technically, it too is an island, thanks to the Cape May Canal, part of the Intracoastal Waterway.

In historical and cultural terms, this small region packs a lot of variety, from quaint old Cape May to noisy, jazzy Wildwood to quiet, wealthy Avalon and Stone Harbor.

Ocean City

Ocean City, blissfully free of false modesty, cheerfully informs everyone that it is "America's Greatest Family Resort." While one or two other Jersey shore towns might believe that they also are contenders for the title, it's true that Ocean City projects an accurate image of middle-class respectability and wholesome fun.

The South Shore region includes all of Cape May County's resorts, from Ocean City to Cape May.

South Shore Beach Facility Profiles

Facility / Phone Number	Accommodations	Amusements	Bathhouses	Beach Fee	Boardwalk	Fishing	Lifeguard	Picnicking	Rafting	Surfing	Tennis Courts	Garden State Parkway Exit
Avalon 609-967-3936	•		•	•	•	•	•	•	•	•	•	130 N,S
Cape May 609-884-5508	•		•	•	•	•	•	•	•	•	•	0
Cape May Point 609-884-8468	•		•		•	•		•	•			0
North Wildwood 609-522-7722	•	•		•	•	•	•	•	•		•	6
Ocean City 800-BEACHNJ	•	•	•	•	•	•	•		•	•	•	30 S, 25 N,S
Sea Isle City 609-263-8687	•	•	•	•	•	•	•	•	•	•	•	17 S
Stone Harbor 609-368-6101	•		•		•	•	•	•	•	•	•	10 N, 10 S
Strathmere 609-628-2011	•				•	•	•	•	•			17
Wildwood 800-WWBYSEA	•	•	•		•	•	•		•	•	•	4 N, 4B-S
Wildwood Crest 800-524-2776	•				•	•		•	•	•		4B-S

Actually, Ocean City's "front door," the most heavily used artery into town, manages to encapsulate that which is important to know about the resort. At the Somers Point traffic circle (traffic circles are a New Jersey invention), a short link from the nearby Garden State Parkway exit intersects with County Route 585, the local designation for a section of the Old Shore Road. State Route 52 leads from the circle across the bay and into Ocean City.

On Somers Point Circle are three key buildings, each of which, in its way, tells much about the character of Ocean City. Somers Mansion, actually a rather modest brick and frame structure, is located on a low bluff overlooking the circle. Built by the family that founded Somers Point, the house dates to 1725, making it the oldest house in Atlantic County. Fully furnished in Colonial style, the mansion is owned and operated by the

New Jersey Department of Environmental Protection's Division of Parks and Forestry. It's open to the public Wednesday through Sunday, and there's no admission fee. For more information, call 609-927-2212.

The Somers family's most famous son was Richard, who became a master commandant in the early days of the U.S. Navy. When the navy was sent to what is now Libya to punish Tripoli's infamous pirates, Somers commanded the USS *Intrepid*. Loaded with explosives, *Intrepid* was to sail into the midst of the enemy fleet and destroy it. The *Intrepid* blew up, perhaps a suicide mission, and indeed did take out much of the Turkish pirate fleet. Somers and a dozen of his men were killed. In commemoration, there has been a fighting ship in the U.S. Navy called the *Intrepid* ever since. Richard Somers was such a famous patriot that George Washington gave him a ring containing a small lock of Washington's hair—a special mark of friendship in those days.

What does Somers Mansion tell us about the seashore in general, and Ocean City in particular? The early settlers did not usually build their houses out on the isolated, windswept beaches. A location on high ground, or at least the highest, best-drained land available, and on the Old Shore Road, was then considered a lot better than one out on a barrier beach. Ocean City wasn't founded until 1879, more than a century and a half after the Somers Mansion was built, illustrating the fact that the barrier beaches originally were considered nearly worthless. They became desirable real estate only when the railroads arrived, linking the sandy beaches with big cities full of would-be vacationers.

A second key building in understanding Ocean City is the Point Diner. Inside, one can enjoy classic American diner food—a varied menu full of satisfying standards like cheeseburgers, meatloaf platters, and pancakes. The décor is a 1950s combination of soft gray and pink Formica, sprinkled with odd little lines and jiggles of contrasting colors. Point Diner serves to reassure us that traditional Middle America is alive and well in greater Ocean City.

The third of the cultural landmarks on the circle is locally famed Circle Liquor Store. Ocean City residents proudly repeat the urban legend that Circle Liquor does the highest volume of business in the entire state. It could well be true, and New Jersey is a thirsty state. Circle Liquor's success is related to the fact that Ocean City, just across the bay, is a dry town. Bone dry. It was founded by three ministers as a Methodist camp meeting. Although Ocean City never was quite as aggressively religious as the North Shore's Ocean Grove, deed restrictions still in force forbid the *selling* of alcoholic beverages, but not the *consumption* of alcoholic beverages. Circle Liquor stands to reassure us that image counts: It's okay to serve your family and guests whatever they'd like, just so long as you don't do

The Point Diner and Circle Liquor Store in Somers Point.

it in public places like those depraved folks in Atlantic City or Wildwood. Ocean City being dry, and liquor being a big part of restaurant profits, means that some of the area's best restaurants are in Somers Point and other Ocean City neighbors.

There are, of course, many excellent restaurants in Ocean City—just don't expect to get a beer or a cocktail with your meal there. Gotta keep that "family" image.

Ironically, this island formerly called Peck's Beach at one time was known among locals as "Party Island." Rowdies from Atlantic City used to go to the island by boat for wild weekend parties that were so boisterous that even Atlantic City's cops would have closed them down.

The Founding of Ocean City

Ocean City includes the entire island once known as Peck's Beach. As with most Jersey shore resorts, the island had few visitors until the railroads made it easy to reach. Back in 1695, long before people had any reason to value the barrier beaches, Thomas Budd wished to purchase some land on the mainland of Cape May County. The proprietors, who were the first legal owners of all the land in the English colony of West Jersey, made him a package deal: buy Peck's Beach at 4 cents an acre, and he could buy mainland property at 40 cents an acre. It was the only way the proprietors could unload the nearly valueless beach lands.

The first permanent resident of Peck's Beach was Parker Miller, in the 1850s. He worked for marine insurance companies and was sent to live on the beach to deter stealing from wrecked ships and protect the shipowners' interests. Miller's last job, in 1881, was to help round up stray cattle as Ocean City began to grow as a resort. His home, the first on the island, was built of timbers salvaged from a wreck. (Sorry, it was demolished long ago.)

To reach Peck's Beach, every visitor took a stagecoach from Camden to Beesley's Point on Great Egg Harbor. From there, a sailboat took them the two miles to the beach. When the railroad from Millville to Cape May reached South Seaville, travelers could leave the train there and take a stage twelve miles over a bad road, and then ferry across to the island. In 1880, a "short line," narrow-gauge railroad was built between Pleasantville, opposite Atlantic City, and Somers Point, opposite the new Methodist temperance resort of Ocean City, a short boat ride away. Finally, in 1884, a railroad from Sea Isle City was extended north across Corson's Inlet into Ocean City. Another railroad was built more directly to Ocean City from Tuckahoe in 1897.

A Princess in Ocean City

Although none of her movies were filmed there, the late Grace Kelly—star of *High Noon* (1952), *Rear Window* (1954), and *High Society* (1956), and later Princess Grace of Monaco—spent every summer of her youth at Ocean City. Her Philadelphia-based building contractor father, John B. Kelly, had a summer home located near the beach at 26th and Wesley. The Kellys are long gone, so don't bother the present owners. Grace and her husband, Rainier, the prince of Monaco, brought their children back to Ocean City on occasion to ride the boardwalk attractions.

The Kellys in Ocean City. Young Grace is on the left. Her mother, Margaret, is behind her, and father, John, is in the center. Siblings Jack and Peggy are behind their father, and Lizanne is in his arms.

Ocean City's founders included three brothers who were all Methodist ministers. Wesley, Ezra, and James Lake's father, a local farmer, mortgaged his mainland farm for $10,000 to help finance their new town. At first the group that was organized to buy Peck's Beach and found a Christian resort was called the New Brighton Association, after the famous English seaside town. Then maybe someone looked up the history of Brighton. It had a reputation as a hard-drinking resort, the kind of place where errant husbands took their mistresses for a naughty weekend. The New Brighton Association was renamed the Ocean City Association one month later, in late 1879. Ocean City was intended to be a tranquil refuge for nondrinking, highly moralistic people who were horrified and repulsed by the hedonistic goings-on at Atlantic City or Cape May.

Today Ocean City has a flourishing, two-and-a-half-mile boardwalk with amusements, although it is a rather sedate promenade compared with Wildwood's. Free concerts are a traditional feature of the Music Pier, rebuilt in 1928. Ocean City is so popular that many of its one-family cottages have been demolished to make room for two-family condominiums, doubling the summer population in many neighborhoods. As this also means doubling the number of cars, Ocean City has some truly monumental traffic and parking problems. A local joke is that restaurants are doing a great take-out business with families stuck in traffic—they enjoy dinner while waiting to cross town! But the beaches and boardwalk are worth the traffic

The last survivor of the many tiny cottages built in the days of the camp meetings.

The boardwalk's Music Pavilion in 1912. Now restored, it is still the site of many family-style entertainments.

jams. On the bayside are many opportunities to rent jet skis, fish, or sightsee. At the southern end of the island is a lovely natural park, Corson's Inlet State Park.

Ocean City Arts Center and Historical Museum

A good rainy afternoon diversion, this nice little museum, at 409 Wesley Avenue, features Ocean City memorabilia, vintage clothing, furniture, dolls, and relics of the famous wreck, the *Sindia*. This four-masted sailing ship, bound for New York from Shanghai, China, by way of Kobe, Japan, was wrecked by a storm in December 1901. The ship's stern rudderpost sits in front of the museum. The hulk still lies beneath the sands off 16th Street. A 1990s estimate of the value of the *Sindia*'s cargo ran to $200 million. The ship's steel hull was loaded with Chinese and Japanese porcelains—dinnerware, figurines, and decorative items—most of which remain in the ship. These century-old collectibles, impervious to water damage, most likely are still in good condition. Now and then there is talk of salvaging the *Sindia*, but every year the hulk works itself deeper into the sand. The ship was built in Belfast, Ireland, by the Harland and Wolff Shipyard, which also constructed an even more famous future wrecked ship—the *Titanic*. While at the museum, also look for the works of local artists and crafts, occasionally on sale upstairs. For information, call 609-399-1801.

〰〰〰〰〰〰〰〰〰〰〰〰〰〰〰〰〰〰〰〰〰〰

The Jersey Devil

Legends of monsters, ghosts, and demons can really boost the tourist industry. Exactly why people are so fascinated by tales of the supernatural or of mysterious, unknown creatures would keep psychologists researching for years, but such fascinations and legends persist. They can even have an effect on the travel trade. It is said, for example, that sightings of Scotland's Loch Ness monster seem to become more frequent in times of economic depression in the Highlands. And the New Orleans tourist trade isn't hurt by stories of ghosts and voodoo happenings.

Ghost and monster stories have a geography. It may be a specific house, as with the Amityville horror; a specific physical feature, such as Loch Ness; or a general region, as with the Mid-Hudson Valley's Headless Horseman. If New Jersey had an official state demon, it would be the famed Jersey Devil. This creature's geography is the eastern edge of the South Jersey Pinelands close to the seashore.

Different versions of the story put the Jersey Devil's birthplace, and favorite haunts, at either Estellville or Leeds Point, both in Atlantic County. Estellville doesn't appear on most maps, being so small as to be almost nonexistent; it's on State Route 50 north of Corbin City. Or maybe, as in other versions of the story, the Devil was born in Leeds Point, off U.S. Route 9 near Smithville.

The confusion might be related to the demon's family name, Leeds. The legend is that early in the nineteenth century, a certain Mrs. Leeds, a mother of twelve, learned, to her distress, that she was again pregnant. She wished, impulsively, that the Devil would take the child, and the Devil accommodated her: She delivered a little devil. Some versions date this as late as 1887. As the story goes, ever since, there have been

Ocean City Special Tours

Go whale and dolphin watching from Ocean City on a sunset cruise on the *North Star,* which also offers day and night fishing trips. The *North Star* leaves from 3rd Street and the Bay. For information, call 609-399-7588.

How about an exciting helicopter ride? Local and Atlantic City tours are available from Ascent Helicopters at Ocean City Airport, Bay Avenue at 26th Street, telephone 609-399-2515.

It seems that ghosts are everywhere, even in Ocean City. The candlelit Ghost Tour, a one-and-a-quarter-hour outdoor walking tour, begins at 8 P.M., departing from 9th Street and Central Avenue. Call 609-814-0199.

A version of the infamous Jersey Devil, based on various, sometimes conflicting, eyewitness accounts from the early twentieth century.

scattered sightings of the demon throughout the state, but mostly in the mainland pine woods from behind Atlantic City down to Cape May. Descriptions vary, but the general consensus is that the Jersey Devil is cloven-hoofed and long-tailed, with the head of a collie, the body of a kangaroo, the wings of a bat, and surprisingly, as some devils in other parts of the county tend to be rather mean-spirited, the gentle disposition of a lamb.

Incidentally, the Jersey Devil seems to have an appetite for chickens, lambs, calves, and other farm animals, stolen in the night. Kids—the goat kind, not the people kind—also are on the menu. The Devil never seems to have actually harmed anyone, other than giving them a really memorable fright. Most sightings occur in woods, on foggy nights, and by people who've had a few libations. The associations of having had too many drinks with sightings of the demon have led some to assert that the Jersey Devil is on the payroll of the Temperance Movement. So if you're driving on a backroad near the southern seashore on a foggy night, and you've had a few drinks, and you hear the sound of large bat wings . . . be sure to tell the local visitors and tourism bureau.

Sea Isle City

Sea Isle City, as originally planned, was to look like Venice with many canals. The bayshore between 42nd Place and 48th Street, including Venicean Place, which leads to the Yacht Club, is the only part of Sea Isle City in which the "Venetian" canals were actually dug. Charles Landis, who earlier had helped found Hammonton and was the founder of Vineland, purchased Ludlam's Beach in 1879. In keeping with his Venetian concept, Landis wanted public fountains in Italian-style piazzas or squares, surrounded by Renaissance-style public buildings and arcades of stores. He wanted a thousand-foot-long pier to accommodate steamboats.

By 1882, a branch of the old West Jersey Railroad reached the new "city," which had one small hotel and ten houses. No sooner had the railroad been extended to Sea Isle City than a violent storm that September swept the tracks away. The railroad was rebuilt, but the Venetian look never quite materialized. The canals on the bayside near downtown remain, but the classical statues that Landis brought have long since disappeared, and the Renaissance public buildings never came to be. Due to the almost simultaneous development of many barrier islands, land sales lagged behind projections. In 1891, Landis offered oceanfront lots for as little as $50. (Don't you wish some of your ancestors had bought a handful?)

Today's Sea Isle City has somewhat more expensive real estate. It's more of a summer cottage community than a motel-dominated resort, a rather quiet place that models itself after Ocean City more than Wildwood. The city's official slogan, "Perfectly natural for families," sums up the community nicely. There are bars and a small amusement center, Fun City. Sea Isle City occupies one of the narrowest barrier beaches on the South Shore and suffered an "overwash" during the infamous March 1962 storm, meaning that the ocean met the bay for a catastrophic few hours. There are boat rentals on the bayside for fishing and crabbing.

The small communities of Strathmere and Townsend's Inlet share Ludlam's Beach with Sea Isle City. Strathmere is in the midst of a development boom, with rising real estate prices.

Ocean Drive, "the flight of the gull," is a forty-four-mile-long highway that includes a series of toll bridges linking the resorts from Longport to Cape May. The bridges offer great scenic views as they cross the inlets between resort islands.

Avalon and Stone Harbor

Avalon and Stone Harbor share the barrier island known as Seven Mile Beach. Actually, most of the barrier beaches along the South Shore are approximately seven miles long. The inlets between the islands allow the tides to move from the ocean into the back bays, and back out again. At tidal ranges of four to five feet along this coast, inlets six to nine miles apart are sufficient to allow this twice-a-day movement of water back and forth. Along the Texas Gulf coast, inlets are much farther apart, and the tidal range is only one to two feet.

Seven Mile Beach was the last of the South Shore's barrier islands to be developed, though only by a few years. The salt marshes lining the baysides of both mainland and barrier island formed a wider belt, and the wider bay channels ("thoroughfares" to locals) were more difficult to cross

The South Shore's best-preserved dunes, in Avalon, have become the most desirable house lots.

A Skeleton that was Unearthed by the Removal of a Sand Dune, at Avalon, N. J.

Even Avalon, pictured here circa 1914, did not always have the wisdom to resist flattening dunes for building lots.

with bridges and causeways. The first railroad onto Seven Mile Beach came across Townsend's Inlet from neighboring Ludlam's Beach (Sea Isle City). That bridge was washed out four times, until an iron bridge succeeded in standing up to the waves and currents.

The lawn-care business must be prosperous in Avalon and Stone Harbor, which resemble well-kept middle-class suburbia—except in real estate

"There's Gold in Them Thar Waves"

Sitting on the beach dreaming of a quick and easy way to become a millionaire? Looking for a hot tip on making big bucks? You're actually looking at a gold mine when you stare out to sea.

The oceans got their salt from the eroding rocks and minerals of the land, carried to sea by rivers and streams. Once delivered to the world's oceans, that salt stays in seawater when evaporation, the only way water can exit the ocean, leaves the salt behind, concentrating it over the millennia.

Salt has been "mined" from seawater since ancient times. During the Revolutionary War, salt was made along New Jersey's coast by evaporating seawater. Magnesium and bromine join table salt as minerals profitably produced from seawater. Magnesium was made from saltwater years ago at a now-defunct plant at Cape May Point.

Just as erosion from land eventually concentrates salt in the ocean, the same process has transported vast quantities of iron, lead, tin, silver, and—yes—gold to the sea.

There are an estimated ten billion tons of gold dissolved in the world's oceans. In the 1920s, a German research vessel was sent on a search for a way to retrieve the gold. Germany was then struggling with a huge war debt and was desperate enough to try anything. The project managed to extract a few dollars' worth of gold from seawater, but there was one catch. There are only 38 pounds of gold in a cubic mile of saltwater, or 0.0004 ounces per million gallons. In contrast, a cubic mile of seawater contains 166 million tons of dissolved salt. The Germans proved that gold could be retrieved. But no one can afford to do it, as so much water needs to be processed for so little gold that it costs more than the gold is worth to get it.

Of course, if you could find a much more efficient and cheaper way to get the gold . . .

values, which would eliminate much of the middle class. Avalon was named after the mythical King Arthur's paradise. Farther down the island from the Townsend's Inlet railroad bridge, Stone Harbor was founded as an equally upscale resort.

Avalon and Stone Harbor are very much alike in two ways. They are peaceful, quiet, mostly residential communities without the commercialized, "fun factory" appearance of the boardwalks at Wildwood, Atlantic City, or Ocean City. Second, and perhaps most significant, is the early realization that environmental preservation is important and worthwhile.

In Avalon are some of the best-preserved dunes this side of Island Beach State Park. At Avalon's south end, the wide beach is backed by six-foot dunes that are about eighty feet wide. The northern end of Avalon has thirty-foot-high dunes with a two-hundred-foot-wide belt of lower dunes in front, facing the beach. Proving the value of dunes in preventing flooding is the fact that the section of town behind these dunes escaped any flood damage in the notorious March 1962 storm. Avalon protects its dunes; walking on them, except on marked paths, destroys the vegetation that holds the sands in place and will cost you a $500 fine—and they mean it. The World Wildlife Fund owns ten thousand acres of marshland at Avalon. This land will never be developed.

Stone Harbor's contributions to ecology include the Wetlands Institute and the town's famous bird sanctuary. Stone Harbor's immaculate and charming downtown has more than one hundred specialty shops.

 **The Wildwoods**

Four towns—Wildwood, North Wildwood, West Wildwood, and Wildwood Crest—are usually grouped together, although their personalities are different. West Wildwood has no beach and occupies a small, low island of its own behind Wildwood; the other three towns share the now joined islands once known as Five Mile Beach (North Wildwood and Wildwood) and Two Mile Beach (Wildwood Crest).

Wildwood is, well, wild. It is known for its classic boardwalk along the lines of those at Atlantic City, Seaside Heights, or the old Coney Island. For those seeking a wonderful variety of mechanical amusements decorated in neon lights, Wildwood is heaven. Nightclubs, bars, and show bars provide a glitzy, noisy, and highly entertaining variety of nightlife. Wildwood, and to a degree, neighboring North Wildwood, could be described as a smaller Atlantic City, but without the casinos. Actually, a few years ago, Wildwood considered a joint effort with a small New Jersey tribe to create an American Indian–sponsored gambling hall. Closeness to the well-established Atlantic City, though, discouraged Wildwood's plan to copy that city's innovative attempt at urban renewal via legalized gambling.

West Wildwood, which lacks an ocean beach, is a quiet, year-round and seasonal residential community, with boating and fishing as its leisure activities. Wildwood Crest also is more residential and quieter in character than its two Five Mile Beach neighbors. Wildwood Crest was once on a separate island, Two Mile Beach. Turtle Gut Inlet, which once separated Two Mile and Five Mile Beaches, closed over in a storm. Other than the array of amusements and nightclubs of Wildwood and North Wildwood,

6073

THE NEW OCEAN PIER AS IT APPEARS FROM THE OLD PIER

An old postcard, circa 1912, documents the long-standing width of Wildwood's beach. Note how far from the waterline bathers can be in shallow water.

Wildwood and its neighboring towns are noted for their extraordinarily wide and gently sloped beaches.

Five Mile Beach's claim to fame is the superb quality of its beaches. While all too many Jersey resorts must cope with beach erosion, the communities of North Wildwood, Wildwood, and Wildwood Crest enjoy wide, gently shelving beaches that are unrivaled anywhere in the world.

While other resorts might fret about losing sand, these beaches, especially at Wildwood and Wildwood Crest (just "the Crest" to locals), are growing. In recent decades, the beach has widened by some 350 feet, necessitating moving the boardwalk seaward and giving the resorts an additional block or two of extremely valuable real estate behind the relocated boardwalk. This exceptional "growth" of beaches is a direct result of the long jetties protecting the entrance to Cold Spring Harbor and the important Coast Guard station there. These jetties trap sand being carried south-southwestward by the alongshore current. Sand that would have naturally replenished Cape May's beaches ended up on Five Mile Island instead. Wildwood's gain is Cape May's loss.

The village of Anglesea, founded in 1884, was renamed North Wildwood in 1910. Holly Beach, which dates to 1882, became part of the city of Wildwood in 1912. Wildwood Crest was founded in 1905. The city of Wildwood dates to 1885; its first name was Florida City.

Wildwood was an accurate name; most of the island once was covered by a tangled growth of holly, maple, oak, magnolia, and cherry trees, together with wild blueberries, blackberries, and even cacti. Poison ivy, which some have suggested should be the official state pest, was abundant also.

The four Wildwoods really began to grow when the West Jersey Railroad, a subsidiary of the Pennsylvania Railroad, began to provide reliable train service in 1889. Just one year later, special excursion trains from Camden's ferry terminal were bringing as many as eight hundred vacationers a day, at $1 for a round-trip ticket. A decades-long boom was under way. By 1904, a long, Atlantic City–style pier, Blaker's, had been built.

CEDAR AVE., WILDWOOD, N.J.

R.W. RYAN, WILDWOOD, N.J.

Boardinghouses were the early-twentieth-century version of today's motels—cheaper and less pretentious than the ornate hotels of some other resorts.

The boardwalk at Wildwood in 1925. Even then, the resort had a reputation for a lively amusement center.

The boardwalk in Wildwood retains its status as South Jersey's best center of amusements and games of chance, a paradise of coasters, Ferris wheels, ski-ball, and cotton candy.

In 1973, rail service to the Wildwoods—and everywhere else on the South Shore, south of Atlantic City—was finally terminated. The grown-up offspring were finally abandoned by the railroads that had created them. Fortunately for the South Shore resorts, the Cape May–Lewes ferry, the Atlantic City Expressway, and the Garden State Parkway had made it easier for vacationers to arrive by car.

By the 1980s, Wildwood had seen better days. Many older guesthouses and hotels looked their age, as did the downtown district, with a number of abandoned storefronts and empty lots. At one time, Wildwood's image had deteriorated to the point that North Wildwood considered reverting to its original name of Anglesea so as to disassociate itself from Wildwood, but better times clearly are on the way. A successful urban renewal program has reversed the trend toward decay. The magnificence of the wide beach has attracted new investment dollars, and the Wildwoods are enjoying a real estate boom once again.

Doo Wop Architecture

When did the Wildwoods reach their pinnacle of fame and fortune? Many would say the 1950s and early 1960s. Wildwood's large-capacity nightclubs—the Surf, the Rainbow, the Hurricane, the Manor, and the Beachcomber—featured all the top entertainers of the day. Calling itself "Little Las Vegas," Wildwood created a special nightclub police unit, the "Downtown Squad," to handle the often noisy crowds attracted by the likes of Tony Bennett, Peggy Lee, Rosemary Clooney, Louis Armstrong, Ella Fitzgerald, Liberace, Jerry Lewis, Al Martino, Dinah Washington, Phyllis Diller, Chubby Checker, Wayne Newton, and yes, Frank Sinatra.

How do you feel about hot, vibrant, perhaps glaring colors? Flamingo pink, pulsating purple, neon red? How about plastic palm trees? Are you in

Wildwood retains a large stock of 1950s-style motels. Space-age themes were popular at the time.

Glorious neon signs line the streets of Wild-wood.

to what Tom Wolfe once called "boomerang modern" shapes? Wildwood and its neighbors are to 1950s and 1960s motel architecture what Cape May is to Victoriana. There is now afoot a serious proposal to have the city's "doo wop" motel district declared a historic district.

Doo Wop Trolley Tours take visitors to see the best chrome-plated and neon sites in the area. The tours run forty-five minutes. For information, call the Mid-Atlantic Center for the Arts, 800-275-4278, or go to www.doowopusa.org. The Doo Wop Museum, at Pine and Pacific Avenues, is run by the Doo Wop Preservation League and features neon art, studios of sign designers, and a research library. Call 609-729-4000.

What self-respecting seafood restaurant doesn't need a fishing boat on the roof?

The Boardwalk and Its Amusement Piers

Wildwood's boardwalk is advertised as "two miles of smiles" and is a modern classic among seashore resorts. Wildwood accurately calls itself the "World Capital of Amusement Piers." Morey's Piers feature more than 150 rides, including seven world-class coasters, and two water parks. Four piers are under the Morey's umbrella: the original Morey's Pier at 25th Street in North Wildwood; Mariners Landing; Wild Wheels, on the former Fun Pier; and the old Hunt's Pier, which was previously Dinosaur Beach. In addition to Sportland Pier, which features small rides and games, and Nichel's Midway Pier, with its Splash Zone water park, Wildwood's amusement piers offer great fun for kids and adults alike.

With world-class roller coasters and water parks, Morey's Piers are at the heart of the World Capital of Amusement Piers.

For History Buffs

The Boyer Historical Museum is a modest but interesting little museum of local history. The museum also houses the National Marbles Hall of Fame, and the National Marbles Annual Championship is held on Wildwood's beach. About a hundred contestants show up each year to compete for $2,000 in prizes and scholarships. The museum is located on the second floor of City Hall, at Spencer and Pacific Avenues at Holly Beach Mall. Admission is free; donations are accepted. For information, call 609-523-0277.

Wildwood Crest has a small museum on Seaview Avenue.

Hereford Inlet Lighthouse in North Wildwood is a functioning Victorian lighthouse built in 1874, surrounded by lovely gardens.

~~~~~~

The Last Roundup

An early use of the sandy islands was for grazing cattle. The wider islands along the southern shore—the future sites of Atlantic City, Ocean City, Avalon, Stone Harbor, and the Wildwoods, in particular—had an abundance of grasses and wooded areas that provided the cattle food and shelter from storms.

The islands had another attractive feature for farmers. Once barged over to the islands for the season—September 1 to June 1, by Colonial law—the cattle could wander freely without any danger of their invading cropfields. It takes sturdy fences to keep determined cattle out of wheat or cornfields; nature's moat around the islands was cheaper than fences.

The Colonial government forbade putting hogs, sheep, or goats on the islands, as those animals were far more destructive of vegetation than cattle or horses. Also, hogs were known to root enthusiastically in the fringing marshes, competing with humans for clams and oysters.

Cattle on the beaches were known to wade out into the surf to escape the notoriously nasty Jersey mosquitoes and greenhead flies. During the Revolution, British warships often anchored out beyond the surf and sent men in small boats onto the islands to slaughter cattle for free roast beef dinners, at the expense of Colonial farmers.

The last roundups took place in the late 1870s and early 1880s, when resorts began to be developed on the islands. Half-wild cattle threatened the newly arrived vacationers. Hotel operators had to hire cowboys to round up the last strays in Wildwood during that resort's early days. The cattle were so bothersome to early guests in Avalon that hunters were hired to shoot them.

Victorian Hereford Inlet Light in North Wildwood was a lower-order light than Barnegat, Absecon, or Cape May, intended only to mark the inlet, not to be seen far at sea.

 Cape May

Cape May is a gem. While every resort along the coast is at least a little different from the others, Cape May is truly unique. It is one of the few Jersey shore towns that have a national recognition and reputation, along with Atlantic City, Long Branch, and Asbury Park. Cape May is also on the very short list of resort towns (Atlantic City is the only other on the Jersey coastline) in which the town itself is an even bigger attraction than the seashore it sits on. Many visitors spend more time admiring the town itself, with its Victorian architecture, than they do sitting on the beach. The architecture and general historic atmosphere of the town have made it a must-see for Americans from every state. Though the beaches at Cape May are not what they once were, they have been improved considerably thanks to the replenishment efforts of the Army Corps of Engineers.

Cape May is the Jersey shore's "cat"; it has led several lives, always bouncing back from problems and disasters that would have done in a less determined and adaptable community. In the steamboat era, Cape May had the ocean beach that was the easiest and fastest to reach from Philadelphia. But the railroads changed the rules when they created Atlantic City in 1854, making it the fastest, cheapest trip from Philadelphia to the shore.

Cape May wasn't reached by the steel rails until 1863, and even then, it was a longer, higher-priced ride than Atlantic City.

The Great Fire of 1878 wiped out the central part of the town, and the 1939 hurricane and the infamous 1962 Ash Wednesday storm temporarily devastated Cape May. Severe beach erosion at one time threatened to carry the town out to sea. But every time, Cape May has landed on its feet. Even though the 1878 fire made empty lots of the heart of town, the soon rebuilt district became uniformly late Victorian in style, making it a visual delight.

Cape May's Early Years

Although North Jerseyans are convinced that Long Branch is the state's (and the nation's) first seaside resort, there is little doubt that Cape May is at least as old a resort as Long Branch. Cape May had become a resort of national repute by the beginning of the Victorian era. In 1844, John Barber and Henry Howe noted in *Historical Collections of the State of New Jersey:* "In the summer months the Island is thronged with visitors, principally from Philadelphia, with which it is in daily steamboat communication. It is estimated than 3,000 strangers annually visit the place. The village is separated by a small creek from the mainland; but its area is fast wearing away by the encroachments of the sea."

By 1851, Cape May had grown big enough to attract over 110,000 visitors per year. It had the largest hotel in the United States, and more were to come. At a time when really large hotels were rare even in great cities, Cape May had some giants. An 1856 listing featured the then-unfinished Mount Vernon at 2,100 rooms; Columbia House, with a 600-guest capacity; Congress Hall, with room for 500; the Mansion House, Atlantic, and United States Hotels, each capable of hosting 300 guests; plus 1,840 more rooms in the many smaller hotels. This impressive stock of hotel rooms reflected a clientele far more broadly based than Philadelphia and southern New Jersey.

Cape May became the first important resort center along the South Jersey coast largely because of its locational advantages. Situated at the southern tip of New Jersey, near the mouth of Delaware Bay, it was convenient by water from Philadelphia, Trenton, Wilmington, and even New York and Baltimore. Before the railroad era, overland travel was by stage or "jersey wagon," which had unusually wide wheels to negotiate the soft sands of the outer coastal plain. Slow and expensive, these were poor alternatives to water travel. Most vacationers went by sailing ship or, after 1830, by steamboat. In short, Cape May's initial advantage was that it was the closest beach point reached by boat to a number of large cities in the Mid-Atlantic region, especially Philadelphia.

"The Stockton." Cape May, N. J.

The Stockton, 1910, was representative of Cape May's tradition of big hotels.

The first railroads just made the steamboats easier to use. Southerners traveled to Cape May by Chesapeake Bay steamer from Baltimore to Frenchtown on Maryland's Upper Eastern Shore, and then by rail across the narrow neck of the Delmarva Peninsula to New Castle via the New Castle and Frenchtown Railroad. At New Castle, they caught the Cape May packet boat outbound from Philadelphia. The New Castle and Frenchtown, opened in 1832, was typical of early railroads in that it was a short link between water routes.

But the railroads soon changed things for Cape May. Once the all-rail route from Camden, the New Jersey terminus of the Philadelphia ferries, to Atlantic City was achieved, Cape May's position of closest seashore resort, as measured in time and cost from Philadelphia, changed forever. The rails reached into Atlantic City in 1854. A branch railroad reached Cape May from Millville in 1863, but it was not until 1879 that the older resort was connected more directly to Philadelphia, with the completion of a link with the West Jersey Seashore Railroad. Although the steamboat connection to Philadelphia continued until 1913, the railroad clearly was preferred by most tourists of the Victorian age, the second half of the nineteenth century.

Atlantic City was in a position to take full advantage of the new set of rules produced by the railroads. Its boosters carefully built an image of the city as a resort that served all social classes, including the rich. Actually,

One of Cape May's many Victorian gems, the Chalfont dates to 1875 and is still a favorite with nostalgic tourists.

early Atlantic City was a working- and middle-class resort, and appearances by persons listed in the various social registers were infrequent. The myth was important, however; the idea that shop girls were sharing the beach with millionaires was good for business. In the meantime, many of the "old money" aristocrats were sunning themselves on Cape May's beach. Cape May was now more expensive to reach, in both time and transport fare; "out-of-the-way" can have a special appeal to the very wealthy. The working class and nouveau riche might crowd one another in Atlantic City; Cape May remained the favorite of the carriage trade into another generation.

In a way, Cape May fossilized. While Atlantic City of the era remained frantically up-to-date, Cape May hotels aged gracefully. There were enough customers to support adequate maintenance, but there was no clamor for garish novelty, no big demand for ever-larger facilities.

The Long, Gentle Decline

The new era of railroads was not Cape May's only problem. The ocean beach was becoming less attractive, less gentle in slope, and less in area. Indeed, it seemed in danger of disappearing entirely.

Concern over erosion and shifting coastlines goes back to the earliest resorts. No two detailed maps of the Jersey shore separated in time by more than a few years will record the identical physical features and locations. Tides and flooding closed major inlets and opened new ones. Large beaches shrank or even disappeared and new beaches were created as the sands shifted.

Cape May has one of the longest histories involving such problems, and it has suffered to a greater degree than most shore resorts. Early in its history, Cape May evidently possessed an ideal beach. According to an 1838 description quoted by Robert Alexander in *Ho! For Cape Island,* "A broad, level and solid beach fronts the island for five miles, almost entirely free of shells or stones which may injure the feet. The beach shelves into the sea with a gradual and easy inclination so that you may meet the breakers at a depth of two feet."

In 1878, the Great Fire destroyed thirty acres of buildings in the city's heart. But rebuilding after that fire was prompt and gave central Cape May an architectural unity that has endured for more than a century.

In 1908, Henry Ford came to Cape May to race his car on the broad, flat beach. At that time, six hundred feet of dunes separated his car from the boardwalk. (According to local legend, Ford sold the car to a local resident, who then became the town's first Ford dealer.)

In 1911, boat owners begged the federal government to build a pair of jetties to protect the inlet at the north end of town from sand filling the channel. These jetties did keep the inlet open, but they also kept sand from replenishing Cape May's beach.

The infamous 1939 hurricane, which brought serious damage along the entire Jersey shore, was particularly hard on relatively exposed Cape May.

A severe storm in March 1962 destroyed many seafront structures and eroded beaches along the New Jersey shore. Thirteen of the fifteen blocks of wooden boardwalk at Cape May were demolished, and the beach, which had been severely eroded even before the storm, practically ceased to exist. The boardwalk was replaced with a rock and concrete seawall.

Preservation and Profit

After the devastation of the 1962 storm, the battered old town's citizens had to rethink their economic base. By the late 1960s, the unified central seafront Victorian skyline was threatened by plans for new structures. The prevailing wisdom was that Cape May was hopelessly behind the times. Sweeping modernization was supposed to be the solution. Maybe the beach was short and steep, and the location the least easily reached from Philadelphia, but at least the visitor accommodations could be glamorously modern. But fortunately for Cape May and its admirers, several key events from 1964 to 1971 helped the city recover from its economic crisis.

In June 1964, the Cape May–Lewes ferry began operations, ending the old resort's "dead-end" status on transportation routes. Then in 1970, the entire central area, with its many Victorian hotels, mansions, and cottages, was placed on the National Register of Historic Places. This act removed tax incentives for demolishing old buildings, making it advantageous to restore them instead, thus preserving much of the city's historic character. Now Cape May was something unique to the South Shore—a mostly intact Victorian urban landscape that could, in itself, attract visitors.

By 1972, an interesting urban renewal experiment, funded by the federal Department of Housing and Urban Development, was completed. The city's main shopping district, Washington Street, was transformed from a narrow, old-fashioned downtown clogged with cars into a pedestrian mall. New streets paralleled the new mall to provide service access and parking close by. The old train station was razed (the last train ran on October 2, 1981) and the tracks torn up to provide more convenient parking at the northeast end of the mall. The 1879 Physick Mansion, designed by noted Philadelphia architect Frank Furness, was rescued from impending demolition and transformed into a museum and arts center. With only a few exceptions, the Victorian ambience of Cape May was delivered from development reasonably intact. In 1976, Cape May was designated a national historic landmark city.

The charm of Cape May's splendidly ornate, exuberantly Victorian architecture has been successful in enticing visitors to travel farther to a

Washington Street Mall, a very successful transformation of a narrow shopping street into a busy pedestrian mall.

Southern-influence architecture. At one time a gentlemen's club, this building had drinking and gambling downstairs and rooms available for brief occupancy upstairs.

rather eroded beach, and to patronize old hotels and guesthouses with atmosphere and antiques rather than modern convenience. In a world of increasingly bland cinderblock and plastic roadside architecture, Cape May's nostalgic urban landscape had undeniable appeal. Resilient Cape May proves that selling history pays.

Victorian architecture strikes several resonant chords in the nostalgic imagery of Americans. A grimmer reality notwithstanding, popular perceptions of this time now beyond living memory are of a simpler, happier period in the nation's history. A supremely self-confident America was pursuing its westward destiny in the midst of an unprecedented flowering of technology and rising standards of living. Lavishly detailed decoration festooned the solid, rather pompous buildings of the Victorian age. There was an unquestioning faith in a bright future with good times.

Historic Architecture

Many visitors to this grand old resort are drawn by the large number of late Victorian hotels and houses. Serious students and admirers of Cape May's magnificent architectural heritage will want to acquire Marsha Cudworth's *Architectural Self-Guided Tours: Cape May, NJ*, available at many local shops. This slim volume has detailed drawings of historic buildings and maps for informed tours of the historic district.

A row of seafront cottages on Cape May's Ocean Drive represents the opulent styles of the nineteenth century. Especially notable is the steamboat gothic style in the center.

Architecture buffs will also find a short trip to Dennisville, a charming little Colonial village, once an important shipbuilding and commercial center, worthwhile. Dennisville is on Delsea Drive (State Route 47), about twenty miles north of Cape May.

Farther afield from Cape May is Bridgeton, about forty miles north on State Route 47 to State Route 55, then west on State Route 49. Bridgeton can boast of an even larger collection of Victorian buildings than Cape May and, for the kids, a free zoo.

Cape May Festivals

More than thirty years old now, the granddaddy of Cape May festivals is Victorian Week. Victorian Week, which actually lasts for ten days, as it includes two weekends, attracts crowds worthy of an August weekend. Every aspect of Victorian life, technology, culture, local history, and the arts is featured in the activities: Victorian feasts, brunches, dinners, and teas; lectures, tours, demonstrations, and exhibits on Victorian arts and traditions; house tours and special presentations in museums, theaters, and historic sites; champagne gourmet brunch and draft beer tasting; a murder mystery dinner; concerts; and a glassblowing demonstration. You will return from Victorian Week much more knowledgeable and appreciative of Victoriana, better supplied with Victorian jewelry and knickknacks, possibly a few pounds heavier, and definitely happier. Victorian Week is held in mid-October, a delightful time of year. Call 609-884-5404 or 800-

275-4278 for a schedule and to reserve your overnight, midweek, or week-end package.

Other festivals include the Spring Tulip Festival, a colorful salute to the Dutch sea captain Mey, the discoverer of Cape May; Confederate Week-end, celebrating Cape May's early visitors from the upper South; and the ever-popular Lima Bean Festival at Cape May Point (honest!). For more information on any of the local festivals, call or write the Mid-Atlantic Center for the Arts, P.O. Box 340, 1048 Washington Street, Cape May, NJ 08204, telephone 609-884-5064, e-mail mac4arts@capemaymac.org.

C'mon Down, the Fishing Is Good

Fishing for a living and fishing for fun—both are important along the shores of New Jersey. Are you a fan of clam chowder? New Jersey lands 80 percent of the nation's catch of ocean quahogs—deeper-water, black-shelled clams—and almost two-thirds of America's surf clams. Although you might think of fish and shellfish as the last important source of food still caught in the wild, nearly half of New Jersey's clam "catch" is farmed. Clams are especially sensitive to pollution, as adult clams simply sit on the ocean bottom and suck in seawater, filtering it for bits of food. Unfortunately for the clams and us, clams concentrate any local pollutants this way. Hard clams are trucked from polluted Monmouth County waters to cleaner Ocean County waters, where they have a chance to flush out bacteria and become safe to eat.

Cape May is the state's most important commercial fishing port, providing 80 percent of New Jersey's total catch. This includes 41 percent of the nation's total catch of sea bass, 37 percent of mackerel, and 20 percent of bluefish. Other important fishing ports include Wildwood, Atlantic City, Belford, Point Pleasant, Barnegat Light, Atlantic Highlands, Belmar, Neptune, and Shark River.

About three-quarters of a million people enjoy ocean sportfishing in New Jersey every year. The typical sportfisher averages seven trips annually. Sportfishers are so successful that they actually catch more bluefish, fluke, and sea bass than do commercial fishermen.

One of New Jersey's largest fishing-fleet docks next to a seafood restaurant at Cape May. It doesn't get any fresher than this.

Southern Belles on Jersey Beaches

Before the Civil War, Cape May hosted at least as many Southerners as Northerners. So strong was the "Confederate connection" to the Jersey Cape that at the onset of the Civil War, there were fears that South Jersey might be a nest of Confederate sympathizers. These fears were groundless, but New Jersey's electoral college votes were denied to Abraham Lincoln in both 1860 and 1864.

When Mason and Dixon surveyed their famous line, they were simply determining the Pennsylvania-Maryland border. But the Mason-Dixon line has become a symbolic dividing line between North and South. If that survey line were continued eastward through New Jersey, something it was never intended to do, it would cross the coast in the vicinity of Harvey Cedars and Loveladies, in Ocean County. Cape May is closer to Baltimore than it is to New York.

In the mid-nineteenth century, wealthy Virginians and Marylanders took steamboats northward up Chesapeake Bay and transferred to a railroad to New Castle, Delaware, where they caught the steamboat for Cape May. Illustrating the longevity of the old Southern tradition of summering at Cape May, Baltimore socialite Wallis Simpson, the future duchess of Windsor, had her social debut at a Cape May hotel. The Southern connection may explain the Dixie appearance of many Cape May hotels and homes, with tall columns, high ceilings, broad wrap-around verandas or porches, and French windows.

Special Places

The Doll House and Miniature Museum, at the Goodman House, 118 Decatur Street, showcases thirty dollhouses, including an antique one from 1885, as well as many miniature furniture and accessory pieces. The museum, which charges an admission fee, is open Thursday, Friday, and Sunday. Call 609-884-6371.

The Emlen Physick Estate, at 1048 Washington Street, home of the Mid-Atlantic Center for the Arts, is a restored 1879 Victorian mansion designed by famed Philadelphia architect Frank Furness. Dr. Physick's (what a great name for a medical doctor!) stick-style house is open for tours; the estate's carriage house is a neat little museum. There are also a tearoom and a museum shop. An admission fee is charged. For information, call 609-884-5404 or 800-275-4278.

Tours and Cruises

Ghost tours (outdoor walking tours) leave from the Haunted Mansion Restaurant at 513 Lafayette Street. Ghost sightings are not guaranteed. There is a fee. Call 609-884-4358.

Half-hour horse and carriage tours leave from Ocean Street and Washington Street Mall. A fee is charged. Call 609-884-4466.

For an enjoyable introduction to the ecology of the salt marshes, sometimes called "New Jersey's equivalent of the Florida Everglades"—without the gators, but with plenty of bird life—take a cruise on the *Skimmer*. The boat holds forty-one passengers and has snacks and drinks available. The *Skimmer* sails from Cape May's Miss Chris Marina (609-884-3100) and occasionally from Stone Harbor's Wetlands Institute. A fee is charged.

Go whale-watching on board the *Cape May Whale Watcher*, a 290-passenger boat with food and beverage service available. Cruises (including a dinner cruise) usually sight humpback, finback, minke, right, or pilot whales, along with dolphins, porpoises, and sharks. A whale sighting is actually *guaranteed*—if you don't see at least one whale, your next trip is free! Miss Chris Marina is your departure point; call 800-786-5445 or 609-884-3100.

If you'd like to go fishing, several "head boats" (so much a head for four-, six-, or eight-hour fishing trips) also leave from Miss Chris Marina.

〜〜〜〜〜〜〜〜〜〜〜〜〜〜〜〜〜〜〜〜〜〜

The Bird-watching Season

Bird-watching has become such a popular event along the shore that enthusiasts have created both spring and fall bird-watching seasons. This activity is especially important at Cape May and Cape May Point. The New Jersey chapter of the National Audubon Society sponsors educational and entertaining programs for bird-watchers throughout the year. These include the Cape May Spring Weekend and the World Series of Birding, both in May, and Cape May Fall Weekend in September. The Cape May Bird Observatory at 707 E. Lake Drive can be reached by calling 609-884-2736.

New Jersey's coastal marshlands have often been compared to Florida's Everglades in both the number and variety of birds to be seen. The South Shore, Atlantic City, and Central Shore regions are also rewarding locations for bird-watching.

~~~~~~~~~~~~~~~~~~~~~~~~~~~~~

The Seashore Goes to War

Long ago, ocean shorelines were avoided as permanent residences because they were dangerous places to be in wartime, or even in peacetime. Pirates, raiders, invaders—think Vikings—once made the seashore hazardous.

New Jersey's seashore has been a relatively safe and peaceful place, at least since the end of the War of 1812. Fort Hancock, on Sandy Hook, was the only significant and long-lived military post along the shore. During the American Revolution, British warships patrolled offshore, landing troops on occasion to burn saltworks (the salt was a necessary ingredient in gunpowder) or steal a few cattle for dinner. Rarely, the British ships would chase American privateers as far as the inlets, which sheltered their smaller, shallow-draft opponents. Toms River and Little Egg Harbor (Tuckerton) were especially busy privateer ports to which the daring Jerseymen brought their captured merchantmen "prizes" of war. A particularly successful privateer was delightfully called "the Skunk."

The War of 1812, essentially a rematch of the Revolutionary War, repeated the minor engagements and general harassment tactics of both sides. The heavy and cumbersome British men-of-war could not safely follow the fast little privateers into the shifting, shallow channels of the inlets and bays. The American privateers played the role of bees stinging the lion, then fleeing retaliation.

The Civil War proved uneventful, militarily, for the Jersey shore—the Union Navy clearly ruled the waves.

During both World Wars, the military took advantage of the seashore's stock of accommodations by setting up training camps and convalescent centers, which utilized some of the big hotels. An interesting sidelight on World War I was the 1914 construction, by a private German company, of the world's then tallest radio tower (840 feet high) at Tuckerton. Supposedly, the message about sinking the *Lusitania* (May 1915) was sent from here to a radio tower in Germany. The torpedoing of the *Lusitania*, which resulted in many American deaths, helped bring about America's declaration of war on Germany. The Tuckerton tower was seized by the federal government at America's entrance into that war.

Wartime censorship clouds the details, but ships were sunk off Long Beach, Atlantic City, and Cape May during World War I. World War II witnessed many tankers sunk on their way from the Gulf coast to North Jersey refineries—so many, in fact, that Jersey beaches were marred by big clumps of sandy "tar," actually crude oil, for years after the end of

Ruins of a World War II gun battery at Cape May Point were once nine hundred feet from the water.

the war. Occasionally, a little crude oil still washes up on beaches, presumably escaped from rusting wrecks offshore. A local myth is that German U-boats, sunk by depth charges or bombs, still lie on the bottom, mostly intact—the ultimate dream goal of amateur divers.

Cape May Point

Cape May Point is a tiny, mostly seasonal residential community. There are no hotels or tourist services; it's just a lovely place to unwind. The Point has had to deal with an almost unbelievable beach erosion problem. Its location at the southernmost tip of New Jersey subjects it to currents moving between the open ocean and Delaware Bay. Near the lighthouse at the Point are the remains of a huge concrete bunker housing an enormous cannon intended to guard the entrance to Delaware Bay. When built in 1942, the structure was nine hundred feet from the water; now it's in the water. More than half the town of Cape May Point, as originally laid out, is gone, a victim of the waves and currents.

Cape May Point was founded in 1875, under the name Sea Grove, as a religious community. A pavilion or tabernacle was to be located at the center, with streets radiating outward from it like spokes of a wheel. President Benjamin Harrison spent several summers at the Point, living in a house given to him by his friend and cabinet member, wealthy department store pioneer John Wanamaker. The Point was a Presbyterian version of the many camp meetings established by Methodists.

The Lighthouse and State Park

At the Point is the picturesque 1859 Cape May Lighthouse, open daily to visitors for a fee from April through November. Climbing the 199 steps to the top brings you to an outdoor gallery with a great view. There's also a small museum with a shop. For information, call 609-884-8656 or 800-275-4278.

Cape May Point State Park, adjacent to the lighthouse, offers sunbathing, surf fishing, and bird-watching—free. Swimming here can be dangerous, though, with fast-moving currents and no lifeguards.

Higbee Beach

Higbee Beach Wildlife Management Area, to the north and west of Cape May Point, is six hundred acres of forest, dunes, ponds, and meadows. Higbee Beach's older name was Diamond Beach, the home of "Cape May diamonds." These are not real diamonds, but quartz crystals, rounded and polished by the sea. They make good souvenirs, and you can pick them up on the beach for free. Most shops in Cape May sell them, polished further by jewelers and mounted.

Lake Lily

A freshwater lake near the ocean at Cape May Point, Lake Lily (also spelled Lake Lilly) has an interesting history. Seamen rowed ashore here from anchored ships to stock up on fresh water. Captain Kidd is known to have visited Lake Lily, and legend has it that he buried treasure somewhere near the lake. Maybe there are real diamonds in the sand along with the "Cape May diamonds." During the War of 1812, Lake Lily's fresh water became important to the British warships patrolling the entrance to Delaware Bay. Local patriots dug a channel between the lake and the ocean so that the lake became salty, denying fresh water to the Redcoats. The channel has since filled in, and the lake's water has been fresh ever since.

The Old Concrete Ship

Located just off Sunset Boulevard in Cape May Point, where the ocean meets Delaware Bay, *Atlantus* (frequently misspelled *Atlantis*) was one of three experimental ships built of concrete during World War I, when steel was in short supply. Yes, it did float. No, it didn't float very well. *Atlantus* was towed to Cape May Point to be sunk and used for the foundation of a ferry terminal. Beached in the wrong place by a storm, it is now a state historic site. There is less and less to see, as the stripped hulk sinks further into the sand.

Nearby Attractions

Historic Cold Spring Village

Located just north of Cape May on U.S. Route 9, this is a restoration and re-creation of a typical South Jersey village of the first half of the nineteenth century. Cold Spring Village includes twenty-five buildings relocated to an outdoor museum. Costumed craftspersons demonstrate various handicrafts of the era, including a blacksmith, weaver, spinner, potter, tinsmith, printer, and bookbinder.

The time is about 150 years ago, the place is a typical country village, the ambience is friendly, and the education afforded visitors is painless. A day or half-day trip here provides a charming respite from tanning on the beach. Many special events and festivals are held here, such as arts and crafts shows, antique shows, antique auto shows, and Civil War and Revolutionary War encampments. There's a fee except for Saturday evening concerts, which are free. The Old Grange Restaurant at the entrance does not require an entrance fee. For information, call 609-898-2300. The village can be reached from Cape May via the Cape May Seashore Lines train. For train information, call 609-884-5300.

Leaming's Run Gardens and Colonial Farm

Located on U.S. Route 9 North in Cape May Court House, about twelve miles north of Cape May, Leaming's Run features twenty acres of gardens and a Colonial farm re-creation built near a 1730 house, one of the oldest in the county. Wear comfortable, sturdy walking shoes to walk the paths to the gardens. There are restrooms and a gift shop. An admission fee is charged. The gardens and farm are open May through October; the gift shop is open till Christmas. For information, call 609-465-5871.

The Wetlands Institute

The Wetlands Institute, on Stone Harbor Boulevard in Stone Harbor, is a six-thousand-acre site owned by a private nonprofit foundation dedicated to advancing the knowledge and appreciation of coastal wetlands ecology. A 150-foot boardwalk over tidal marsh lets you observe marsh life without getting your feet wet. Bird-watchers will appreciate the observation deck atop the institute.

An entrance fee (free to members) also includes salt marsh hands-on exhibits, the award-winning film *Secrets of the Salt Marsh*, and a turtle display. There also are a library, gift shop, and restrooms. Not included in the entrance fee are back bay birding tours on a pontoon boat, the *Skimmer*; wetlands kayaking; and summer classes on nature and on painting nature. For information, call 609-368-1211.

Bird Sanctuary

Bird-watchers will enjoy Stone Harbor's municipal bird sanctuary, located on 3rd Avenue between 111th and 117th Streets. Egrets, herons, and ibises abound on these twenty-one acres. The relatively small area is said to host ten thousand birds during the high season from late July to early August. Avalon also has a small but well-populated bird sanctuary at Armacost Park, on Ocean Drive between 71st and 74th Streets.

The Cape May–Lewes Ferry

To cool off on a hot day, ride the Cape May–Lewes, Delaware, ferry round-trip as a foot passenger. There is ample free parking at the Cape May terminal, six miles from downtown Cape May at Sandman Boulevard and Lincoln Drive, North Cape May. For schedules, call 609-880-7200. For an extra few dol-

The easternmost officially sanctioned, permanent rodeo, Cowtown is a day trip from the South Shore or Atlantic City that is worth the distance. Where else can you see professional rodeo in the Northeast?

lars, get a ticket that includes shuttle service to historic Lewes's downtown and to the Rehoboth Outlets, a 140-store complex including Disney, Brooks Brothers, J. Crew, Lenox, Coach, Eddie Bauer, Liz Claiborne, Royal Doulton, and Waterford Wedgwood. *Shoppers' alert:* Not only is this a shoppers' paradise, but Delaware has *no* sales tax! Enjoy.

Nostalgic Train Rides

Although Cape May no longer has train service to Philadelphia or New York, the newly formed Cape May Seashore Lines is a tourist short line offering nostalgic trips in authentically restored cars. The trains leave from Lafayette and Ocean Streets Terminal, near the north end of Washington Street Mall, on jaunts to Cold Spring Village, Cape May Court House, and the 4-H Fairgrounds at the County Park and Zoo. Special trains are scheduled for special events. Treat yourself to an English-style tea/lunch on the 2 P.M. *Sun Tan,* or to a gourmet dinner on the 5 P.M. *Sea Breeze* or 8 P.M. *Twilight,* Saturdays only. Meals are served in an authentic Santa Fe dining car, the *Epicurus.* For information, call 609-884-2675.

Cowtown Rodeo

Admittedly, this is stretching the definition of "nearby," but this attraction is unique to New Jersey. Here's something different for your Saturday night on the South Shore—a genuine, professional rodeo contest sanctioned by the Professional Rodeo Cowboys Association. It's great fun, and the only chance to see authentic rodeo in New Jersey. "Cowtown" is not a town; it's just the rodeo and a daytime flea market with great buys. Located on U.S. Route 40 about two miles west of Woodstown. For information, call 609-769-3200.

Belleplain State Forest and Lake Nummy

Lake Nummy is the central focus for recreation in this Cape May County state forest. Swimming, boating, picnicking, camping, and bird-watching can all be enjoyed here. State licenses are required for hunting and fishing. Open daily, year-round. There's a fee for parking in summer. For information, call 609-861-2404.

Tuckahoe Wildlife Management Area

Located on the edge of the Pinelands, this expanse of salt marsh and tidal creeks, freshwater pond, and pine-oak forest provides a variety of habitats for wildlife. An eight-mile loop gives hikers easy access to these wildlife areas. From Seaville, take State Route 50 north to County Road 631; turn right to Gravel Road. For information, call 609-628-2103.

Bridgeton and Greenwich

Bridgeton, about fifty-five miles from Cape May, is an undiscovered gem of a day trip from Cape May County seashore resorts. Take U.S. Route 9 to State Route 47, to Route 55, to Route 49. The town is an unrestored but generally well-preserved inland version of Cape May—a fine collection of late Victoriana.

The Woodruff Indian Museum, located in the Bridgeton Public Library at 150 E. Commerce Street, has the best collection of Lenni-Lenape artifacts in the state. It's open Monday through Friday afternoons. For information, call 856-451-2620.

In Bridgeton's City Park, the Nail House Museum on West Commerce Street has exhibits on the local nail industry. For information, call 856-455-4100. The Cohanzick Zoo, a free municipal zoo open year-round, is a charming little zoo the perfect size for young children—an hour or so does it. For information, call 609-455-3230. The New Sweden Farmstead Museum is an outdoor re-creation of a seventeenth-century Swedish Colonial farm. An admission fee is charged.

While you're in the neighborhood, head southwest on County Route 650 about eight miles to Greenwich (pronounced "Greenwitch" by locals), a beautifully preserved, tiny Colonial port that staged its own "tea party," Boston-style, during the Revolution. It's a rewarding and easy walking tour.

Wheaton Village and the Museum of American Glass

The soil in much of the Pinelands that lie between the seashore to the east and big cities to the west is almost pure silica sand—not especially good for farming. Silica sand is the major ingredient in making glass, however, and there were glass factories in southern New Jersey before the American Revolution. Wheaton Glass was started in 1888 and is still a major producer of scientific and cosmetics glassware.

The Museum of American Glass is the centerpiece of Wheaton Village, where reproduction Victorian-era buildings create a nineteenth-century small-town atmosphere. The village has a one-room schoolhouse from 1876 and many Victorian-period shops and craft facilities. With well over seven thousand items, this is one of America's largest museums dedicated to the history of glass. Exhibits range from ancient Roman glass to Venetian glass to modern television picture tubes. You'll see glass bottles of all kinds, including the world's largest, as well as glass toys, paperweights, and decorative glass, all made at Wheaton Village's own glass factory.

Glassblowing demonstrations are offered in a re-created 1888 glass factory. Don't miss the opportunity to watch glass being made and hand-blown into pitchers, vases, bottles, paperweights, and decorative items. You can even make an appointment to create your own paperweights under the watchful eye of a veteran glassmaker.

There are many interesting, quaint little shops selling glass objects along with a variety of other handicrafts, antiques, and one-of-a-kind items handmade by contemporary glass artisans. You'll be tempted by the magically beautiful paperweights, many of them made at the glass furnace. Adjacent are a restaurant and pub, and the Down Jersey Folklife Center.

The village is open year-round, and many special events are held throughout the year, including glass and nonglass antiques, craft fairs, and a delightful Christmas exhibit. An admission fee is charged. This large, nationally known museum is located just off Exit 24 of State Route 55 in Millville. For information, call 856-825-6800.

Cape May County Park and Zoo

The shady, wooded Cape May County Park's main attraction is a free accredited zoo. In addition, there are picnic areas, playgrounds, paths, bike trails, and a pond for fishing. At the zoo, visitors follow a boardwalk through natural settings, including an "African savanna," visit the reptile house and aviary, and view a wide variety of animals, from big cats to monkeys to deer. A café and souvenir gift shop are open. From Cape May, take the Parkway north to Exit 11, turn left on Crest Haven Road, and follow to Route 9. From the north, take Exit 11 off the Parkway, turn right on Crest Haven Road, and follow to Route 9. For information, call 609-465-5271. This attraction can be reached via the Cape May Seashore Lines railroad; call 609-884-2675.

Port Norris and Bivalve

Visit the villages of Port Norris and Bivalve, formerly home to a large fleet of oyster boats that once supplied both New York and Philadelphia. Go for a bay tour aboard the 115-foot schooner *A. J. Meerwald,* New Jersey's official "tall ship." The *Meerwald,* launched in 1928, is the last of the oyster schooners once common on the bay. For schedules of public cruises, call 856-785-2060.

The Delaware Bayside

Like the North Shore, the South Shore also has "another shore" on the coasts of Delaware Bay. The Delaware Bay shores were never as important in resort development as the towns along Sandy Hook and Raritan Bays, however.

The Delaware Bay shoreline of New Jersey, from Bayside to Miami Beach (not to be confused with Florida's Miami Beach), consists of very narrow beaches backed by extensive marshlands. Only Cape May County's lower bayshore has better-drained uplands fronting the water. The sand is coarse and the surf nonexistent. Seldom are the waves higher than a few feet. Though surfers will be disappointed, toddlers might find the bayside waters less intimidating than ocean surf.

As on the North Shore's "other shore," boating and fishing are more important than swimming. Delaware Bay has been cleaned up considerably in recent years, and the fishing is much better now than just a few decades ago. There is a state marina at Fortescue, and many private docks.

Where the beach is backed by extensive marshlands, further development is severely restricted by the Wetlands Act, which prohibits disturbance of marshlands (there isn't much development "upbay" from Miami Beach to Wildwood Villas anyhow). Erosion has been nibbling away at Cape May County's bayshore at an average rate of four feet a year for nearly two centuries.

Visitor facilities range from basic to none. The hotels and restaurants once found in places like Fortescue and Money Island are long gone. There are several bayshore campgrounds in Lower Cape May County, which cater to the budget-minded from as far away as Montreal. Contact the Cape May County Visitor Information Center, 609-465-7181.

Information Sources

State of New Jersey Office of Travel and Tourism
20 W. State St., P.O. Box 820, Trenton, NJ 08625-0820; 609-777-0885;
fax 609-777-4097; www.visitnj.org; for free travel guides,
call 800-VISITNJ, ext. 0922

Department of Environmental Protection, Division of Fish and Wildlife
P.O. Box 400, Trenton, NJ 08625-0400; 609-292-2965;
www.njfishandwildlife.com

Department of Transportation
609-530-2000; www.state.nj.us/transportation

Atlantic City Expressway
609-965-6060; www.acexpressway.com

Garden State Parkway
732-442-8600; www.gspkway.state.nj.us

New Jersey Turnpike
732-247-0900; www.state.nj.us/turnpike

Amtrak
800-872-7245; www.amtrak.com

New Jersey Transit
Northern New Jersey, 800-772-2222; southern New Jersey, 800-582-5946;
out of state, 973-762-5100; www.njtransit.com; www.njtransit.state.nj.us

Cape May–Lewes Ferry
609-889-7200; www.capemay-lewesferry.com

New York Fast Ferry
Ferry service between Jersey City, Hoboken, Weehawken, Keyport, and
New York City: 800-693-6933; www.nyff.com

New York Waterway
Ferry service between Jersey City, Hoboken, Weehawken, and New York City: 800-53-FERRY; www.nywaterway.com

Seastreak
Ferry service between Atlantic Highlands, Highlands, and New York City: 732-872-2628; www.seastreakusa.com

Atlantic City International Airport
609-645-7895; www.acairport.com

JFK International Airport
718-244-4444; www.panynj.com

LaGuardia International Airport
718-426-5000; www.panynj.com

Newark International Airport
973-961-6000; www.panynj.com

Philadelphia International Airport
215-937-6800; www.philadelphia-phl.com

North Shore

Monmouth County Department of Economic Development and Tourism
800-523-2587; fax 732-294-5930; www.visitmonmouth.com/tourism

Central Shore

Ocean County Public Affairs and Tourism
721-929-2000; fax 732-506-5370; www.oceancountygov.com

Atlantic City and Its Neighbors

Greater Atlantic City Tourism Council
609-748-0498; fax 609-748-0497; www.actourism.org

Atlantic City Expressway Welcome Center
609-965-6316

Greater Atlantic City Convention and Visitors Authority
888-ACVISIT; www.atlanticcitynj.com

South Shore

Southern Shore Tourism Council
800-227-2297; 609-463-6415; fax 609-465-4639;
www.njsouthernshore.com

Cape May County Department of Tourism
609-463-6415; www.thejerseycape.com

Bibliography

Alexander, Robert. *Ho! For Cape Island.* Cape May: Self-published, 1956.

Armstrong, Harry, and Tom Wilk. *New Jersey Firsts: The Famous, Infamous and Quirky of the Garden State.* Philadelphia: Camino Books, 1999.

Barber, John, and Henry Howe. *Historical Collections of the State of New Jersey.* New York: Tuttle, 1844.

Bennett, D.W. *New Jersey Coastwalks.* Sandy Hook, Highlands, NJ: American Littoral Society, 1981.

Bishop, Gordon. *Gems of New Jersey.* Englewood Cliffs, NJ: Prentice Hall, 1985.

Boucher, Jack. *Absegami Yesteryear.* Egg Harbor City, NJ: Laureate Press, 1963.

Boyle, William. *A Guide to Bird Finding in New Jersey.* New Brunswick, NJ: Rutgers University Press, 1985.

Brown, Michael. *New Jersey Parks, Forests and Natural Areas: A Guide.* New Brunswick, NJ: Rutgers University Press, 1997.

Burton, Hal. *The Morro Castle.* New York: Viking Press, 1973.

Cappuzzo, Michael. *Close to Shore: A True Story of Terror in an Age of Innocence.* New York: Broadway Books, 2001.

Carson, Rachel. *The Edge of the Sea.* Boston: Houghton Mifflin, 1955.

Cudworth, Marsha. *Architectural Self-Guided Tours: Cape May, NJ.* New York: Lady Raspberry Press, 1997.

Cunningham, John T. *The New Jersey Sampler: Historic Tales of New Jersey.* Upper Montclair, NJ: New Jersey Almanac, 1964.

———. *The New Jersey Shore.* New Brunswick, NJ: Rutgers University Press, 1958.

———. *This Is New Jersey.* New Brunswick, NJ: Rutgers University Press, 1978.

Davis, Ed. *Atlantic City Diary.* McKee City, NJ: Atlantic Sunrise Publishing, 1980.

Deford, Frank. *The Life and Times of Miss America.* New York: Viking Press, 1971.

Dilonno, Mark. *New Jersey's Coastal Heritage.* New Brunswick, NJ: Rutgers University Press, 1997.

Dorwart, Jeffery. *Cape May County, NJ: The Making of an American Resort Community.* New Brunswick, NJ: Rutgers University Press, 1992.

Dowd, Gregory. *The Indians of New Jersey.* Trenton, NJ: New Jersey Historical Commission, 1992.

Eadington, William, ed. *The Gambling Papers: Proceedings of the Fifth National Conference on Gambling and Risk-Taking.* Vol. 8, *Issues in Casino Gambling: Nevada and Atlantic City.* Reno: University of Nevada, 1982.

Federal Writers' Project. *New Jersey: A Guide to Its Present and Past.* New York: Viking Press, 1939.

Fernicola, Richard. *Twelve Days of Terror.* Guilford, CT: Lyons Press, 2001.

Field Guide to the Birds of North America. Washington, DC: National Geographic Society, 1983.

Francis, David, Diane Francis, and Robert Scully. *Wildwood by the Sea: The History of an American Resort.* Fairview Park, OH: Amusement Park Books, 1998.

Funnell, Charles. *By the Beautiful Sea: The Rise and High Times of That Great American Resort, Atlantic City.* New York: Alfred A. Knopf, 1975.

Gottmann, Jean. *Megalopolis: The Urbanization of the Northeastern Seaboard of the United States.* New York: Twentieth Century Fund, 1961.

Hawkins, Michael. "The Atlantic City Experience: Casino Gambling as an Economic Recovery Program." In William Eadington, ed. *The Gambling Papers: Proceedings of the Fifth National Conference on Gambling and Risk Taking.* Vol. 8, *Issues in Casino Gambling: Nevada and Atlantic City.* Reno: University of Nevada, 1982.

Heide, Robert, and John Gilman. *O'New Jersey: Day Tripping, Back Roads, Eateries and Funky Adventures* (rev. ed.). New York: St. Martin's Press, 1992.

Hudson, Kenneth. *Air Travel: A Social History.* Totowa, NJ: Rowman and Littlefield, 1972.

Jakle, John. *The Tourist: Travel in Twentieth-Century North America.* Lincoln: University of Nebraska Press, 1985.

Kelland, Frank, and Marylin Kelland. *New Jersey: Garden or Suburb?* Dubuque, IA: Kendall Hunt Publishing, 1978.

Kraft, Bayard. *Under Barnegat's Beam: Light on Happenings along the Jersey Shore.* New York: Privately printed, distributed by Appleton, Parsons & Co., 1960.

Lehne, Richard. *Casino Policy.* New Brunswick, NJ: Rutgers University Press, 1986.

Lencek, Lena, and Gideon Bosker. *The Beach: The History of Paradise on Earth.* New York: Viking, 1998.

Lloyd, John. *Eighteen Miles of History on Long Beach Island.* Harvey Cedars, NJ: Down the Shore Publishing, 1986.

———. *Six Miles at Sea.* Harvey Cedars, NJ: Down the Shore Publishing, 1990.

Luff, William. *The Story of the Ocean City Tabernacle.* Ocean City, NJ: Ocean City Tabernacle, 1995.

Mahon, Gigi. *The Company that Bought the Boardwalk.* New York: Random House, 1980.

Mappen, Marc. *Jerseyana: The Underside of New Jersey History.* New Brunswick, NJ: Rutgers University Press, 1992.

McCloy, James, and Ray Miller. *The Jersey Devil.* Wallingford, PA: Middle Atlantic Press, 1976.

McPhee, John. *The Pine Barrens.* New York: Ballantine Books, 1971.

Meyer-Arendt, Klaus, and Rudi Hartmann. *Casino Gambling in America: Origins, Trends and Impacts.* Elmsford, NY: Cognizant Communication Corporation, 1998.

Nasaw, David. *Going Out: The Rise and Fall of Public Amusements.* New York: Basic Books, 1993.

Nelson, William, ed. *The New Jersey Coast in Three Centuries.* New York: Lewis Historical Publishing Co., 1902.

New Jersey's Barrier Islands: An Ever-Changing Public Resource. New Brunswick, NJ: Rutgers University Center for Coastal and Environmental Studies, 1983.

Nordstrom, Karl, Paul A. Gares, Norbert P. Psuty, et al. *Living with the New Jersey Shore.* Durham, NC: Duke University Press, 1986.

Peterson, Roger. *A Field Guide to the Birds of Eastern and Central North America.* 4th ed. Boston: Houghton Mifflin, 1980.

Pike, Helen-Chantal. *Greetings from New Jersey: A Postcard Tour of the Garden State.* New Brunswick, NJ: Rutgers University Press, 2001.

Radko, Thomas. *Discovering New Jersey.* New Brunswick, NJ: Rutgers University Press, 1982.

Ricciuti, E. *The Beachwalker's Guide: The Seashore from Maine to Florida.* Garden City, NY: Doubleday, 1982.

Roberts, Russell. *Discover Hidden New Jersey.* New Brunswick, NJ: Rutgers University Press, 1995.

Roberts, Russell, and Rich Youmans. *Down the Jersey Shore.* New Brunswick, NJ: Rutgers University Press, 1993.

Rose, T. F. *Historical and Biographical Atlas of the New Jersey Coast.* Philadelphia: Woolman and Rose, 1878.

Russell, Don. "Atlantic City's Bet on Gambling: Who Won What?" *Atlantic City Magazine* 11, no. 1 (January 1987).

Salvini, Emil. *The Summer City by the Sea: Cape May, New Jersey.* Belleville, NJ: Wheal-Grace Publications, distributed by Rutgers University Press, 1995.

Santelli, Robert. *The Jersey Shore: A Travel and Pleasure Guide.* Charlotte, NC: Fast and McMillan Publishers, 1986.

––––––. *Short Bike Rides in New Jersey.* Chester, CT: Globe Pequot Press, 1988.

Scheller, William. *New Jersey off the Beaten Path.* Chester, CT: Globe Pequot Press, 1988.

Skolnik, Jerome. *House of Cards: The Legalization and Control of Casino Gambling.* Boston: Little Brown, 1978.

Smith, James. "The Premium-Grind: The Atlantic City Casino Hybrid." In William Eadington, ed. *The Gambling Papers: Proceedings of the Fifth National Conference on Gambling and Risk-Taking.* Vol. 8, *Issues in Casino Gambling: Nevada and Atlantic City.* Reno: University of Nevada, 1982.

Somerville, George. *The Lure of Long Beach, New Jersey.* (Reprint of a 1914 volume.) Harvey Cedars, NJ: Down the Shore Publishing, 1987.

Stansfield, Charles A., Jr. "Atlantic City and the Resort Cycles." *Annals of Tourism Research* 5 (1978): 238–51.

––––––. *An Ecological History of New Jersey.* Trenton, NJ: New Jersey Historical Commission, 1996.

––––––. "From East Coast Monopoly to Destination Resort: The Geographic Context of Atlantic City's Transformation." In Klaus Meyer-Arendt and Rudi Hartmann, eds. *Casino Gambling in America: Origins, Trends and Impacts.* Elmsford, NY: Cognizant Communication Corporation, 1998.

––––––. *A Geography of New Jersey: The City in the Garden.* New Brunswick, NJ: Rutgers University Press, 1998.

Sternlieb, George, and James Hughes. *The Atlantic City Gamble.* Cambridge, MA: Harvard University Press, 1983.

Stilgoe, John. *Alongshore.* New Haven, CT: Yale University Press, 1994.

––––––. *Metropolitan Corridor: Railroads and the American Scene.* New Haven, CT: Yale University Press, 1983.

Studley, Miriam. *Historic New Jersey through Visitors' Eyes*. Princeton, NJ: Van Nostrand Co., 1964.

Teal, John, and Margaret Teal. *Life and Death of the Salt Marsh*. New York: Ballantine Books, 1969.

Wacker, Peter O. *Land and People*. New Brunswick, NJ: Rutgers University Press, 1975.

Wilson, Harold. *The Story of the New Jersey Shore*. Princeton, NJ: D. Van Nostrand Co., 1964. A condensation and revision of the author's classic study, *The Jersey Shore* (2 vols.). New York: Lewis Historical Publishing Co., 1953.

Zatz, Arline. *New Jersey's Special Places: Scenic, Historic and Cultural Treasures in the Garden State*. Woodstock, VT: Countryman Press, 1990.

Zehnder, Leonard. *Florida's Disney World: Promises and Problems*. Tallahassee, FL: Peninsular Publishing, 1979.

Index

About the Author

Charles Stansfield has been writing about seashore resorts for nearly forty years. His doctoral dissertation studied the growth of early seaside resorts in England and New Jersey. The author of a dozen textbooks on geography, he has taught at Rowan University in South Jersey for more than thirty-five years.

Taken on childhood summer vacations to Cape May, Wildwood, and Atlantic City by his parents, who had honeymooned in Atlantic City, Charles fell in love with the seashore. He also fell in love at the seashore—his wife's parents had a house in Ocean City. His most memorable summer job as a college student was as a temporary patrolman with the Wildwood Police Force.

The author and his wife, Diane, at Ocean City, 1963.